The Efficient House Sourcebook

1739 Snowmass Creek Road
Snowmass, Colorado 81654-9199
(303) 927-3851
Fax: (303) 927-4178

Cover illustration by Sheri Tolhurst, courtesy of Integral Energy Systems, Nevada City CA.

Printed on recycled paper

"Knowledge is of two kinds. We know a subject ourselves, or we know where we can find information upon it."

Boswell, Life of Johnson (1775)

Table Of Contents

Please Note: Some of the most helpful publications in this sourcebook are out of print. Be resourceful! They can usually can be found in a local library.

What is the use of a house if you haven't got a tolerable planet to put it on?
Henry David Thoreau

Illustration by Sheri Tolhurst, courtesy of Integral Energy Systems, Nevada City CA.

1. Introduction

Our homes can make a powerful statement about our values, goals, and lifestyles. They tangibly show, among other things, how we can, or cannot, live in harmony with nature. Though most "modern" American homes provide us with unprecedented comforts, supplying these often wastes precious, non-renewable resources and wreaks havoc on the environment. Fortunately, we now have the knowledge and technology to rectify this. By building or renovating our homes to be resource-efficient, responsive to their surroundings and sensitive to this planet's finite resource base, we can not only live comfortably while honoring the other lives that share our world, but can also instill in our homes a sense of beauty, richness, and spirit. Bringing this to fruition, however, requires that we, in architect Tom Bender's words:

> ...put heart into our homes....Part of a building's power to move our hearts, derives from its rightness to its place and time, the clarity with which it draws us into the web of natural rhythms and qualities in which it is embedded. Every region has a different climate, geography, and community of living things. Out of these patterns emerges the unique spirit of each place, and, as well, a particular kind of human being and human community. Our homes connect us to or isolate us from this spirit of place. They take on (or ignore) the special qualities of snow country, desert, prairie, piedmont, or bayou, and can nurture us with the unique possibilities of growth inherent there.

Because a house is a microcosm of life, consisting of interconnected elements, this guide addresses the subject of resource-efficient housing from many perspectives. These include, for example, energy efficiency, economics, land use, health, food production, indigenous building materials, water use, waste disposal, environmental quality, and transportation. This book gives you access to all the practical information you'll need to create and manage a truly resource-efficient house. Though most of the information presented is of a nuts-and-bolts and how-to nature, this does not mean that technical fixes are sufficient *alone* to solve the environmental or energy crises, or make our world a safe or secure place to live. Still, it's a good way to start. Making efficient use of resources—doing more with less—benefits both the household and society. And little actions add up. The energy saving "industry" now "delivers" two-fifths more energy each year than the oil industry, and it does it cheaper! Since 1979, millions of individual decisions to save energy have given this country more than ten times as much new energy as all net expansions of energy supply put together. Of those expansions, more new energy has come from sun, wind, water, and wood than from oil, gas, coal, and uranium. Decreasing energy imports reduces a major source of potential foreign conflict. By providing us with greater comfort and security at less cost, resource efficiency also makes it possible, if we choose, to share the "global pie" more equitably without compromising our standard of living.

Because a house is a microcosm of life, consisting of interconnected elements, this guide addresses the subject of resource-efficient housing from many perspectives.

New developments in house design, materials, and appliances are advancing with dizzying speed; many of the best resource-efficient building techniques and technologies in use today did not exist a year ago!

Finding smart, gentle, efficient ways to harness and work with the natural resources present at a site are perhaps the most important keys to household resource efficiency. Most households rely on distant life-support systems for their energy supply, food production, water delivery, waste disposal, and other basic needs. A resource-efficient household strives, where feasible, to provide these by making productive and efficient use of the natural resources—sun, wind, rain, plants, trees, soil, etc.—available within its borders. It also substitutes environmentally benign household products for toxic ones and recycles valuable "wastes" rather than throwing them away. To the extent that we clean up our act at home, where we have the greatest control, we reduce damage globally.

There are many ways to be resource efficient. Many of the most effective techniques incorporate sophisticated yet elegantly simple technologies. Figuring out what the best options are for your particular home situation—site, climate, budget, aesthetics, lifestyle, etc.—can, however, be formidable, even overwhelming. New developments in house design, materials, and appliances are advancing with dizzying speed; many of the best resource-efficient building techniques and technologies in use today did not exist a year ago! Information on what the best buys are, where to get them, how to shop for them, and the most efficient ways to install them remains a critical need, heightened by change so fast it demands "looseleaf" minds.

Thousands of people faced with this dilemma write to Rocky Mountain Institute each year; they want to make their homes more resource efficient, but don't know where to begin. *The Efficient House Sourcebook* is our response. It reviews and lists hundreds of informative resources which can help you identify and make the most of whatever household resource-efficiency opportunities exist for you, whether you live in a suburban ranch style house, an urban high-rise, a country bungalow, an inner-city row-house, a mountainside chalet, a mobile home, or a house just now being created on an architect's drafting board. The periodicals, books, energy offices, schools, appropriate-technology information services, alternative energy associations, and other helpful resources cited represent many of the best sources of information, advice, and training that the staff at RMI knows of. In addition to recommending where to turn for specific resource-efficient housing assistance, this publication also contains much informative background material within its introductions, reviews, and excerpts.

Three basic sources of information are presented in the guide: periodicals, books, and organizations. Each of these can help you in different ways. **Periodicals** represent the best way to keep up with or tune into the state-of-the-art in resource-efficient housing. Because of periodicals' limited space and, sometimes, "jump-the-gun" reporting, however, they rarely tell you everything you want or need to know about a subject. If an article does appear to "tell all," be forewarned: you may be a guinea pig. **Books**, on the other hand, can provide you with more comprehensive and, in general, definitive (as of its printing, that is) coverage on both the theory and practice of any given subject. As you'd expect, however, they can be and often are somewhat dated by the time they roll off the press. Use them as primary references, checking with appropriate periodicals to verify that you're not missing out on some potentially "latest and greatest" opportunity to improve upon whatever project you're working on. Last, the diverse **organizations**—energy offices, schools, research centers, information services, etc.—listed here can offer you invaluable access to both general and very specialized information specifically tailored to your site, region, or project. They may also offer training or referrals to local designers, contractors, and product suppliers. The staff at local organizations can be particularly helpful in this regard, since the successful application of many resource-efficient technologies can require detailed knowledge of local microclimates and on-site professional help with design and installation.

Don't feel that you must buy or subscribe to any of the references in this guide—especially not before you've reviewed their worth firsthand. Most libraries can get you practically any book through interlibrary loan; be prepared to wait, though, this service usually takes several weeks. You can order most of the books in this guide through your neighborhood bookstore, supporting a local business and probably saving postage and handling charges. For a fee (check with the publisher), you can order sample copies of practically all the magazines reviewed here. Better yet, see if you can borrow a copy from a local architect, builder, engineer, contractor, or alternative energy professional.

The Efficient House Sourcebook offers you access to the best resources we could find. No doubt, however, better or complementary ones exist. When you come across these, please let us know so we can add them to the next edition. There is a form at the back of the book that you can use to submit your comments.

The resources listed can help you identify and wisely invest in those household resource-efficiency opportunities which make the most sense for your particular situation. No matter what projects you pursue, these resources can also help ensure that you get them done as smoothly and cost-effectively as possible. Much of the advice they offer was learned the hard way. As a master builder friend of ours once said, "If you can't afford to do it right the first time, how come you can afford to do it twice?" Take heed, and you'll get improvements and new creations done right the first time.

Robert Sardinsky
Old Snowmass, Colorado

No matter what projects you pursue, these resources can also help ensure that you get them done as smoothly and cost-effectively as possible.

Rocky Mountain Institute facility.

Illustration by David Gross, Public Image, Boulder Colorado.

1A. Acknowledgements

Dozens of people have made major contributions to this sourcebook, and to earlier editions. Linda Baynham coordinated the revision of this edition, with assistance from James Johnson, Judd Hirsch, Michael Shepard, Brady Bancroft, and Scott Chaplin. Others who have assisted with various editions over the years include Bartlett, Colleen Burkhardt, Pam Dyer, Ted Flanigan, Alison Gold, Barbara Heckendorn, Catherine Henze, Dave Houghton, Pat Kiernan, John Klusmire, Amory Lovins, Hunter Lovins, Laura Maggos, Meredith Miller, Kate Mink, Chris Myers, Pattie Norton, MaryKay Parker, Sharon Troyer, and Barb Walss.

We are especially indebted to J. Baldwin and his colleagues at Whole Earth Review/Catalog for giving us invaluable and inspirational publications which have been used as models and for generously letting us use a number of their reviews.

The staffs at the National Appropriate Technology Assistance Center and the Conservation & Renewable Energy Inquiry Service helped us track down many useful resources.

Colleagues throughout the country recommended their favorite sources of specialized and hard-to-find information, and many of them reviewed these for us. They include: Neils Andersen, Jordan Energy Institute; Earle Barnhart, New Alchemy Institute; Tom Bender, architect/author; Joe Carter, Rodale Press; Jeffrey Cook, Architect; Chan Dawson, Home magazine; Christine Donovan, energy consultant; John Dunlop, Interstate Solar Coordination Council; Tom Enos, San Luis Valley Solar Energy Association; Dr. Philip Fairey, Florida Solar Energy Center; Jerry Germer, energy and building writer; Susan Hassol, environmental author; Martha Hewett, Minneapolis Energy Office; Bion Howard, Alliance to Save Energy; Dr. Russell Jaffe, director and fellow of Health Studies Collegium; Brian Kent, Maine Tomorrow; Dr. Henry Liers, fellow of Health Studies Collegium; Joe Lstiburek, Building Engineer Corp.; Mac McCoy, Renew America; Maureen McIntyre, Home Resource magazine; Tad Montgomery, waste water systems researcher; John Morrill and Steve Nadel, American Council for an Energy-Efficient Economy; Ned Nisson, Energy Design Update; Robert Roy, Earthwood Building School; Larry Sherwood, American Solar Energy Society; Dr. William Shurcliff, Harvard University; Bill Smith, Maine Audubon Society; Jane Sorensen, land use planner; Malcolm Wells, Architect/Author; Alex Wilson, West River Communications; and Bill Yanda, Brother Sun. Thanks also are offered to the many others who contributed in small but significant ways.

All reviews not otherwise attributed are by Rocky Mountain Institute staff.

Rocky Mountain Institute gratefully acknowledges research and outreach grants in support of this publication from The Educational Foundation of America, the W. Alton Jones Foundation, and the Albert A. List and Evergreen Foundations. In addition, general support from the Compton Foundation, the Golden Rule Foundation, the Grainger Foundation, the James Ford Bell Foundation, the Joyce Mertz-Gilmore Foundation, the Harder Foundation, the William and Flora Hewlett Foundation, the Kane Family Foundation, Pew Charitable Trusts, the Rockefeller Family & Associates, the Tides Foundation, and the Lawson Valentine Foundation assisted in the production of this work and is gratefully acknowledged.

Illustration from proceedings of *The Village as Solar Ecology*, courtesy of John and Nancy Todd, New Alchemy Institute.

2. Resource-Efficient Housing Periodicals

Magazines and newsletters are perhaps the best way to keep informed about the state-of-the-art in resource-efficient housing. Because a large array of "new and improved" products continuously floods the marketplace, simply identifying those worth considering for your needs, much less figuring out each one's suitability for any particular job, is a monumental task. Fortunately, a few periodicals track and report on such developments.

Though coverage in the following periodicals often overlaps, each offers unique insights and perspectives. Therefore, whether you're sorting new product fact from fiction, seeking dream-house inspirations, or searching for the best materials, tools, and techniques to carry out a project, you can get a more complete picture by consulting several of these publications. But mind you, no such reporting should be accepted as the final word on any housing innovation unless it has held up under real-world experience. Credible periodicals, in fact, routinely devote considerable space to "mopping up" and rectifying previous articles which proved unduly optimistic. Such corrections are important information for you to heed.

In addition to popular newstand-type periodicals, there are a number of specialized "layperson-friendly" trade publications for you to consider. These typically get the word out first and in greatest detail about new housing developments.

Don't feel like you must subscribe to all, or any, of the periodicals on our recommended list in order to keep up with the-state-of-the-art in resource-efficient housing. Instead, see whether a local library, college, architect, builder, engineer, or alternative-energy professional subscribes to the ones you'd like to examine. If all else fails, get sample copies from the publishers, and be sure to get their annual subject indexes too. Back issues often contain long-forgotten gold mines of information which just may answer those "I'm-gonna-go-crazy-if-I-don't-get-the-straight-scoop-on-this-soon" sorts of questions.

Magazines and newsletters are perhaps the best way to keep informed about the state-of-the-art in resource-efficient housing.

2A. Periodicals Which Regularly Report on State-Of-The-Art Developments In Resource-Efficient Housing

The Earthwise Consumer
(formerly Everything Natural)
Box 279
Forest Knolls CA 94933
$20/year (8 issues)

How do you keep up with and choose the best green products? Read *The Earthwise Consumer*. Philosophical around the edges but practical in focus, it is filled with advice and insights both on the availability of everyday products which are better for our health, the earth, and living in harmony with nature in our daily lives. A typical issue contains an interesting sampling of reader correspondence—questions, tips and experiences, in-depth articles on products and alternative methods, interviews with experts, book reviews, new brand-name products, mail order catalogs, and much more. Recent issues have featured articles on such subjects as "Toxic Carpets," "Renewable Energy," "Electromagnetic Fields," Water Efficiency," "Organically Grown Skin Care Products," and "Recycling Paper."

Best Selling Home Plans
$3.50 at newstands
Hachette Magazines
1633 Broadway
New York NY 10019
(800)526-4667

This bimonthly magazine features 175 plans from various architects and designers. Each issue includes plans for about 30 homes incorporating passive solar features such as greenhouses, clerestories and masonry storage walls. Some include earthberming, superinsulation and active solar systems. Blueprints for the homes shown can be ordered plus questions about the plans can be answered by calling the toll-free number.

Custom Builder: The Monthly Magazine of Quality Home Construction
(formerly Progressive Builder and, before that, Solar Age)
Subscription Services
38 Lafayette Street
Yarmouth, ME 04096
$38.00/2 years (12 issues)
(207)846-0970

This not-too-technical trade magazine informs residential builders, architects, engineers, and housing subcontractors about the latest in innovative products, construction techniques, and business practices, with special emphasis on energy efficiency. Each issue is full of useful hands-on information and practical advice, much of it valuable to homeowners as well as to professionals. Features range from "What's New In Sunspaces" and "The True Cost of Conservation" to "Heat Recovery the Right Way" and "Views On Insulating Foundation Walls." The December issue includes a product directory.

Garbage: The Practical Journal for the Environment
P.O. Box 51647
Boulder CO 80321-1647
$21/year (6 issues)
(303)447-9330

One of a new breed of first-rate environmental magazines, *Garbage* informs you how to set up and maintain your household in a healthy fashion with minimum harmful impact on the environment. Each issue explores how common household practices can negatively affect the environment, and offers sound information and resources on environmentally sound alternatives. This generously illustrated magazine addresses the subject in straight talk, with a refreshing twist of good humor. Recent feature articles include "Combatting Household Pests Without Chemical Warfare," "Natural Lawn Care," "Home Energy," "Bottled Water: Fads and Facts," "Kitchen Design for Recycling," and "Toilets: Low Flush/No Flush."

Design Spirit
438 Third St.
Brooklyn NY 11215
$16/year (3 issues)

Design Spirit is a fascinating magazine supporting "architecture that harmonizes with nature." Updates on non-toxic building materials, feng shui (the Chinese art of building in harmony with nature), earthquake-proof building, and traditional timber framing were featured in the Winter 1990 premier issue. The magazine has a creative edge—factual information intermingles with topics such as "the spiritual impulse that informs great art and the contemporary exhibition." It emphasizes the artistic—the marriage of art, architecture, and the environment—and should be of interest to architects and laypeople alike.

Energy Design Update
Cutter Information Corp.
37 Broadway
Arlington MA 02174-5539
(617)648-8700
$157/year (12 issues)

Comprehensive yet concise technical reporting on the latest building research and construction news fills *Energy Design Update*. The state-of-the-art in both new and retrofit energy-efficient housing is addressed in a newsletter format. Each issue is packed with design and construction tips, new product reviews, case studies, survey results, and insightful commentary on such issues as indoor air quality and vapor-barrier detailing in superinsulated buildings. Articles take on the smallest to largest subject areas. For example, the Split Hairs Department reports on "The Effect of Sheathing Nails on Wall Thermal Performance" while the Feature Department covers "Air-to-Air Heat Exchanger Update: News, Research, Questions and Myths." *EDU* is especially useful for designers, builders, and others already familiar with general house design, construction terminology, and techniques who don't have much time for reading, but want to keep abreast of the most innovative design, hardware, and construction options.

Fine Homebuilding

The Taunton Press
P.O. Box 5506
Newtown CT 06470-5506
(800)243-7252
$26/year (7 issues)

Striking color photos, beautiful illustrations, and spirited text make *Fine Homebuilding* magazine captivating reading. Each issue is filled with a diverse assortment of articles which span every facet of new construction and building renovation. Architects, contractors, and owner-builders tell you first-hand about their often one-of-a-kind houseraising and remodeling experiences. All building media and architectural styles are fair game. While this is unequivocally a magazine for any connoisseur of fine homes, its coverage isn't elitist. Homes of both the rich and the more modestly endowed are covered, showing each as a unique reflection of its creator. Stories on a custom, low-cost home being built from prefab metal parts appear next to ones on the painstaking remodel of a 17th-century French farmhouse. There are numerous articles on resource-efficient housing which explore superinsulated building techniques, home energy myths, air-to-air heat exchangers, sunspace design, rammed-earth forming techniques, and more. *Fine Homebuilding* also gives equal attention to practical matters. How-to articles report on everything from selecting and using screw guns and laying brick floors without mortar to building timber bowstring trusses and scribe-fitting a log house.

Home Energy

(formerly Energy Auditor & Retrofitter)
2124 Kittredge, #95
Berkeley CA 94704
(510)524-5405
$49/year (6 issues)

This friendly trade magazine focuses on all facets of residential energy efficiency—issues, trends, analytic techniques, hardware, and retrofit methods—for existing homes. It primarily serves as a timely forum for the exchange of information and ideas among professionals. Virtually every issue contains useful, easy-to-understand information on new energy conserving techniques and hardware which is useful to anyone interested in making a home more resource-efficient. Practical, clearly written and often humorously illustrated, the articles make for informative and entertaining reading. Articles address everything from retrofitting mobile homes and the kerosene-heater controversy to efficient appliances for the home and using a blower door.

Home Power

P.O. Box 130
Hornbrook CA 96044
$10/year (6 issues)
(916)475-3179

Home Power magazine is the best source of up-to-date, practical, and friendly information on designing and living with alternative energy systems for those striving to supply their own power. It's a true labor of love written by folks who work and live with independent power systems—photovoltaic power, wind power, water power, etc., day in and day out. Admirably, they freely share their hard learned knowledge, including "trade secrets," in each issue. The magazine is packed with stories about working home power systems which are set up throughout the country and the people behind them, product reviews, installation tips, where-to-find it information, technology assessments, question and answer dialogue, and lots more. Excellent supporting graphics, downhome style and presentation, and an inspirational let's-take-charge spirit give *Home Power* character, while its content makes the magazine a great resource.

The Journal of Light Construction

(formerly New England Builder)
P.O. Box 686
Holmes PA 19043
$27.50/year (12 issues)
(800)345-8112

The Journal of Light Construction is a great tabloid for anyone involved in building or restoring houses. Each issue offers a wealth of practical, interesting, and at times entertaining information. Features have included: energy-wise construction; water problems/water cures; renovation and remodeling; interior construction and design; exteriors; and the construction, restoration, and repair of roofs. Experienced practitioners report on everyday and controversial building matters, often with refreshing insights on design, technique, aesthetics, safety, health, energy efficiency, and cost-effectiveness. Lots of bold illustrations, lively reader/editor dialogue, and "gee-whiz-that's-neat" sorts of tidbits give *The Journal of Light Construction* zesty character.

Northeast Sun

Northeast Sustainable Energy Association
23 Ames Street
Greenfield MA 01301
(413)774-6051
$30/year (4 issues) includes NESEA membership

Northeast Sun, the quarterly magazine of the Northeast Sustainable Energy Association, is a great resource for anyone concerned about energy use and environmental degradation. *Northeast Sun* fosters responsible energy use for a clean environment by bringing issues and nuts and bolts information to a broad audience of builders, architects and engineers of residential, commercial, and industrial buildings, energy management consultants, designers and builders of solar and electric vehicles, as well as the general public. Experienced professionals on the cutting edge of energy-efficient technology bring an insightful and inspirational look to such topics as energy-efficient lighting, global warming and building design, technologies and utility programs for commercial buildings, photovoltaics, practical solar, and electric cars for everyday use. Quarterly columns include the Northeast Reporter energy news clips, Northeast Calendar of Events, and local and regional association news.

Popular Science

Box 54965
Boulder CO 80322-4965
$13.94/year (12 issues)

A particularly good article on advanced technology, "State-of the-Art Houses" (in the January 1990 issue), is typical of the sort of well-researched information you'll find when *Popular Science* explores the latest in housing technology. Occasionally, this "what's new" magazine reports on such matters as part of its broad coverage of science and technology. Features on a wide variety of laboratory and field developments in resource-efficient housing look at innovations in construction, hardware, appliance, and renewable energy systems for both the scientifically informed lay reader and the handyman. Though there's lots of high-tech talk, good balance is attained by including practical home improvement projects, energy-efficient house plans, and home energy management information.

Practical Homeowner
(formerly New Shelter)
P.O. Box 58977
Boulder CO 80322-8977
(800)525-0643
$13.97/year (9 issues)

This slick, nicely illustrated magazine gives average homeowners good advice for making the most of everything they have within their borders—from landscaping to a healthy home environment, from home finances to product evaluations and recommendations, and much more. Most articles focus on practical, cost-effective ways to increase your home's comfort, beauty, and value. Energy-related coverage shares equal space with the rest of these subjects, exploring everything from "Home Heating Options? Gas, Oil, Electric, Wood and Solar" and "Smart Energy Savings" to "Prefab Sunspaces" and "The Conservation Revolution."

Solplan Review: The Independent Newsletter of Energy Conservation, Building Science, and Construction Practice
The Drawing-Room Graphic Services Ltd.
Box 86627
North Vancouver, British Columbia V7L 4L2
Canada
(604)689-1841
$36/year for U.S. subscriptions, $30/year for Canadian subscriptions (6 issues)

This newsletter reports on energy-efficient housing construction practices and technical issues that have not quite been resolved by the building industry. Geared toward house designers, builders, and energy auditors/retrofitters working in colder climates, each issue contains short news announcements, commentary, and analysis on a sampling of new building products, survey results, research findings, and construction techniques. Recent coverage has addressed everything from incremental costs of energy conservation, efficient household appliances, gas fireplace alert, and preserved wood foundations. Though its reporting and packaging are fairly dry, the *Solplan Review* earns its keep by providing authoritative information on a variety of building matters hard to find covered elsewhere in the far north. While the newsletter's reporting focuses on Canadian building issues, much of its coverage is useful to people living in the northern U.S.

Traditions Southwest: The Adobe Journal
P.O. Box 7725
Albuquerque NM 87194
$15/year (4 issues)
(505)243-7801

This well-designed, interesting, and informative magazine appears quarterly. It deals specifically with adobe, rammed earth and pressure block construction, including architecture, construction, and preservation, and will in the future develop discussions of appropriate solar design and low-cost housing.

2B. Periodicals Regularly Featuring General Resource-Efficient Housing Information

Cost Cuts
505 American City Building
Columbia MD 21044
(301)964-1230
Free—contributions welcome (9 issues)

Cost Cuts is published by The Enterprise Foundation's Rehab Work Group to provide cost cutting techniques for low-income housing construction and rehabilitation. Options are discussed in the context of codes, type of dwelling, prevailing local construction practice, and the use of sweat equity.

Country Journal
P.O. Box 392
Mt. Morris IL 61054-9957
(800)435-9610
$16.95/year (bimonthly)

Authoritative and engaging writing, beautiful photographs and illustrations offer *Country Journal* readers a nice blend of practical advice and experience with unique insights into many of the focal points of country life including: gardening, houseraisings, cooking, natural history, community events, and rural enterprises, to name a few.

Harrowsmith Country Life
Ferry Road
P.O. Box 1000
Charlotte VT 05445-9984
$24/year (6 issues)

This beautifully presented and intelligently written magazine covers all facets of country living. Coverage spans a wide range of subjects including cold-climate gardening, rural architecture, cooking, and environmental politics.

HOME
1633 Broadway
New York NY 10019
$18/year (12 issues)
(800)526-4667

Clear editorials and handsome photography fill this compendium of creative ideas for people interested in enhancing their home environment. Architecture, remodeling, interior design, landscaping, finance, and other home-related subjects are covered.

Permaculture Activist
P.O. Box 3630
Kailua Kona HI 96745
(808)929-9463
$13/year (4 issues)

This quarterly newsletter reports on innovative ideas for creating self-sustaining agricultural systems which are adaptable to both backyard and large scale rural and urban sites. These permaculture systems integrate trees, plants, animals, buildings, and human activities in the design of energy-efficient, low-maintenance landscapes, with the ultimate goal being ecological diversity and stability. Besides covering the latest in permaculture research and field experiences, each *Permaculture Activist* includes updates from regional and international permaculture groups. One dollar of each subscription is donated to a tree-tithe fund.

Mother Earth News
P.O. Box 3015
Harlan IA 51593-4255
$13.95/year (6 issues)

Originally the inspiration for many a back-to-the-lander, this slick but folksy magazine shares many first-hand experiences about self-sufficiency, low-cost living, do-it-yourself housing, and alternative energy.

2C. Consumer Protection Periodicals

Consumer Reports/Buying Guide
Box 53015
Boulder CO 80321-3015
$20/year (12 issues, including the Buying Guide issue)

And

Consumers Union News Digest
Consumers Union
256 Washington Street
Mount Vernon NY 10553
(914)667-9400, Ext. 251
$48/year (24 issues)

Has an appliance sales person ever sweet-talked you into buying the "deal of the century," which promptly self-destructed the day after its warranty expired? If so, you're not alone. Millions of consumers spend more effort deliberating between decorator colors and auto-this-and-that options than examining what's "under the hood." Whether you are shopping for a washing machine, automobile, or practically any other consumer good (or service), the nonprofit *Consumers Union* research staff can help you avoid such pitfalls. They offer wise shoppers three unbiased sources of valuable information and advice: *Consumer Reports; Consumer Reports Buying Guide* (each year's work is summed up in the annual *Buying Guide* issue, printed in pocket size so you can take it shopping with you. It may also be purchased separately for $6.95); and *Consumers Union News Digest* (The Digest brings you the latest consumer information as it breaks.)

These publications can alert you to the many details and features which you should consider while evaluating new product options. Before running off to make new purchases, check out their analyses and surveys. Then you'll be prepared to ask salespeople not only about color options, but also about product performance, quality, reliability, warranty, energy/water consumption, etc. And when it comes time to talk price, you'll know whether you are in fact getting the "deal of the century," since *CU* lists the average "real-world" retail pricing for all the products it evaluates. A few examples of resource-efficient products *CU* has reported on are instantaneous water heaters, low-flow showerheads, heat pumps, air-to-air heat exchangers, and woodstoves.

Please note that in addition to *CU*'s studies, there are a number of other sources of consumer information which you should examine when shopping for new appliances and cars. They are *The Most Energy Efficient Appliances* (reviewed in section 9A) and *The Car Book* (reviewed in section 15).

Illustration from proceedings of *The Village as Solar Ecology*, courtesy of John and Nancy Todd, New Alchemy Institute.

3. Organizations Providing Information, Advice, and Referrals on Resource-Efficient Housing

Finding the information and advice you need to think through or carry out a resource-efficient housing project can be a major stumbling block. Fortunately, there are hundreds of organizations—government agencies, nonprofit research and education groups, utility companies, etc.—located throughout the country which can help you overcome such hurdles. Some of these offer comprehensive consumer assistance services, manned by full-time professional staff, while others provide more limited, yet valuable, support through informal networks of volunteers.

In addition, check with the colleges, universities, and other nonprofit education organizations in your area to see if any offer courses, workshops, and seminars which touch on household resource efficiency, such as energy-efficient architecture, solar architecture, earth-sheltered house design, alternative energy systems, appropriate technology, energy management and audits, human ecology, energy conservation, daylighting, energy-efficient heating, ventilation, and cooling, environmental studies, and natural resource management. While most of these programs are set up to provide career training, some also, or exclusively, give less formal evening, weekend, and seasonal educational programs. These are mostly offered through community colleges, the continuing education departments of universities, and small appropriate technology research and education centers. Such organizations can offer you not only a wide variety of formal or continuing education studies, but also an excellent pool of resource people to draw upon. Many teachers and researchers will answer inquiries or refer you to other appropriate sources of assistance. (In general, these folks will be most responsive when you ask them for specific information which you haven't been able to get elsewhere. Questions such as "What can you tell me about solar energy?" will be met with less enthusiasm.)

Also, check with your State/County Agricultural Extension office for programs and publications related to housing/resource/and community development topics. Some County extension offices, for example, conduct programs on residential water quality, radon detection and control, and management of hazardous household wastes. Programs will vary from state to state, county to county.

This section lists a variety of organizations that cater to national, regional, or state audiences; most provide low-cost or no-cost information and referral services. Call or write them to find what resources they offer.

This section lists a variety of organizations that cater to national, regional, or state audiences; most provide low-cost or no-cost information and referral services.

3A. Federal Information Services

Conservation And Renewable Energy Inquiry And Referral Service (CAREIRS)
P.O. Box 8900
Silver Spring MD 20907
(800)523-2929

The U.S. Department of Energy funds CAREIRS to provide basic consumer information on the full spectrum of renewable energy technologies—solar, wind, hydro, photovoltaic, geothermal, and bioconversion—and on household energy conservation techniques. The service can, for example, help you figure out how to build a solar greenhouse, choose what type of heat pump to buy, identify local groups that can advise you about alternative energy technologies, determine what indoor air pollutants you should be concerned about in a tightly sealed house, and decide what glazing options are best for your windows.

National Appropriate Technology Assistance Service (NATAS)
P.O. Box 2525
Butte MT 59702-2525
(800)428-2525
(800)428-1718 in Montana

NATAS provides three primary services: 1) tailored information responses, 2) engineering/scientific technical assistance, and 3) commercialization technical assistance. NATAS is available to assist anyone in the United States through a toll-free number. However, it should prove most useful to energy innovators, homeowners, small businesses, farmers, state and local governments, nonprofit organizations, and educational institutions. NATAS works closely with federal, state, and local programs to coordinate technical assistance activities. One of the more innovative aspects of NATAS is its commercialization technical assistance. The service helps entrepreneurs develop the business side of energy-related appropriate technologies with advice on marketing, business planning, and funding.

National Center for Appropriate Technology (NCAT)
P. O. Box 3838
Butte MT 59702
406-494-4572

"En-Cat" (National Center for Appropriate Technology) publishes its research findings as inexpensive booklets (most less than $5). The subject matter is aimed at ordinary folks who wish to know more about subjects common to the appropriate tech field: solar water heaters, composting toilets, biogas, weatherizing a mobile home, and lots more. Its publications tend to summarize the baffling amount of information available elsewhere—a very useful service. Write NCAT for a publications list.

Reviewed by J. Baldwin in The Essential Whole Earth Catalog

Appropriate Technology Transfer for Rural Areas (ATTRA)
University of Arkansas
P.O. Box 3657
Fayetteville AR 72702
(800)346-9410

American agriculture is in the midst of many changes, brought on by spiraling production costs, unstable market prices and increasingly difficult environmental problems. While scientists and farmers search for solutions, ATTRA serves as a bridge between rapidly changing farming technologies and farmers on the land. Funded by the U.S. Fish and Wildlife Service, Department of the Interior, ATTRA is managed by the National Center for Appropriate Technology. They offer cost-free information and technical assistance to farmers, county extension agents, agricultural support groups and agribusiness.

While ATTRA is interested in all aspects of agriculture, their efforts at providing information are limited to low input and sustainable agriculture practices. These agricultural practices allow farmers to reduce adverse impacts on the environment, produce high-quality food and maintain good profit levels. Each request for information is referred to a Technical Specialist, who reviews literature in the ATTRA Resource Center, contacts research agencies, farmers and other specialists in that field, and searches available databases and other networks for information. Time allowed for research on each question is usually limited to three or four hours and it may take two to four weeks for information to reach you. ATTRA is not able to respond to questions which require overnight responses, as some pest and weed problems do. Extension agents, crop scouts, and on-farm consultants are recommended for problems which require immediate assistance.

3B. National Listing of:

▲ State Energy Offices
■ Renewable Energy Associations
● Research and Education Centers
◆ Energy Extension Services
△ Regional Power Authorities
❑ Schools
○ Other Helpful Organizations

Alabama

▲ **Alabama Dept. of Economic and Community Affairs, Science, Technology and Energy Division**
401 Adams Avenue
PO Box 5690
Montgomery AL 36103-5690
(205)242-5100
(800)392-8098 within AL

■ **Alabama Solar Energy Association**
The Johnson Research Center
University of Alabama in Huntsville
Huntsville AL 35899
(205)895-6745

Alaska

▲ **Alaska Dept. of Community & Regional Affairs**
Rural Development Division
Energy Programs
333 W. 4th Ave., Ste. 220
Anchorage AK 99501-2341
(907)563-1073
(800)478-4636 within AK

Arizona

▲ **Arizona Energy Office**
Dept. of Commerce
3800 N. Central, Suite 1200
Phoenix AZ 85012
(602)280-1430
(800)352-5499 within AZ

■ **Arizona Solar Energy Association**
Diana Pfaff
PO Box 26
Scottsdale AZ 85252
(602)965-7608

Arkansas

▲ **Arkansas Energy Office**
1 State Capitol Mall, Suite 4B-215
Little Rock AR 72201
(501)682-1370

● **Energy Rated Homes of America**
100 Main, Ste. 404
Little Rock AR 72201
(501)374-7827

California

❑ **Cabrillo College**
Construction & Energy Management
6500 Soquel Drive
Aptos CA 95003,
(408)479-6201, Ext. 235

▲ **California Energy Commission**
1516 Ninth Street, MS-25
Sacramento CA 95814-5512
(916)654-4064
Energy Hotline (800)772-3300 within CA

❑ **California Polytechnic State University**
Mechanical Engineering Dept.
San Luis Obispo CA 93407
(805)756-1334

■ **Northern California Solar Energy Association**
P.O. Box 3008
Berkeley CA 94703

❑ **Orange Coast College**
P. O. Box 5005
Costa Mesa CA 92628-0120
(714)432-4011

❑ **Santa Rosa Junior College**
1501 Mendocino Avenue
Santa Rosa CA 95401
(707)527-4011

❑ **Sierra College**
Solar Energy Technology
5000 Rocklin Road
Rocklin CA 95677
(916)624-3333

❑ **Sonoma State University**
Energy Management and Design Program,
School of Environmental Studies and Planning
Rohnert Park CA 94928
(707)664-2306

❑ **University of California**
Division of Environmental Studies
Davis CA 95616
(916)752-3026

❑ **University of California**
Energy and Resources Group
Room 100, Building T-4
Berkeley CA 94720
(415)642-1640

❑ **University of California**
Graduate Group in Ecology
Davis CA 95616
(916)752-6751
Also serving California:

△ **Bonneville Power Administration**
Office of Energy Resources-R
Box 3621
Portland OR 97208
(503)230-5311 or 5489

Colorado

■ **American Solar Energy Society**
2400 Central Avenue, Unit 6-1
Boulder CO 80202-4613
(303)443-3130
Contact for information on state chapters.

▲ **Colorado Office of Energy Conservation**
1675 Broadway Suite 1300
Denver CO 80202-4613
(303)620-4292
Energy Conservation Hotline: (800)632-6662
within Colorado
(Metro (800)620-4284)

(Woodstove Emissions)
○ **Colorado Air Quality Control Commission**
4210 East 11th Avenue
Denver CO 80220
(303)331-8597

■ **Denver Solar Energy Association**
7123 Arapahoe Avenue
Boulder CO 80303
(303)442-4277

❑ **The Energy Office**
128 South 5th Street
Grand Junction CO 81501
(303)241-2871

◆ **Energy Resource Center of the Pike's Peak Region**
Box 267
Colorado Springs CO 80901
(719)591-0772

❑ **Red Rocks Community College**
Instructional Services
13300 W. 6th Avenue
Lakewood CO 80401
(303)988-6160, ext. 369 or 380

● **Rocky Mountain Institute**
1739 Snowmass Creek Road
Snowmass CO 81654-9199
(303)927-3851

◆ **Roaring Fork Energy Center**
242 Main Street
Carbondale CO 81623
(303)963-0311

❑ **Solar Technology Institute**
PO Box 1115
Carbondale CO 61623-1115
(303)963-0715

△ **Western Area Power Administration**
1627 Cole Blvd., Bldg. 18
Golden CO 80401
(303)231-1500

● **The Windstar Foundation**
2317 Snowmass Creek Road
Snowmass CO 81654
(303)927-4777

Connecticut

▲ **Office of Policy and Management**
Energy Division
80 Washington Street
Hartford CT 06106
(203)566-2800

Delaware

▲ **Dept. of Administrative Services**
Div. of Facilities Management Energy Office
O'Neill Building
P.O. Box 1401
Dover DE 19903
(302)739-5644
(800)282-8616 within DE

District Of Columbia

● **The Alliance to Save Energy**
1725 K Street NW, Suite 509
Washington DC 20006-1401(202)857-0666

● **American Council for an Energy-Efficient Economy (ACEEE)**
1001 Connecticut Avenue NW, Suite 801
Washington DC 20036
(202)429-8873

(Trade Association)
○ **The American Wind Energy Association**
777 N. Capitol Street, Suite 805
Washington DC 20002
(202)408-8988

(Indoor Air Pollution)
○ **The Consumer Federation of America**
1424 Sixteenth Street NW, Suite 604
Washington DC 20036
(202)387-6121

▲ **District of Columbia Energy Office**
613 G Street NW, Suite 500
Washington DC 20001
(202)727-1800

○ **Passive Solar Industries Council**
1090 Vermont Avenue Suite 1200
Washington DC 20005
(202)371-0357

● **Renew America**
1400 Sixteenth Street NW, Suite 710
Washington DC 20036
(202)232-2252

(Trade Association)
○ **Solar Energy Industries Association**
777 N. Capitol N.E., Suite 805
Washington DC 20002
(703)524-6100

(Trade Association)
○ **Wood Heating Alliance**
1101 Connecticut Avenue NW, Suite 700
Washington DC 20036
(202)857-1181

Florida

▲ **Florida Energy Office**
Dept. of Community Affairs
2740 Centerview Drive
Tallahassee FL 32399-2100
(904)488-6764

● **Florida Solar Energy Center**
300 State Road, #401
Cape Canaveral FL 32920-4099
(407)783-0300

Georgia

▲ **Georgia Office of Energy Resources**
254 Washington Street SW, Suite 401
Atlanta GA 30334-8502
(404)656-5176

(Household Environmental Quality)

○ **Human Ecology Action League**
P.O. Box 49126
Atlanta GA 30359
(404)248-1898

● **The Southface Energy Institute**
Box 5506
Atlanta GA 30307
(404)525-7657

Hawaii

▲ **Dept. of Business / Economic Development**
Energy Division
335 Merchant Street, Room 110
Honolulu HI 96813
(808)587-3812

Idaho

❑ **University of Idaho**
Dept. of Architecture
Moscow ID 83843
(208)885-6272

▲ **Bureau of Energy Resources**
Resources Analysis Division
Dept. of Water Resources
State House
1301 N. Orchard
Boise ID 83706
(208)327-7900
(800)334-7283 within ID

Illinois

(Trade Association)
○ **The Association of Home Appliance Manufacturers**
20 North Wacker Drive
Suite 1500
Chicago IL 60606
(312)984-5800

(Community Economic Development/ Energy Conservation)
○ **Center for Neighborhood Technology**
2125 W. North Avenue
Chicago IL 60647
(312)278-4800

▲ **Dept. of Energy and Natural Resources**
325 West Adams, Room 300
Springfield IL 62704-1892
(217)785-2800

❑ **Sangamon State University**
Environmental Studies
Springfield IL 62794-9243
(217)786-6720

● **Small Homes Council Building Research Council**
University of Illinois at Urbana-Champaign
One East Saint Mary's Road
Champaign IL 61820
(217)333-1801

Indiana

❑ **Ball State University**
Energy Dept.
2000 W. University Avenue
Muncie IN 47306-0170
(317)285-1135

● **Center for Energy Research/Education/Services (CERES)**
Ball State University
Muncie IN 47306-0170
(317)285-1135

▲ **Indiana Dept. of Commerce Office of Energy Policy**
Indiana Commerce Center
One North Capitol, Suite 700
Indianapolis IN 46204-2288
(317)232-8940
Energy Hotline (800)382-4631 within IN

Iowa

▲ **Iowa Dept. of Natural Resources**
Energy Bureau
Wallace State Office Building
900 East Grand
Des Moines IA 50319
(515)281-5145

Kansas

▲ **Garden City Community College**
801 Campus Drive
Garden City KS 67846
(316)276-7611

▲ **Kansas Corporation Commission**
Energy Conservation Programs
1500 S.W. Arrowhead Road
Topeka KS 66604-4027
(913)271-3170
Energy Hotline (800)332-0036 within KS

▲ **Kansas State University**
Dept. of Architecture
211 Seaton Hall
Manhattan KS 66506
(913)532-6026

● **The Land Institute**
2440 E. Water Well Road
Salina KS 67401
(913)823-5376

❑ **Pittsburg State University**
Pittsburg KS 66762
(316)235-4393

Kentucky

▲ **Center for Applied Energy Research**
University of Kentucky
3572 Iron Works Pike
Lexington KY 40511-8433
(606)257-0305

Louisiana

▲ **Dept. of Natural Resources**
625 N. Fourth Street
Baton Rouge LA 70802
(504)342-4500

■ **Louisiana Solar Design Association**
Dr. Jason Shih
Box 21540
Baton Rouge LA 70893

Maine

❑ **College of the Atlantic**
Bar Harbor ME 04609
(207)288-5015

▲ **Dept. of Economic and Community Development**
Energy Conservation Division
State House Station No. 53
Augusta ME 04333
(207)289-6000

■ **Maine Solar Energy Association**
RFD Box 751
Addison ME 04606
(207)497-2204

Maryland

(Energy Information Service)
○ **Conservation And Renewable Energy Inquiry and Referral Service (CAREIRS)**
P.O. Box 8900
Silver Spring MD 20907
(800)523-2929

(Housing Rehab/Energy Conservation)
○ **The Enterprise Foundation**
505 American City Building
Columbia MD 21044
(301)964-1230

▲ **Maryland Energy Office**
Dept. of Housing and Community Development
45 Calvert Street Suite 201
Annapolis MD 21401
(301)974-3751

Massachusetts

■ **Boston Area Solar Energy Association**
P.O. Box 44-1017
Somerville MA 02144
(617)868-7450

▲ **Division of Energy Resources**
100 Cambridge Street, Room 1500
Boston MA 02202
(617)727-4732

● **Massachusetts Audubon Society**
South Great Road
Lincoln MA 01773
(617)259-9500
Environmental Helpline (800)541-3443 within
MA

■ **North East Sustainable Energy
Association**
23 Ames Street
Greenfield MA 01301
(413)774-6051
Serves other Northeastern states

Michigan

❑ **Grand Rapids Junior College**
151 Fountain N.E.
Grand Rapids MI 49503-3263
(616)456-4965

■ **Jordan Energy Institute**
155 Seven Mile Road
Comstock Park MI 49321
(616)784-7595

❑ **Lansing Community College**
P.O. Box 40010
Lansing MI 48901
(517)483-1957

❑ **Macomb Community College**
14500 Twelve Mile Road
Warren MI 48093
(313)445-7455

▲ **Michigan Dept. of Commerce**
Michigan Public Service Commission
Office of Energy Programs
P.O. Box 30221
Lansing MI 48909
(517)334-6272

❑ **Oakland Community College**
2900 Featherstone Road
Auburn Hills MI 48326
(313)340-6525

Minnesota

▲ **Dept. of Public Service**
Energy Division
150 E. Kellogg Boulevard
St. Paul MN 55101-1496
(612)296-5175
(800)652-9747 within MN

● **Underground Space Center**
790 Civil and Mineral Engineering Building
500 Pillsbury Drive, SE
University of Minnesota
Minneapolis MN 55455
(612)624-0066

Mississippi

▲ **Dept. of Economic and
Community Development**
Energy and Transportation
510 George Street
Jackson MS 39202
(601)359-6600
Energy Hotline (800)222-8311 within MS

Missouri

❑ **Crowder College**
Solar Dept.
Neosho MO 64850
(417)451-3223

▲ **Dept. of Natural Resources**
Division of Energy
Box 176
Jefferson City MO 65102
(314)751-4000
(800)334-6946 within MO

■ **Missouri Solar Energy Assoc.**
15510 Olive Street Road, Suite 202
Chesterfield MO 63017
(314)537-0881

Montana

■ **Alternative Energy Resources
Organization (AERO)**
44 North Last Chance Gulch, #9
Helena MT 59601
(406)443-7272

▲ **Dept. of Natural Resources &
Conservation**
Energy Division
1520 E. Sixth Avenue
Helena MT 59620-2301
(406)444-6697

● **National Center for Appropriate Technology (NCAT)**
P.O. Box 3838
Butte MT 59702
(406)494-4572

● **National Appropriate Technology Assistance Service (NATAS)**
Box 2525
Butte MT 59702-2525
(800)428-2525
(800)428-1718 within MT

Nebraska

■ **Nebraska Solar Energy Society**
Engineering Building, Room 114
University of Nebraska at Omaha
Omaha NE 68182-0176
(402)554-3276

▲ **Nebraska State Energy Office**
Box 95085
Lincoln NE 68509-5085
(402)471-2867

Nevada

▲ **Nevada Office of Community Services**
400 W. King, Suite 400
Carson City NV 89710
(702)687-4990

❑ **Sierra Nevada College**
P.O. Box 4269
Incline Village NV 89450
(702)831-1314

New Hampshire

■ **Energy Association of New Hampshire**
George Malette
P.O. Box 657
Manchester NH 03105
(603)895-0726

▲ **Governor's Energy Office**
2-1/2 Beacon Street, Second Floor
Concord NH 03301-4498
(603)271-2711
(800)852-3466 within NH

New Jersey

○ **Center for Energy and Environmental Studies (CEES)**
H-102 Engineering Quadrangle
Princeton University
Princeton NJ 08544
(609)258-5446

▲ **New Jersey Board of Public Utilities**
Office of the Secretary/Customer Assistance
Two Gateway Center
Newark NJ 07102
(201)622-6103
(800)492-4242 within NJ

New Mexico

▲ **Energy and Minerals Dept.**
2040 S. Pacheco
Santa Fe NM 87505
(505)827-5950

■ **New Mexico Solar Energy Association**
P.O. Box 8507
Santa Fe NM 87504

● **Southwest Technology Development Institute**
New Mexico State University
Dept. 3 SOL
Box 30001
Las Cruces NM 88003-0001
(505)646-1846

New York

(Indoor Air Quality)
○ **The American Lung Association**
1740 Broadway
New York NY 10019
(212)315-8700

❑ **Long Island University**
Southampton Campus
Southampton NY 11968
(516)283-4000, Ext.206

▲ **New York State Energy Office**
Empire State Plaza
Agency Building 2, 10th Floor
Albany NY 12223
(518)473-4376
(800)423-7283 within NY

■ **New York Metropolitan Solar Energy Society/Solar Coalition**
Jon Naar
PO Box 6696
New York NY 10163
(212)752-4625

North Carolina

❑ **Appalachian State University**
Dept. of Technology
Boone NC 28608
(704)262-3111

❑ **North Carolina Agricultural and Technical State University**
Greensboro NC 27411
(919)334-7780

● **North Carolina Alternative Energy Corporation**
P.O. Box 12699
Research Triangle Park, NC 27709
(919)361-8000

▲ **North Carolina Dept. of Economic and Community Development**
Energy Division
430 N. Salisbury Street
Raleigh NC 27611
(919)733-2230
(800)662-7131 within NC (A.M. only)

▲ **North Carolina Solar Center**
North Carolina State University
Box 7401
Raleigh NC 27695-7401
(919)515-3480
(800)33-NC SUN within NC

(Community Energy/Recycling)
○ **Sunshares Recycling**
1215 Briggs Avenue, Suite 100
Durham NC 27703
(919)596-1870

North Dakota

▲ **North Dakota Energy Office**
Office of Intergovernmental Assistance
State Capitol, 14th Floor
600 E. Boulevard Avenue
Bismarck ND 58505-0170
(701)224-2094

Ohio

▲ **Dept. of Development**
Office of Energy Conservation
P.O. Box 1001
Columbus OH 43266-0101
(614)466-6797

● **Housing Resource Center**
1820 West 48th Street
Cleveland OH 44102
(216)281-4663

Oregon

△ **Bonneville Power Administration**
Office of Energy Resources-R
Box 3621
Portland OR 97208
(503)230-5311 or 5489
Also serves Washington , Idaho, and Montana

❑ **Energy Extension Program**
Oregon State University
Batchellar Hall 344
Corvalis OR 97331-2405
(503)737-3004

▲ **Oregon Dept. of Energy**
625 Marion Street NE
Salem OR 97310
(503)378-4040
(800)221-8035 within OR

(Woodstove Emission Standards)
○ **Oregon Dept. of Environmental Quality**
811 SW Sixth Avenue
Portland OR 97204-1390
(503)229-5177

❑ **Portland State University**
Portland OR 97207-0751
(503)725-4292

■ **Solar Energy Association of Oregon**
Scott Lawrie
2637 SW Water Avenue
Portland OR 97201
(503)224-7867

Pennsylvania

▲ **Pennsylvania Energy Office**
116 Pine Street
Harrisburg PA 17101
(717)783-9982
Energy Hotline (800)692-7312 within PA

❑ **Carnegie-Mellon University**
Engineering And Public Policy
Schenley Park, Pittsburgh PA 15213
(412)268-6115

❑ **Pennsylvania State University**
The Fayette Campus
P.O. Box 519, Route 119 North
Uniontown PA 15401
(412)430-4100

❑ **Pennsylvania State University at Harrisburg**
The Capital College
Middletown PA 17057
(717)948-6116

Rhode Island

▲ **Governor's Office of Housing, Energy and Intergovernmental Relations**
275 Westminster Street, 3rd Floor
Providence RI 02903
(401)-277-3370

■ **R.I. Solar Energy Associates**
Dominic Bucci
42 Tremont Street
Cranston RI 02920-2543
(401)942-6691

South Carolina

▲ **South Carolina Energy Office**
Governor's Division of Energy, Agriculture and
Natural Resources
1205 Pendleton Street
Columbia SC 29201
(803)734-1740
(800)851-8899 within SC

South Dakota

▲ **The Governor's Office of Energy Policy**
217 W. Missouri, Suite 200
Pierre SD 57501-4516
(605)773-3603

Tennessee

▲ **Dept. of Economic and Community Development**
Energy Division
320 Sixth Avenue North, 6th Floor
Nashville TN 37243-0405
(615)741-2994
(800)342-1340 within TN

● **Appropriate Technology Transfer for Rural Areas (ATTRA)**
P.O. Box 3657
Fayetteville AR 72702
(501)442-9824
(800)346-9140 within AR

■ **Tennessee Solar Energy Association**
Tennessee Energy Education Network
Jackson State Community College
2046 N. Parkway
Jackson TN 38301
(901)664-4316

△ **Tennessee Valley Authority**
400 W. Summit Hill Drive
GRN1S124E
Knoxville TN 37902
(615)632-2101
Serves other Southeastern states

Texas

● **Center for Maximum Potential Building Systems**
8604 F.M. 969
Austin TX 78724
(512)928-4786

▲ **Division of Emergency Management**
Energy Program
Box 4087
Austin TX 78773-0001
(512)465-2138

■ **Texas Solar Energy Society**
Russell Smith
P.O. Box 14541
Austin TX 78761-4561
(512)339-8562

■ **Texas Renewable Energy Industries Association**
P.O. Box 16469
Austin TX 78761-6469
(512)339-8562

❏ **University of Texas at Austin**
Center for Energy Studies, Conservation and Solar Division
W. 100 Burnt Road, Building 133
Austin TX 78712
(512)471-7792

Utah

▲ **Utah Energy Office**
3 Triad Center, Suite 450
355 West North Temple
Salt Lake City UT 84180-1204
(801)538-5428
Hotline (800)662-3633 within UT

■ **Utah Solar Energy Society**
1477 East Cedro Circle
Sandy UT 84093
(801)561-8484

Vermont

▲ **Energy Efficiency Division**
Public Service Dept.
120 State Street
Montpelier VT 05620-2601
(802)828-2393
(800)642-3281 within VT

○ **Vermont Energy Investment Corp.**
7 Lawson Lane
Burlington VT 05401
(802)658-6060

Virginia

(Trade Association)
○ **Air Conditioning and Refrigeration Institute**
1501 Wilson Boulevard, Suite 600
Arlington VA 22209
(703)524-8800

(Trade Association)
○ **The Gas Appliance Manufacturers Association**
1901 N. Moore Street
Arlington VA 22209
(703)525-9565

▲ **Virginia Division of Energy**
2201 West Broad Street
Richmond VA 23220
(804)367-1310

■ **Virginia Solar Energy Association**
Watt Bradshaw
107 South Main
Harrisonburg VA 22801
(703)434-3016

Washington

❏ **Edmonds Community College**
Energy Management
20000 68th Avenue W.
Lynnwood WA 98036
206)771-7406

■ **Energy Outreach Center**
503 Fourth West
Olympia WA 98501-1009
(206)943-4595

❑ **Evergreen State College**
LAB 1
Olympia WA 98505
(206)866-6000, Ext. 6750

(Research, Consulting, Design)
○ **Ecotope, Inc.**
2812 E. Madison Street
Seattle WA 98112
(206)322-3753

❑ **University of Washington**
Dept. of Architecture
Gould Hall JO-20
Seattle WA 98195
(206)543-4180

▲ **Washington State Energy Office**
809 Legion Way SE
MS FA-11
Olympia WA 98504
(206)956-2000
(800)962-9731 within WA

West Virginia

(Alternative Wastewater Treatment)
○ **The EPA National Small Flows
Clearinghouse**
P.O. Box 6064
West Virginia University
Morgantown WV 26506-6064
(800)624-8301

▲ **West Virginia Fuel and Energy
Office**
1204 Kanawha Boulevard East, 2nd Floor
Charleston WV 25301
(304)348-8860
(800)642-9012 within WV

Wisconsin

▲ **Division of State Energy**
Dept. of Administration
Box 7868
Madison WI 53707
(608)266-8234

❑ **Energy Efficient Building
Association**
Northcentral Technical College
100 Campus Drive
Wausau WI 54401
(715)675-6331

❑ **University of Wisconsin**
Institute for Environmental Studies
550 North Park Street, Room 70
Madison WI 53706
(608)263-4373

● **University of Wisconsin:
Extension Service**
College of Engineering
432 N. Lake Street
Madison WI 53706
(608)262-2061

Wyoming

▲ **Wyoming Energy Conservation
Office**
Dept. of Economic Development & Stabilization
Herschler Building
2nd Floor West
Cheyenne WY 82002
(307)777-7284

3C. Utility Companies

The majority of the nation's largest utility companies and many smaller ones have established programs to promote the efficient use of electricity at home. Such efforts, of course, help reduce, or keep in check, household electric bills. But thanks to regulatory reforms in many states, they also represent an exciting opportunity for utilities to make more money at less risk, and serve their customers more reliably at lower cost. How so? By helping its customers get the same desired energy services (heat, light, refrigeration, etc.) from technologies that use less electricity, a utility can generate "negawatts" (saved electricity). In most cases, the cost of generating "negawatts" is less than the cost of building new power plants to increase capacity, and many times it costs less to save electricity than generate it in existing power plants. Many gas utilities have embarked on efficiency programs for similar reasons.

Ask your utility what energy efficiency programs it offers. To varying degrees, many private and public utilities offer valuable consumer services. Some will, for example, carry out a home energy audit, solar water heating analysis, gas heating system analysis, economic analysis of mechanical cooling strategies, and a rate comparison and load management analysis to help you plan the most cost-effective ways to manage your energy use. Some utilities' customers also receive monthly energy updates and can request a variety of informative topical consumer energy conservation publications on such subjects as summertime cooling, appliances, energy savings for renters, mobile homes, homebuyers energy considerations, fireplaces, woodburning stoves, and portable heaters. Other utilities offer low-cost financing for household energy improvements, arrange for qualified contractors to carry out the weatherization work on your home, distribute energy-efficient appliance buying guides, and give rebates on the purchase of certain energy-efficient appliances. Please note that, if your utility can't provide you with the energy conservation information you need, many others will send you their consumer publications.

3D. Selected Organizations Concerned With Resource-Efficient Housing

American Council for an Energy Efficient Economy
1001 Connecticut Avenue, NW, Suite 801
Washington D.C. 20036
(202) 429-8873

One of the leading energy policy and analysis organizations, ACEEE also provides timely information for consumers, builders and energy auditors through *Home Energy Magazine* and their excellent book, *Consumer Guide to Home Energy Savings*.

Rocky Mountain Institute
1739 Snowmass Creek Road
Snowmass CO 81654
(303) 927-3851

Rocky Mountain Institute (RMI), the publisher of this book, is a non-profit research and educational foundation with a vision across boundaries. Its mission is to foster the efficient and sustainable use of resources as a path to global security. The Institute's work reveals new solutions to old problems—mainly by harnessing the problem-solving power of market economics and of advanced techniques for resource efficiency. Founded in 1982 by Amory and Hunter Lovins, RMI has organized its research and outreach into five strongly interrelated programs – in Energy, Water, Agriculture, Economic Renewal, and Security. RMI's headquarters, located high in the Colorado Rockies, is a functioning example of resource efficiency and renewable energy. The structure has no heating system in a climate that gets as cold as -47°F, and costs about $5 a month for household electricity. Its energy savings paid for themselves in ten months. Yet it sets high standards of enjoyment, convenience, and beauty, and has already welcomed some 20,000 visitors. RMI is constantly churning out information, and has several publications available on home energy and water savings, including *Practical Home Energy Savings* listed in section 5C. See the end of this book for more information.

Smart House
400 Prince George's Boulevard
Upper Marlboro MD 20772-8731
(301) 249-6000

The Jetsons have come home, and they're living in a Smart House. The Electric Smart House is propelling energy usage into the 21st century. Sophisticated wiring systems and communication between electrically powered devices intelligently control energy use. Most of the innovations are in convenience—a television in every room and an air conditioner that turns itself off. The Smart House concept alone may not be a big energy saver, but combined with energy-efficient technologies, the potential for 50% savings on energy costs may become reality.

Intelligent Buildings Institute
2101 L. Street, N.W. Suite 300
Washington D.C. 20037
(202) 457-1988

An increasing number of commercial structures are using intelligent building systems. They are being retrofitted with electronic equipment that controls the use of advanced technology in the building's systems (electrical, HVAC, lighting, etc.). These systems minimize energy consumption by controlling energy use with precision without decreasing comfort. Paying attention to efficiency also pays off financially—reduced energy use means substantial cost savings for commercial buildings.

Energy Efficient Building Association
Northcentral Technical College
1000 Campus Dr.
Wausau,WI 54401
(715)675-6331

EEBA fosters the development and dissemination of technical information relating to the design, construction, and maintenance of energy-efficient buildings. They sponsor annual international conferences and expositions, organize technical seminars and workshops, including their "domicile" tour each year to countries which are leaders in energy-efficient house construction, and distribute a variety of publications on energy-efficient house design and construction. Write for a publications list. The Association can also provide referrals to sources of energy-efficient house plans.

Small Homes Council-Building Research Council
University of Illinois at Urbana-Champaign
One East Saint Mary's Road
Champaign IL 61820
(217)333-1801

The Council carries out research on and educates the public about all facets of house design and construction. Much of its work has focused on simplifying construction techniques and on adapting large-scale building techniques to the needs of the small builder. Efficient space utilization and energy conservation are key concerns. Findings are available through concise, nicely illustrated, and inexpensive booklets and reports. Write for a publications list, which includes a host of practical references that cover a wide variety of house construction and energy management topics. A few examples of these are: Heat Pumps, Summer Comfort, Illinois Lo-Cal House, Cooling Systems For The Home, Room Heaters, and Current House Construction Practices. Before ordering any publications, however, check when they were published; many are dated, though they still provide good background information.

Center for Maximum Potential Building Systems ("Max's Pot")
8604 F.M. 969
Austin TX 78724
(512)928-4786

"Max's Pot" works with clients throughout the western hemisphere to develop bioregionally sensitive land planning and building design with an emphasis on indigenous resources. This non-profit corporation has particular expertise in earthen building materials (adobe, rammed earth, caliche, and others), but has practical experience with a host of innovative techniques, some of which they originated. The Center offers ecological land planning and indigenous architectural design, product design and fabrication, laboratory analysis of earthen and other indigenous building materials, and is designing a demonstration resource-efficient farm for arid climates in collaboration with the Texas Department of Agriculture and Laredo Junior College. Call for a publications list.

Renew America
1400 Sixteenth Street, NW
Suite 710
Washington DC 20036
(202)232-2252

Renew America provides a focal point for the collection, evaluation, and dissemination of information that allows private and government agencies to identify and pursue solutions to environmental problems. It fosters the rapid, efficient expansion of successful environmental programs, and encourages cooperation among environmental interests. Issues covered in their *Searching for Success: Meeting Community Needs Through Environmental Leadership* ($10.00) include air pollution reduction, food safety, pesticide contamination reduction, and transportation efficiency. Other publications available for $10.00 include *Communities at Risk: Environmental Dangers in Rural America* and *Sustainable Energy*.

Illustration courtesy of *Tools For a Change*, proceedings of the Northeast Regional Appropriate Technology Forum.

4. Catalogs and Source Books Which Provide Access to Resource-Efficient Housing Information and Tools

This section highlights catalogs and sourcebooks which collectively provide access to thousands of products, publications, ideas, information, and insights that can help you use resources more efficiently.

Whole Earth Ecolog
The Best of Environmental Tools and Ideas
27 Gate Five Road
Sausalito CA 94965
October 1990

Brought to you by the talented and diverse crew of experts who produced *The Essential Whole Earth Catalog* (see below), *Ecologue* is a "Whole Earth Catalog" focused on environmental and ecological matters...a "snapshot" of applied ecology. Like its complementary companions, *Ecologue* is captivating, pushes the cutting edge, and is chock-full of where-to-find-it, did-you-know?, and who's-doing-good-work sorts of information.

The Essential Whole Earth Catalog
1986; 416 pp.
$20 postpaid from:
Whole Earth Review
27 Gate Five Road
Sausalito CA 94965
(415)332-1716

Like its contemporary-classic predecessors, this latest edition of *The Whole Earth Catalog* provides easy access to a vast array of subjects that reflect a wide range of human interest—from psychological self-care, building your own home or managing and operating a small business to beekeeping; and from grasslands preservation to desktop publishing, mysticism, ultralight aircraft, blacksmithing, and city restoration. These topics and more are covered in ten all-encompassing sections: whole systems, land use, community, household, craft, livelihood, health, nomadics, communications, and learning.

The Essential Whole Earth Catalog is an extraordinary evaluation and access tool. It helps users discover what is worth getting and how to get it. According to staff notes in its "Essentials" section, "*We're here to point, not sell. We have no financial obligation or connection to any of the suppliers listed. We only review stuff we think is great. Why waste your time with anything else? An item is listed in this Catalog if it is deemed: useful as a tool, relevant to independent education, high quality or low cost, and easily available by mail. The listings are continually revised and updated according to the experience and suggestions of Catalog users and staff. Latest news can be found in our magazine,* Whole Earth Review *(available from address cited above for $20/year (4 issues)*".

Furthermore, Stewart Brand, editor emeritus, says, "Of the 1962 items recommended here, 1086 are books, 297 are magazines, 579 are mail order suppliers. Each is an opportunity to learn a skill. In times even more in transition than the times that were a-changin' in the '60s, there is no safer and more rewarding strategy than the routine acquiring and use of new skills." Profusely illustrated and endlessly useful, *The Essential Whole Earth Catalog* is a timely encyclopedia for living in the modern world.

Ecologue: The Environmental Catalogue and Consumer's Guide for a Safe Earth

Bruce N. Anderson
September 1990
$18.95 postpaid from:
Order Services
Prentice Hall, a division of Simon & Schuster
1230 Avenue of the Americas
New York NY 10020

Noted *Solar Home Book* author Bruce Anderson's latest project is *Ecologue*, a catalogue for environmentally conscious consumers. *Ecologue* is the only book currently available that reviews, compares, and evaluates the cost, performance, energy efficiency, and effect on the environment of a wide range of products, many of them well-known brands, and tells readers where to get many hard-to-find items.

Ecologue is organized according to product use, such as Groceries, Household Cleaners, Clothing, Personal Care Items, Baby Care, Appliances, Transportation, and includes the most up-to-date information on recycling, disposing of hazardous waste, water conservation, photovoltaics, sunspaces, and environmental construction.

Appropriate Technology Sourcebook: A Guide To Practical Books For Village And Small Community Technology

Ken Darrow and Mike Saxenian
1986; 800 pp.
$17.95 paperback, $26.95 hardbound postpaid from:
Appropriate Technology Project
Volunteers in Asia
Box 4543
Stanford CA 94305
(415)326-8581

Though written primarily for people doing appropriate technology and community development work in developing countries, this densely packed, abundantly illustrated reference book will help folks living almost anywhere find sources of practical information for carrying out a great variety of small-scale technology projects. The *Sourcebook* reviews many of the most useful appropriate technology references—1,150 including publications, articles, and plans—from around the world. Price and ordering information are given for each. A diverse range of topics covered, including renewable energy, water supply and sanitation, agriculture, aquaculture, crop drying, preservation and storage, forestry, housing and construction, local communications, and transportation. The authors provide access to a wealth of how-to information in each of these areas, such as building a bridge, designing a cookstove to save fuel, surveying a field for irrigation, constructing a water-pumping windmill, replanting a forest, and installing a solar water-heating system. References featuring low-cost tools and techniques and the use of indigenous materials are emphasized.

Alternative Energy Engineering

1991-92 Catalog & Design Guide
P.O. Box 339
Redway CA 95560
(800)777-6609

From the "Alternative Living Capital of the World", Northern California, comes this wonderful little catalog. The suppliers live like they sell—in "the heart of what is left of redwood country", off the grid, and the owner even powers a solar car with the PV panels on the roof of the store. Because of the hands on experience of its producer, this catalog is able to provide excellent technical support and wisdom. Great for anyone interested in becoming self-sufficient.

Real Goods Alternative Energy Sourcebook

1991; 399 pp.
$14.00 from:
Real Goods
966 Mazzoni Street
Ukiah CA 95482-3471
(707)468-9214

Possibly the most complete reference for low energy, water and other resource use gadgets. From solar bumper stickers to water distillation equipment, solar-powered motorcycles to inverters, this book has what you need. Explanations of various technologies and essays on energy complete this resource. If you're wondering about where you can actually apply solar technologies, this book can give you ideas you never dreamed of. *Country Life* calls it "The Sears Catalog for people who live off the grid."

Real Goods Catalog

Quarterly; 71 pp.
Free from:
Real Goods
966 Mazzoni Street
Ukiah CA 95482-3471
(707)468-9214

A less overwhelming version of Real Goods *Alternative Energy Sourcebook*, this catalog offers up-to-date equipment for independent energy users. Subscribers to *Real Goods News* ($25.00) will receive the catalogs, quarterly issues of the *News*—more products plus articles on recent technologies, plus a copy of the *Sourcebook*.

Builders Booksource Catalog

Free from:
Builders Booksource
1817 4th Street
Berkeley CA 94710
(800)843-2028

Oh boy, a bookstore just for people who build things. The catalog is very comprehensive, covering every aspect of building with at least one good book, and usually with several—each with a review. The store carries many more titles (4000 in all) than are in the catalog. If you have special needs, ask for a reference. They'll probably have it.

Reviewed by J. Baldwin in *The Essential Whole Earth Catalog*

Illustration courtesy of Malcolm Wells, <u>An Architect's Sketchbook of Underground Buildings.</u>

5. Resource-Efficient Housing Design, Construction, and Retrofit

When we live close to our natural surroundings, we come to know and love them deeply and to build in ways which reflect our sense of joy in being a part of them. Our buildings come to connect us to rather than isolate us from the natural forces of the place, and they take their own form from the special spirit of the region which arises from its unique climate, geography and community of living things. Such buildings vent or hoard heat as needed in each climate. They shade or welcome the sun and wind, depending on the needs of each particular place. Their palette of color is attuned to the space-filling white light of snow country, the pastels of fog country, the green light of forest, or the golden sunsets of the tropics. They know their world and are fully a part of it.

Tom Bender in *In Context Magazine*, Autumn 1986

This section can help you identify those resource-efficient strategies which are most appropriate for your site, climate, budget, needs, and aesthetic preference.

There are a great many ways to incorporate resource efficiency into existing and new homes. Whether you are considering simply tightening up a drafty older home or undertaking the building of a superinsulated, passive-solar, or earth-sheltered new one, the references and organizations reviewed in this section can help you identify those resource-efficient strategies which are most appropriate for your site, climate, budget, needs, and aesthetic preference. In addition, they can guide you step-by-step through the decision making and design processes as well as the actual execution of the work.

5A. Primers On Resource-Efficient Housing Design

The Natural House Book
David Pearson
1989; 287 pp.
$19.95 paper
Simon & Schuster/Fireside
Rockefeller Center
1230 Avenue of the Americas
New York NY 10020
(201)767-5937

This book exalts a holistic approach to creating shelter with rich text and magnificent photographs and illustrations; the unique ideas and images inspire fresh thinking. *The Natural House Book* emphasizes ecologically sound homes which are also aesthetically pleasing and good for our personal well-being. The author recommends materials which are renewable and abundant, nonpolluting, energy efficient, durable, time-tested, low waste, and capable of being reused and recycled; such sustainable materials include earth, stone, and timber. Home design is discussed in terms of "systems" and "spaces" rather than the usual "rooms." A connection to history is felt throughout, as a return to simplicity of design and materials is stressed. This is a book that belongs in everyone's library, or better still on coffee tables where it is sure to be picked up, read, studied, and admired. Don't miss it.

Reviewed by Susan Hassol

Excerpts:

➤ *The home and its setting in the landscape symbolize our relationship with nature. A building can be constructed in such a way that it supports the natural ecology of the area—the vegetation, water, and wildlife—or it can be disruptive and damaging. Most buildings have a major impact on the local environment and unless the degree of disturbance is carefully controlled and the land restored afterward, the delicate ecological balance could be destroyed.*

➤ *For your home to be comfortable yet use as little energy as possible, working with nature rather than against it is the fundamental principle. The location, siting, and orientation are all vitally important if you are to gain the maximum benefit of winter sun but also make the most of shelter given by hills and trees against any prevailing winter winds and summer overheating. A well-sited, energy-efficient home will use the natural features of the locale and, therefore, will never have to draw on as much supplementary energy as one built without any regard for its surroundings.*

➤ *Think in fresh ways about the things you do at home—how you do them and why. Think "activities" and "processes" rather than "rooms." Think "spaces"—living spaces, sleeping spaces, kitchen spaces, bathing spaces, health spaces, and greenspaces.*

A Pattern Language (Towns, Buildings, Construction)

Christopher Alexander, Sara Ishikawa, and Murray Silverstein
1977; 1,169 pp.
$49.95 postpaid from:
Oxford University Press
2001 Evans Road
Cary NC 27513
(800)451-7556

This project is overwhelmingly ambitious—to establish a language for talking about what people really need from buildings and communities, drawing from many epochs and cultures, but focusing on our own. The genius of Alexander, *et al.*, is that they simply ignore the stylistic fad-mongering that passes for architectural thought, and get on with sensible, useful, highly distilled wisdom about what works and what doesn't. They're not shy about laying down rules of thumb ("Balconies and porches which are less than six feet deep are hardly ever used")—often with research citations to back them up, and charming, pointed illustrations.

The most important book in architecture and planning for many decades—a landmark whose clarity and humanity give hope that our private and public spaces can yet be made gracefully habitable.
Reviewed by Ernest Callenbach in *The Essential Whole Earth Review*

Excerpt:

➤ *In principle, any window with a reasonably pleasant view can be a window place, provided that it is taken seriously as a space, a volume, not merely treated as a hole in the wall. Any room that people use often should have a window place. And window places should even be considered for waiting rooms or as special places along the length of hallways.*

Green Architecture, Design for an Energy-Conscious Future

Brenda and Robert Vale
1991; 192 pp.
$40 hardback from:
Bulfinch Press
Little, Brown and Company
ISBN 0-8212-1866-2

The architecture of our buildings reflects our attitudes about the natural world and its resources, argue Brenda and Robert Vale. Thoreau's hut on Walden Pond, for example, came from a very different mindset on nature and resources than Philip Johnson's Glass House. *Green Architecture* outlines some of the environmental problems generated by current building practices, and presents a strong case for resource-efficient design. The Vales outline six principles: conserving energy, working with climate, minimizing new resources, respect for users, respect for site, and holism. The buildings used as examples of the six principles are from a refreshing mixture of cultures and climates. Descriptions of homes, offices, schools and other buildings are illustrated with plans, drawings, and photographs. Energy and other resource efficiency measures are discussed, although you'll need to brush up on metric units to translate some of the numbers. The authors go on to argue for the design of green cities and the development of a new attitude toward architecture and the natural environment. *Green Architecture* might not be directly useful for some homeowners, but it's a welcome addition to any library on environmentally responsive design.

Excerpts:

➤ *It is not just a question of respecting the site. For the green architect the site is the whole planet.*

➤ *The energy content of a material is clearly connected to its closeness to the earth; the more it is refined, the more energy it contains. However, it has to be remembered that the figures are in energy content per kilogram, and the the "low energy" materials are largely those that are used in bulk. Steel, while high energy, is not a mass material, but one used in carefully sized section to provide structural efficiency.*

> The 'green' approach to architecture is not a new approach. It has existed since people first selected a south-facing cave rather than one facing north to achieve comfort in a temperate climate. What is new is the realization that a green approach to the built environment involves a holistic approach to the design of buildings; that all resources that go into a building, be they materials, fuels or the contribution of the users, need to be considered if a sustainable architecture is to be produced.

How To Build An Underground House
Malcolm Wells
1991; 96 pp.
$12 postpaid from:
Malcolm Wells
673 Satucket Road
Brewster MA 02631
(508)896-6850

In his fourth book, Malcolm Wells once again, with wit and passion, takes us into another realm of architecture. "This is not a book of construction plans," states Wells. "It's more a scenario for the construction, written so you'll know what to expect when you decide to accept earth's invitation." Using more than 25 years experience with underground buildings, he presents the lessons and considerations that are involved in the design and construction of an underground house.

How To Build An Underground House, follows the construction of a single house. Through this process, Wells presents ideas that both increase the environmental responsiveness of the home, and make it a better, more beautiful place to live. Considerations about siting, structural systems, insulation, waterproofing, heating, cooling, plumbing, electrical systems, landscaping, and interiors are included. Discussing the various building elements with both a design/construction and an environmental view makes this book relevant for almost any new construction or work on existing homes.

Excerpts:

> Spend an imaginary year at your new house. Think of the seasons, the holidays, vacationtime shutdown, raging storms, the hottest time, the coldest. Picture carrying (reusable cloth) bags of groceries into the house during a raging rainstorm. Did you provide enough shelter at the door? Would someone in a wheelchair get soaked while you searched for the key? Are all the pipes and wires accessible? Do all this and walk the site, too, all in your mind, and your design will begin to evolve organically.

> "How much earth should I put on the Roof?" That's question no. 2. I've had success with a total of 2 feet: 18" of subsoil, and 6" of topsoil ... then some mulch. I've also had success, where no topsoil was available, by using town-collected street leaves placed directly on barren subsoil. The result was spectacular: a jungle. But then we had a lot of rain that year. You'll get good advice on rooftop soil depth from a local landscape architect or horticulturalist.

> If your windows are of the very best kind, if you've built a really tight house, and if you ventilate it by using a heat exchanger, you'll need little fuel indeed.

> A bit of stained glass in a high window will cast bands of colored light across the walls, illustrating the rotation of the earth.

Gentle Architecture

Malcolm Wells
1987; 178 pp.
McGraw-Hill
$19.95 postpaid from:
Malcolm Wells
673 Satucket Road
Brewster MA 02631
(508)896-6850

"American architecture is wandering aimlessly, producing pink and green buildings, and copies of temples! It is incredibly wasteful and destructive. *Gentle Architecture* starts with the land and tries to accommodate all creatures, not just the human one." That is how author/architect Malcolm Wells sums up his book, which is a concise, visionary, and philosophical volume on instilling in architecture a sense of responsibility for its impact on the environment. Wells mounts a scathing attack on the architectural trends of the day and proposes to counter those trends with enactment of a simple law: "leave the land no worse than you found it." Anyone interested in land use, planning, or architecture will find in this book the philosophical and theoretical underpinnings of why we, as a people, must start building with respect and even reverence for the planet we inhabit.

Excerpts:

➤ *Take away all governments and armies, take away all businesses and industries, take away cars, houses, cities, hospitals, schools and libraries; take away electricity, clothes, medicine and police; take away everything in fact, but the green plants, and most of us would survive. But take away the plants and we would all die. That's how important they are.*

➤ *Now, wouldn't you think that something that important—that vital—would have been communicated to the architects and engineers of America at some time during their education? Wouldn't you think that the value of land and the health of plants, each more precious than gold, would have been made the two top considerations by anyone about to tamper with the surface of the earth? You'd think so, all right, but in all the talk about planning and environment those central facts are almost never heard.*

➤ *Few construction practices today are based on reverence for life, but the next architecture of America will have to be. Its central rule will be this: Improve the land when you build, or don't build there.*

Climatic Design

Donald Watson AIA and Kenneth Labs
1983; 280 pp.
McGraw-Hill Book Co.
Manchester MO 63011
(Out of print; borrow from a library)

Climatic Design is attaining nearly biblical status among energy-conscious designers and architects. It's valuable as a reliable and comprehensive reference to anyone, but it's not bedtime reading. Much of the book is organized as a series of specific maxims, replete with text and drawings, that form parts of broad bioclimatic strategies such as "promote earth cooling" and "minimize infiltration." Some of the theory is obtuse and hard to use, but the bulk of the book is excellent background for those thinking about a new house in the broadest terms: site, orientation, and rough floor plans.

Reviewed by David Godolphin in *The Essential Whole Earth Catalog*

Excerpts:

➤ *A house can be made more energy efficient simply by designing the plan so that the order of rooms in which the normal daily sequence of activities occurs "follows" the path of the sun. This strategy is* complemented by, and most effective when combined with, partitioning the interior into separate heating and cooling zones, as recommended in subsequent techniques. By relating zones to sun movement, solar energy can be put to use when it is most available by direct orientation, and the call for mechanical heating or cooling can be minimized.

➤ Projections from the surface of the building shell can be used to increase the volume and velocity of air flow into the structure and to alter the flow pattern of air as it enters and travels through the interior. Appendages to the building shell are not a substitute for proper site planning and orientation, but these devices can enhance the building's ventilating ability under both normal and less than ideal conditions.

Modest Mansions: Design Ideas For Luxurious Living in Less Space
Donald Prowler
1985; 276 pp.
Rodale Press
(Out of print; check your local library)

You don't have to build a mansion to feel like you live in one. Taking the "smaller is better" credo to heart, *Modest Mansions* shows you how to get the most out of every nook and cranny in your home. Most homes today are poorly designed: they make inefficient use of space (unnecessarily raising already hefty price tags); are not particularly comfortable or fun to live in; and are costly to heat and cool. This book is filled with many great ideas for designing new smaller homes or remodeling existing ones to make them more attractive, affordable, space-efficient, and energy-efficient. Thoughtful attention is paid to almost every aspect of planning, constructing, and completing the compact house as well as to improving your present home. Perhaps most important, Prowler focuses on the principles and details of compact-house design which can help you truly make smaller homes beautiful, practical, and desirable. Lots of illustrative drawings, photographs, and case studies reinforce the book's principles.

Excerpts:

➤ To create a successful illusion of depth, a mirror should encompass an entire surface, covering a wall from corner to corner and from floor to ceiling. In this way, the mirror will reflect the edges of the room continuously, emphasizing the effect of perspective lines receding into the distance. A mirror that occupies only a part of a wall will be "read" as a mirror, for the wall upon which it is hung will serve as a reference, allowing us to judge the boundaries of the room.

➤ Too often, homeowners equate large rooms with comfort. This is unfortunate, because some of the most pleasant rooms of all are modestly sized and modestly furnished. Think, for example, of a sunlit breakfast nook, a cozy sleeping loft, or a cool screened porch. Home designers must learn to capture the spirit of these spaces for tomorrow's high-quality compact dwellings.

➤ The dynamic quality of natural light has the psychological effect of expanding the boundaries of a small room. The variability of the light connects us to the vast natural cycles—the diurnal and seasonal migration of the sun across the sky. In a modest mansion, enough window area can easily be included to give adequate general illumination throughout the house.

Tiny Houses: or How to Get Away From It All
Lester Walker
1987, 220 pp.
$27.95 postpaid from:
Overlook Press
Lewis Hollow Road
Woodstock NY 12498
(914)679-6838

Besides being very endearing, tiny houses occupy little space, use fewer resources to construct and maintain, and can be built for a pittance. Though "tiny" may be too claustrophobic for most people, author Lester Walker's insightful exploration into 40 tiny houses (the largest one featured is 365 square-feet) offers practical inspiration and guidance for those considering building a shelter for home, work, or get-away, on a modest scale. "Resource-efficiency" is integral to many of the designs, but emphasis is placed on space use.

Tiny Houses revels in the beauty of design where economy of space is paramount, without compromise of function. Tour the subject through history, from Henry David Thoreau's cabin on Walden Pond and George Bernard Shaw's writing hut to a contemporary portable shelter cart designed for the homeless city dweller and a "cottage in the woods" for the wilderness recluse. There are tiny houses featured here for the urban and rural setting, tiny houses designed for just eating, sleeping, meditation, drafting, and wood working, and tiny nomadic shelters for mobile people, just to name a few.

Over 1,000 friendly and informative line drawings and 100 black and white photographs bring the subject to life, illustrating construction sequences, birds-eye cut away perspectives, floor plans and furniture layouts, design details, and more. Just enough information is presented to rouse one to create their own tiny house and help get them started, but no complete blueprints or construction documentation are provided. You'll have to work out many of the details on your own and in the process will likely create a tiny house which best suits your individual needs. *Tiny Houses* speaks to the dream in those who want a special, intimate place in their lives for retreat.

Excerpts:

➤ *George Bernard Shaw, perhaps the most significant British playwright since the seventeenth century, wrote his most creative works, including his plays Pygmalion, Heartbreak House, Back to Methuselah, and Saint Joan, in a little writing hut at the bottom of his garden at his home in England. Shaw designed the hut himself as a tiny office built on a central steel-pole frame so that it could be manually rotated to follow the arc of the sun. He worked alone and loved his privacy; he even adjusted his telephone for outgoing calls only.*

➤ *By far, the least expensive method of siding a house is to use tar-impregnated building felt-tar paper. This type of cladding is usually viewed as an interim technology, used to protect the building until enough money is raised to install a more proper siding material over the tarpaper . However, as shown here, tarpaper can be an effective and somewhat pleasing finish material. Its life-span is about six years, varying with the climate, and if properly battened, it can last longer. Its advantages, beyond cost, are easy installation (staple gun) and heat absorption (the black color will gain heat from the sun).*

➤ *Egan describes his design problem as an architectural question: "Assuming a person must live temporarily on the sidewalk, how can we provide shelter that begins to offer the dignity each member of society deserves? His solution combines the symbols of an urban community (like the steep entrance steps, intended to create a personal "stoop") with the minimal function and material requirements of a portable, all-weather shelter. His resulting cart design grows from the basic concerns defined by the homeless themselves: shelter from climate extremes, safe storage of personal belongings, personal hygiene facilities, and privacy. The Portable Shelter Cart is one way to address a societal problem that demands discussion and a solution. It is included here because it is a tiny home that is a compassionate and thoughtful response to a most difficult and complex dilemma.*

Making Space: Design For Compact Living

Rick Ball
1989; 132 pp.
$18.90 postpaid from:
Overlook Press
Lewis Hollow Rd
Woodstock NY 12498
(914)679-6838

Small homes are more resource-efficient, but how small is too small? This book methodically reviews all facets of making the most of small living spaces or creating more space in larger ones. *Making Space* explores people's physical and psychological needs for space using fascinating examples through history, different cultures, and present day dwellers. Learn about space use in living quarters ranging from high-tech submarines and space shuttles, traditional, simple Japanese homes and the tents of nomadic Sahara desert dwellers, to contemporary New York City apartments.

Roughly half the book covers such subjects in academic detail while the rest addresses practical concerns, considerations, and solutions to a wide array of specific issues, such as one-room living, noise control, lighting, storage, decorating, and renovation. Walk through each living area and learn, through many nitty gritty details, the possibilities for best utilizing that space. The book encourages you to inspect what you have, tinker with that on the drawing board, and execute a well-thought-out renovation.

The book is liberally illustrated with diverse and intriguing photographs and drawings, which lighten up the book and make for fun browsing.

Excerpts:

➤ *Probably the most important lesson to be learned from the travelers and professional designers is to be aware of yourself and the way you live. The most underused small space of all, we are often told, is the human brain. It can be interesting and profitable to fire up a few brain cells on your design problem, and no one stands more chance of getting it right than you do. The whole point of designing and decorating your own space is to end up with a result that works for you and that you like living with.*

➤ *The eye is taken beyond the limits of a little room by painting the window frame in a bright color.*

➤ *Beware of gadgetry. Manufacturers of kitchen appliances have consistently reduced the versatility of utensils. Many can now perform only one specialized task—cooking only hot dogs or pancakes for example. These are a waste of space in small kitchens, unless you exist on hot dogs and pancakes. The great all-purpose kitchen was the servant, although people complained constantly about them not working properly. Servants made Georgian houses such flexible spaces. Servants running around the house carrying things to where they were needed meant no fixed services were necessary.*

➤ *The mirror's ability to reflect light can be used to brighten a dark room. Mirrors on the wall opposite the window reflect light back into the room.*

➤ *The sliding screen is one of the most inexpensive and effective ways of redefining your small space. Screens will provide instant visual privacy, for example, to create a temporary guest-room or to cut off the sight of a kitchen littered with the remains of dinner. Screens and doors that slide and fold are much easier to erect than permanent partition walls, and perhaps more importantly, they give you greater flexibility than solid walls, as they can be removed instantly when you want to open up the room to its maximum size.*

Regional Guidelines For Building Passive Energy Conserving Homes
AIA Research Corporation
1978; 312 pp.
(Out of print; available from the "government
documents" section of major libraries)

A house designed to operate energy-efficiently in Texas likely won't work well in Maine, which is the reason for this book. Depending on where you live, different climatic conditions—temperature, humidity levels, wind speeds, and sunshine—can be a liability or an asset in meeting your home heating or cooling needs. This fascinating book breaks down the country into 13 distinct climatic regions and reviews various strategies for designing and constructing passive, energy-conserving homes which are responsive to the environmental conditions found in each region. All the general principles and guidelines presented are reinforced with an abundance of excellent illustrations and numerous case-studies. Please note, however, that the climatic data presented here is representative for large regions; your microclimate may differ significantly. Use this book as a general reference and fine tune it with your own or other locals' firsthand experience.

Excerpts:

➤ *In summary, houses in the Appalachian climate should be well insulated against consistently cold temperatures. Compact floor plans, buffer spaces on exterior walls, and insulating shutters or drapes prevent unnecessary heat loss in winter. Massive or heavy building materials such as stone, brick, concrete or even logs should be used in combination with exterior insulation to store internal heat gains and temper outside temperature extremes. The house orientation, in addition to well placed openings and basement and attic vents, should allow the use of prevailing summer breezes for ventilation around and through the home.*

➤ *When these priority guidelines are successfully followed, several secondary guidelines can ensure the efficiency of the passive energy conserving home. Windows should be sized and placed to collect the southern sun in winter, but they should also be shuttered to prevent heat loss at night and shaded to prevent overheating in summer. Deciduous trees and proper overhang design allow the low winter sun to penetrate south-facing windows for passive solar heating but block the higher summer sun. Evergreen trees, earth berms and tight construction can prevent unnecessary infiltration from the northwest while allowing for the blessings of summer breezes from the south and southwest.*

➤ *All entrances should be sheltered from the cold winter winds by proper placement, wing walls or the addition of airlock vestibules. Finally, home designs should avoid creating additional humidity through the addition of pools of water or heavy planting in the direction of the prevailing winds, and maximize the use of desiccation and natural ventilation systems for non-mechanical comfort.*

More Other Homes And Garbage: Designs For Self-Reliant Living

Jim Leckie, Gil Masters, Harry Whitehead, and Lilly Young
1981; 370 pp.
$14.95 postpaid from:
Sierra Club Books
730 Polk Street
San Francisco CA 94109
(415)923-5600

More Other Homes and Garbage is a comprehensive reference on the theory and application of home resource efficiency and small-scale renewable energy use. The book covers alternative architecture, small-scale generation of electricity, solar heating principles, waste handling and water supply systems, and home gardening and aquaculture. Both practical and philosophical aspects are addressed. Its authors, all engineers, have done a credible job translating sophisticated technical concepts into understandable language. Although parts of the book contain more engineering calculations, charts, maps, and tables than the average reader will need (they are there for people who want to understand the science or engineering behind the application), the clear text and outstanding illustrations keep things on solid, comprehensible ground. Though many new technologies have emerged since this book was published, it still serves as a valuable primer and detailed reference for those who want to make their home more resource efficient.

Excerpts:

➤ *We cannot turn our backs on the fact that we live in a highly industrialized society. Where sophisticated technologies serve our goal and can be used effectively to reduce the depletion of resources, they should become a part of our alternative architecture. But we advocate an architecture that relates to its environment in the same way that primitive architecture does: symbiotically. To reduce energy and material waste, we must design simpler, smaller structures that use less highly processed building materials, that reuse discarded materials, and that make more permanent use of both...Above all, we must be willing to adjust our habits, physiology, and psychology, opening ourselves to the wonders and limits of the earth where we abide our little while.*

➤ *There has evolved a hierarchy of strategies for dealing with the maintenance of a comfortable thermal environment within a building. The first priority is energy conservation. Until the heating requirement for a residence is reduced to its lowest practical value, it makes little sense to attempt to derive a significant fraction of that demand with solar techniques. It is generally easier and cheaper to control heat losses than to supply solar gains. The same is true on the cooling side. The best single element in a cooling strategy is simply not to let the sun and heat into the building in the first place.*

Building an Environmentally Friendly House

Nadav Malin and Alex Wilson
1991; 41 pp.
$5.00 from:
Massachusetts Audubon Society
Lincoln MA 01773
(617)259-9500

A no-nonsense publication that describes the most effective actions needed to live in an environmentally friendly house. All the steps in building or living in a house are addressed, from choosing a site to reducing garbage. The bulk of the book builds on materials from a previous publication on superinsulation, and the resulting issues, such as moisture control, proper ventilation, are not left to chance. This book is short on frills but is full of resource efficiency common sense.

Excerpts:

➤ *During the construction process, a great deal of solid waste is produced, much of which can be salvaged or recycled. Although it may not be cost-effective to have a builder spend a lot of time dealing with waste reduction because of the high labor costs, it might be a good way for the homeowner to get involved. If you want to help with the waste disposal process, ask your builder which piles of debris are on their way to the dump and if they'd mind your sorting through them. Better yet, you might offer to sort all their construction waste into different piles for reuse, recycling and disposal by type. There might be insurance concerns to consider, so respect the builder's requests.*

➤ *In an ordinary, leaky house, air exchange varies widely from day to day, depending on such variables as wind speed, outdoor temperature, and how often you open doors. Ventilation tends to be excessive on cold windy days, and it may be inadequate on very calm days. Far more effective is a deliberately planned and controlled ventilation system.*

➤ *If you've chosen to build a new house on previously undeveloped land, there are a number of steps you can take to minimize damage to the local environment. Although it is common practice for builders to clear a large area around the house site, more and more contractors are becoming aware of the value of preserving existing vegetation wherever possible. Preservation of trees and shrubs protects indigenous plants and wildlife habitats, in addition to providing valuable shade and shelter for you.*

The Integral Urban House: Self-Reliant Living In The City
Helga Olkowski, Bill Olkowski, Tom Javits, and the Farallones Institute Staff
1979; 484 pp.
$14.95 postpaid from:
Sierra Club Books
730 Polk Street
San Francisco CA 94109
(415)923-5600

You don't have to live in the country to adopt a self-reliant lifestyle. This inspiring book proves that point by describing dozens of little and big ways in which city dwellers, primarily those living in single-family houses or low-rise apartments with at least a tiny bit of land around them, can reduce their dependence on centralized systems to provide their basic needs. The book's main focus is the Integral Urban House, a pioneering research project in Berkeley, California, established to demonstrate the viability of a urban residence integrating its inhabitants' life-support systems in ways that conserve energy and resources and provide a healthy, thriving living environment. This comprehensive reference explores the fundamental design and lifestyle issues central to any such effort. Its pages are filled with clear and interesting ecological, philosophical, and practical information on conserving energy and water resources, managing wastes, using solar energy, establishing indoor and outdoor food gardens, raising small livestock, managing pests and wildlife, and dealing with the links between the House and the neighborhood. It includes lots of handsome and useful illustrations, tables, and charts.

Excerpts:

➤ *We advise people to develop an overall plan for the total integrated system but when beginning the actual work to start small. Choose to develop first those areas of life-support that have immediate economic rewards, that are easiest to establish and manage, and for which you either already possess or can easily obtain the expertise. Gradually build towards greater self-reliance as the initial projects prove successful. If you start by conserving the energy and resources you already have, your efforts will make an immediate difference and give you a base from which to approach the more difficult tasks of producing your own food or the more glamorous ones of creating and installing hardware of solar technology.*

➤ *Urban dwellers tend to become insensitive to the microclimate variations of their habitat in a way that farmers can never afford to do. When you begin to raise some of your own plants, particularly* when these plants are to produce food that will sustain you, you become aware of your outdoor living spaces in a new way. How the sunlight and shade move and the winds blow are once again significant. Small, warm, protected areas are cherished. It becomes a challenge to make productive use of cool, shady, or otherwise "wasted" spaces. Compost bins and dry-leaf storage areas may fit with the corner of a sunny balcony with containers of tomatoes. Because of the small scale involved, you will discover a great many ingenious methods for modifying temperature, humidity, and wind that would require far too much labor and too many materials for the farmer.

Breaking New Ground
John N. Cole and Charles Wing
1986; 237 pp.
Little, Brown and Company
(Out of print; borrow from a library)

Witty and accurate, this book is a collection of lengthy letters between Cole, a writer building his dream home, and his friend Wing, a physicist and one of the fathers of the U.S. owner-builder movement. The letters are great. Stories, jokes, and romantic visions of the perfect home are interspersed with very useful and practical information. The dialogue between the two friends covers most aspects of building a home. Siting, materials, foundations, framing and sheathing, insulation, windows, solar heating, wiring, and plumbing are tackled as the men trade questions and insights. These two authors covered much of the same ground in their 1976 book, *From the Ground Up* and in Wing's 1979 work, *From the Walls In*. But the style and format of *Breaking New Ground* breathes a new life into the information and gives you an idea of what kinds of decisions, problems, and options you will be facing once you begin building your own home; it reveals that building a home that is harmonious with nature and meets your needs entails much more than figuring out how to run drainpipes to the second-story bathroom.

Excerpts:

➤ *We want style, aesthetics, ease of maintenance, enough contact with nature to extend our horizons, and enough flexibility to allow for the return of some of those now-grown children when they visit. We also want a place that has a strong sense of order and simplicity, is easy to clean, and is convenient to put in secure limbo if we decide to take a trip for a week or so. And, in addition to all that, we want a home that can respond to each of the definite seasons that bless us north of the fortieth parallel.*

➤ *After getting this far with the new home, I've decided that what I've always said about building houses is more true than ever: A building is enclosed space with more decisions than nails holding it together.*

➤ *For every dimension of every design of every space there are dozens of options and thus hundreds of dozens of decisions, because the builder, owner, designer has to choose from combinations of options. And guys like you, with your bushels of detailed information, can sometimes make the process more difficult. After all, think how simple a foundation/basement choice might be if we were ignorant of each alternative.*

➤ *There are tremendous thermal benefits to be gained from insulating outside a concrete wall with rigid extruded polystyrene. First, counter to intuition, concrete is a lousy insulator. A single inch of foam insulation has the same thermal resistance as 5 feet of concrete. As a result, 15 to 25 percent of the winter heat loss of a typical home occurs through its concrete foundation. Second, large quantities of heat energy can be stored in a concrete wall with small changes in temperature. The thermal mass of the wall acts like a flywheel, holding the building at a constant temperature. As a result, the interior living space of the building becomes less responsive to swings in outside temperature.*

5B. Building Science

A house is a complex system of interrelated elements. It typically incorporates hundreds of building materials and products, dozens of structural assemblies, numerous space conditioning and domestic appliances, and a host of personal furnishings and consumer goods. The choice and assembly of these elements determines not only what the structure costs to build, but also its ongoing operation and maintenance costs, its comfort, its indoor environmental quality, and ultimately its longevity. Learning about the science of building technology—the characteristics, applications, and performance of each building element, individually and in concert with each other—can help create the most cost-effective, energy-efficient, healthy, and durable houses possible. The construction of energy-efficient housing has, in particular, raised many concerns about indoor air quality and building longevity—poorly detailed or ventilated building shells can lead to rotting problems. The following resources can help you avoid such problems and others by giving you a fundamental understanding of many building science basics.

Residential Indoor Air Quality & Energy Efficiency
Peter du Pont and John Morrill
1989; 267 pp.
$24.50 from:
American Council for an Energy-Efficient Economy
1001 Connecticut Ave. NW, Ste. 801
Washington DD 20036
(202)429-8873

This fairly technical book dispels the myth that tight, energy-efficient construction must necessarily lead to indoor air quality problems. After explaining the principles of infiltration and mechanical ventilation in homes, it devotes separate chapters to the sources and health effects of radon, combustion pollutants, organics and asbestos, and moisture and biological contaminants. The two final chapters cover monitoring and mitigation techniques. Lots of charts and graphs give the technical data behind the conclusions. There is no better source that cuts across all the major indoor pollutants.

Excerpts:

➤ *Two premises are central to this handbook. The first is that, as a human health issue, indoor air quality is much more important than outdoor air quality. The second premise results from research over the past decade into the primary causes of indoor air pollution: pollutant sources in or under the home, rather than changes in the ventilation rate, are the major cause of indoor air pollution.*

➤ *A tight house will not have a pollution problem unless there are strong pollutant sources—and not even then if appropriate measures are taken. Conversely, a leaky house will not necessarily contain healthy air if there are substantial pollutant sources present.*

➤ *Formaldehyde is used as a component in the glue that binds pressed-wood building materials (plywood and particleboard) and in some consumer products. Unfortunately, formaldehyde gas gradually escapes ("offgases") from these products into indoor air and can cause a variety of health effects even at the low levels typically found indoors.*

Building Science/Moisture Control Handbook

Joseph Lstiburek
1991; 250 pp.
$40 postpaid from:
Building Science Corporation
273 Russett Road
Chestnut Hill MA 02167
(617)323-6552

This unique construction and renovation manual authoritatively challenges many popular approaches to building houses in both cold and hot climates and offers alternatives based on the fundamentals of building science. Lstiburek chronicles the changes in construction techniques and materials over the last 50 years which have had major impacts on buildings' performance and durability. The recent development of better insulated and tighter homes, he notes, has created a myriad of problems affecting building durability and indoor air quality. The handbook explores these problems in depth and then clearly explains how to construct new homes or renovate existing ones to get durable, healthy, problem-free results. North America is broken down into three broad climatic zones—heating, cooling, and mixed, with specific construction practices recommended for each. The theory behind each technique described and much of its practical, nuts-and-bolts detail is covered in the text and excellent supporting illustrations.

The book's treatment of the fundamentals of building envelope design is the best we've seen anywhere. For example, eight principles required to construct a durable building envelope are outlined. Likewise, there is other comprehensive, hard-to-find information which can help you answer questions about vapor-barrier detailing, insulation placement, and ventilation requirements, to name just a few topics. A series of classic papers on theoretical building science wraps up the book and lends credence to previous discussions. Though more in-depth than most people may care to pursue, this book contains information that is particularly valuable to anyone considering upgrading or building a home.

Excerpts:

➤ *Significant material durability problems exist with currently utilized polyethylene films in the residential construction industry. These problems include UV degradation, thermal oxidation, thermal degradation, chemical attack, biological attack and built-in manufacturing process "pre-aging."*

➤ *Any material or system of materials may be used as an air barrier if the following requirements are met:*
1) The material, or system, must be continuous.
2) The material, or system, must be impermeable to air (allowing not more than .1 litres of air to pass through the system per second per square meter at 75 Pascals).
3) The material, or system, must be able to withstand the air pressure loads which act on it. That is, in addition to the influence of mechanical systems and stack action, the local minimum wind loads must be taken into account.
4) The material or system must be adequately stiff or rigid to maintain pressure equalization behind exterior cladding in order to control rain penetration under fluctuating wind pressures.
5) The material, or system, must be durable and easy to maintain over the service life of the building.

➤ *The entire combustion air/make-up air issue [for gas-oil-and wood-burning appliances] can be dealt with by the application of a single principle: aerodynamically uncouple all combustion equipment from the influence of house interior air pressures. The only acceptable method of accomplishing this is to install equipment that is not sensitive to interior air pressure variations. Such equipment includes induced draft gas furnaces, condensing gas furnaces, sealed combustion equipment, balanced flue devices, and pulse combustion equipment. While induced draft devices require combustion air from within the house, they have power fans to mechanically exhaust the products of combustion. That is, such devices mechanically induce a draft to occur and as such do not require draft control air to operate nor do they have a tendency to backdraft from negative pressures that may occur within the house enclosure, since they are not influenced by interior house pressures.*

Builder's Field Guide to Energy Efficient Construction
Produced for the Bonneville Power Administration by the
Oregon State University Energy Extension Program
1991; 140 pp.
Contact:
New Residential Section
Bonneville Power Administration
RMRB
P.O. Box 3621
Portland OR 97208
(503) 230-5630

The Northwest has it's act together when it comes to energy efficiency. This book helps builders comply with the region's above average energy code. Detailed drawings accompany instructions for installing the nitty gritty of energy efficiency—insulation, vapor barriers, efficient HVAC systems, etc. Somewhat tailored to the Northwest builder, it is nonetheless an excellent publication for people who build buildings anywhere.

Excerpt:

➤ *Water heaters on a basement slab on grade (in a garage, for instance) must have a non-compressible insulated pad of R-10 or better placed under them. The R-10 pad is typically two inches of blue, pink or green extruded polystyrene foam insulation. If you use white expanded polystyrene, you'll need a three-inch pad since it has a lower R-value per inch. White bead board also has less compressive strength and may provide less stability than the blue, pink and green products.*

➤ *To achieve a high wall R-value, you may need to apply rigid foam sheets over the wall framing in addition to the cavity insulation. If the foam sheeting is applied to the interior surface of a wall, a few extra steps can create a continuous wall air barrier. The advanced air leakage control package is complete when the wall air barrier is finally connected to the floor and ceiling air barrier.*

Residential Building Design & Construction Workbook
Second Edition
J.D. Ned Nissan
1988; 347 pp.
$95.00 from:
Cutter Information Corp.
37 Broadway
Arlington MA 02174-5539
617/648-8700
800/888-8939

This nitty gritty workbook was created to "provide the practicing field professional with a working manual of construction techniques and background information." The first section reviews the principles of superinsulated housing. Subsequent sections cover the brass tacks of building an efficient house. Each section presents the theory—how do air, moisture, and heat pass through and interact with various building components—and then covers the materials and construction details for addressing those issues. Wondering how to do airtight drywall? what Tyvek is and how to install it? how densely cellulose insulation should be blown into walls to avoid settling? how to frame a corner that can be well insulated? how to select and install a window or a mechanical ventilation system? This book has it all, including appendices that list manufacturers. The book is not slick: it's comb bound, and some of the chapters are inserted directly from other publications with different graphic and type styles. It's also not current on gas-filled superwindows, but we know of no better nuts and bolts construction guide.

Excerpts:

➤ *Install the ceiling air/vapor barrier before the interior partitions. The advantage of this sequence is that the air/vapor barrier can be installed quickly and easily, in a few large pieces, with little or no cutting and sealing around partition top plates.*

➤ *Some builders express concern that insulating a foundation wall increases the hazard of damage from frost heave because there is no longer enough heat escaping from the foundation to keep the ground from freezing. There is absolutely no evidence to support this fear. The way to prevent this problem, however, is not to warm the soil with heat from the house, but rather to properly drain the soil around the foundation.*

Canadian Building Digest
250 issues in print
Whole set price: $50

and

Building Practice Notes
62 issues in print
Single copies vary, between $5 and $25 per issue

Both available from:
Institute For Research In Construction
National Research Council
Montreal Road
Ottawa, Ontario, K1A0R6,
Canada
(613)993-2054
Write for publication list and current pricing

Canadian Building Digest is an extraordinary serial encyclopedia of practical building science broken down into 250 or so topical areas which are concisely reviewed in handy 3-6-page guides. Each *Digest* covers a specific building material, construction technique, design methodology, maintenance procedure, climatic force, indoor health issue, or environmental factor affecting human comfort. Coverage spans houses to skyscrapers and is so clearly presented that both building professionals and laypeople will, for the most part, find it interesting and useful. There is lots of hard-to-find, nitty-gritty information in *Canadian Building Digest* relevant to resource-efficient housing. Emphasis is, as you'd expect, on Canadian climate and buildings, but most of the Guides are every bit as applicable in the States. New Guides are added on occasion and outdated ones (the series was started in 1960) dropped. Examples of a few *Canadian Building Digest* titles are: Airtight Houses and Carbon Monoxide Poisoning, Buildings and Life-Cycle Costing, Principles of Solar Shading, Fire and Plastic Foam Insulation Material, Ground Temperatures, Moisture Problems In Houses, and Interior Lighting Design and Energy Conservation.

Building Practice Notes is very similar to *Canadian Building Digest*, but each issue is more lengthy (typically 8-60 pages), comprehensive, and oriented toward the design professional. Topics covered run the gamut from The Principles and Dilemmas of Designing Durable House Envelopes For The North and How To Reduce Noise Transmission Between Apartments to The Installation, Practice And Reliability of Add-On Heat Pumps and Recognizing and Controlling Termites And Carpenter Ants.

Foam-Core Panels & Building Systems
Steve Andrews
1988; 130 pp.
$49.00 from
Cutter Information Corp.
37 Broadway
Arlington MA 02174-5539
(617)648-8700
(800)888-8939

The 1980s saw a rapid proliferation in the use of prefabricated foam-core panels to form part of the exterior envelope of buildings. Foam-core panels are used in everything from low-cost modular housing to the most elegant custom built adobe and timber-frame homes. This book provides all the theory and practical advice needed to sort through the various systems on the market, and offers labor-saving tips, case studies, cost information, and a product directory. The current volume is a bit dated, particularly on product listings, but a new edition is due out in 1992.

Excerpts:

➤ *Nearly every manufacturer claims that its product leads to tight construction. . . It should be noted, however, that tightness is not an automatic feature. Achieving a degree of tightness will still require good caulking and air sealing at critical locations and times during construction.*

➤ *Panel placement starts at one corner. Getting the first one level and fully seated is worth a small fortune in avoided problems. Keep checking for level as you nail off both the inside and outside facings at the base plate. Thereafter, leveling every panel is just as critical. Keep a pry bar and sledge hammer handy.*

Reducing Home Building Costs with Optimum Value Engineered Design and Construction
1977; 133 pp.
$10 from:
National Association of Home Builders Research Center
400 Prince George's Blvd.
Upper Marlboro, MD 20772-8731
(301)249-4000

Commissioned by the U.S. Department of Housing and Urban Development, this modest little book contains a wealth of labor and material cost cutting techniques for typical wood frame construction. The book claims to offer savings of 12% compared to conventional practice by designing the house on 2-foot modules to minimize material waste, clustering plumbing facilities, and eliminating or reducing the size of components that typically exceed code requirements. The book does not focus on energy-saving opportunities, but its suggestions can certainly be adapted to energy-conscious designs.

Excerpts:

➤ *Many building codes and standards specifically permit 2x4 studs to be spaced up to 24 inches on center in single story homes and in the second story of two-story homes. The 2-foot spacing reduces the number of framing members to be handled in the field by one-third compared to the traditional 16-inch spacing.*

➤ *The use of 2x3 studs spaced at 24 inches on center for nonloadbearing partitions is acceptable under most building codes. The useable floor area is increased perhaps 12 to 14 square feet in a typical home, and occupants are generally unaware of any difference compared to a traditional 2x4 wall.*

5C. Weatherizing / Retrofitting Existing Houses

Part of every household dollar you spend on electricity, gas, oil, or firewood doesn't pay for what you actually *use,* but for what you *waste.* Few people deliberately waste energy, but when it comes to energy efficiency, few of us do as well as we could.

Energy "leaks" from homes in dozens of ways. Some of these leaks are lifestyle choices: standing in front of open refrigerators trying to decide which leftovers to grab; leaving lights on all over in the house while reading the evening paper; and neglecting to maintain heating and cooling systems in top operating condition. Other energy-wasters, though, are built right into homes and appliances. Single-pane glass and poorly insulated walls and roofs do an inadequate job of keeping homes comfortable. Fireplaces suck out more heat than they contribute. The little heaters sandwiched in refrigerator walls keep them frost-free, but contribute to energy bills.

How many hard-earned dollars go to pay for such energy leaks? If you and your home are modestly energy-conserving—neither better or worse than most others—a year's worth of wasted energy could pay for a new television, a plush living room couch, or maybe even a vacation. Fixing up your home to be more energy-efficient will save money through *avoided* electricity and fuel bills. Investing in energy efficiency can offer better returns than money-market funds or certificates of deposit. And besides saving money, your investment will enhance your home's comfort.

The publications in this section can show you many ways to upgrade the energy efficiency of your home. The techniques range from simple weatherstripping of doors and windows or "tune-ups" of existing appliances to the all-out superinsulated retrofit of a house's shell or replacement of its heating system. One strategy to consider for doing this work is to undertake the easier, less expensive options first, then use the resulting savings on your utility bills to finance the larger, more expensive retrofits.

547 Tips for Saving Energy in Your Home
Roger Albright
1990; 120 pp.
$5.95 from:
Storey Publishing
P.O. Box 445
Schoolhouse Road
Pownal VT 05261
(800) 827-8673

For the homeowner who wants to save energy *now,* this publication is full of practical, down-to-earth energy advice. Quick, easy-to-read tidbits explain each action, why it will save you energy, and how much it will reduce your energy bills. According to the author "the first idea you try will more than pay for this book—all the rest of your savings will be pure profit." The wide range of topics cover conserving home energy room-by-room, saving hot water, gardening for energy efficiency, and saving automobile energy costs. A chapter is devoted to helping apartment and condominium dwellers cut energy consumption. A very straightforward and practical book, you'll have no reason not to start saving energy and money right now.

Excerpts:

➤ *More than 70% of home energy costs consists of heating space and water, making them the "hot spots" for energy conservation.*

➤ *An open chimney damper on a fireplace or woodstove not in use will exhaust more heat than an open window.*

➤ *Sunshine is not only a source of warmth, but also, of course, a source of light at the same time. Flicking on the light switches in the daytime may be a habit you can break just by rearranging the furniture.*

➤ *Do you need to talk yourself into a lower thermostat setting? Here's an argument. Your plants are healthier in the cooler air.*

Cut Your Electric Bill In Half
Ralph Herbert, Ph.D.
1986; 152 pp.
Rodale Press
(Out of print; check your local library)

Cussing about skyrocketing electricity bills won't help save you any money, but this step-by-step, how-to guide can. It outlines practical, straightforward approaches to slashing household electric costs without sacrificing comfort or convenience. Herbert reviews the typical energy performance and operating costs of the electricity-consuming tasks carried out in homes: space and water heating, air conditioning, refrigeration, lighting, cooking, clotheswashing, dishwashing, and others. He then clearly lays out strategies for accomplishing each job more efficiently, discussing any significant limitations which may be involved. The costs and benefits of a variety of simple as well as more involved options are covered. For example, he discusses using existing appliances more efficiently, replacing them with new energy-saving ones, and, where appropriate, substituting renewable-powered devices—solar collectors, woodstoves, etc. Efficiency is treated as the first essential step in all of Herbert's recommendations. Following his advice can in fact save up to 80% on electric hot water, air conditioning, and space heating costs and up to 50% on lighting, cooking, and refrigeration costs. Given the extraordinarily rapid development of new energy-saving technologies, however, it is possible to take even greater strides today by using newly-available devices which are more efficient than those Herbert describes. His survey is thus no longer state-of-the-art in all departments, but nonetheless extremely useful as a broad introduction to the subject.

Excerpts:

➤ *Running electricity through a high-resistance coil in order to heat air or water makes very little sense, and recognizing this is a first step toward trimming your monthly electric bill. The appropriate use of electrical energy is that of running motors and solid-state equipment. Thus, for $1, you will probably get a year's use of your blender—44 hours—or 18 hours of work out of your automatic clothes washer. You will only get about 2 hours from your water heater, however, and only about 3.5 hours from your oven for the same dollar. It could easily cost you $1 to $1.50 to cook a Sunday roast, and it will cost $2 to $2.50 at future rates.*

➤ *When selecting a gas-fueled water heater, look for "regulated power combustion," which gives a better fuel/air mixture and a more efficient burn. With an electronic ignition, you will not need a constantly burning pilot light and this will also mean fuel savings.*

Practical Home Energy Savings
David Bill and Rocky Mountain Institute Staff
1991; 51 pp.
$8.00 postpaid from:
Rocky Mountain Institute
1739 Snowmass Creek Road
Snowmass CO 81654-9199

Can we toot our own horn and say this is perhaps the most *useful* publication RMI has ever written? This booklet is a truly down-to-earth, nuts-and-bolts guide to energy savings for the average man and woman on the street—or in the mountains, or on an island. *Practical Home Energy Savings* contains a cornucopia of savings tips. The book is clearly, even humorously, written. Yet, there is enough detail so that all the homeowner or renter needs besides this book in order to actually achieve incredible energy savings is a trip to the hardware store. Sure, there are some high-tech suggestions here— but they are recommended only after the unglamorous solutions are exhausted— solutions like caulk, water-heater blankets, and curtains. The appendices are as valuable as the text, and include sources—such as state energy offices, mail-order outfits, and federally funded information sources—and a comparison chart of energy-efficiency measures, which lists cost, savings per year, avoided emissions of CO_2, and payback period. *Practical Home Energy Savings* is a sure bet for homeowners, renters, or folks building a new home.

Excerpts:

➤ *Practical Home Energy Savings is designed to give you the information you need to cut your energy bills and reduce the impact of your home or apartment on the environment.*

➤ *To us, "practical" means simple and cost-effective (within a five-year payback period). While many cost-effective measures like installing solar panels and major retrofits of new energy saving devices enhance your home's efficiency, what you'll find as you read this book are the simple measures you can do. If you're interested in pursuing energy efficiency further, we've cited references and "1-800" numbers you'll find helpful.*

➤ *Implementing the technologies described in this booklet allows you to be part of the solution. You can invest $20 in one low-flow showerhead and save $35-75 per year or take the whole house on.*

➤ *"Insulate an apartment I'll live in for six months max?" We hear it again and again: "But I rent!" Of course you're not about to put your next paycheck into storm windows for the apartment your landlord owns. But aren't you paying the utility bills? Aren't you the one who has to live with drafts and frost on the INSIDE of the window? It's a set up for inefficient and wasteful housing. The landlord buys the cheapest refrigerator available, which is likely to be the least efficient, and you pay the electrical bills. Break the cycle. You do have a stake in efficient housing. So does your landlord who'll find it easier to rent the more cozy and energy-efficient apartment.*

➤ *Make tightening the skin of your home or apartment your first priority. An average house in the U.S. has about five square feet of air leaks which account for 30-40% of the heating and cooling bill.*

➤ *It's a cinch to replace your existing showerhead with a low-flow model. For $10—$20, you can cut conventional showerhead use by one half or more—without sacrificing the quality of your shower. Don't settle for "flow restrictors," which are special washers fit between the shower head and arm— these deliver something more like a Northwest drizzle than a satisfying downpour.*

➤ *Would you believe that as Americans we buy 45 million appliances each year to cool our beer, heat our chili, clean our laundry, squash our garbage, and dehumidify our air?*

➤ *Heating water accounts for some 90% of the energy consumed by a clothes washer. Short of washing your clothes less often (which might not hurt either), use the warm wash cycle, rinse in cold water, and wash full loads (or use the low water-level setting). If you're in the market for a new one, buy a front loader. These use about half the energy of top loaders, because they need less water to clean the same load of wash.*

> Efforts such as yours mean our nation's energy bills today are about $150 billion less than they would have been if we still used energy as inefficiently as we did in 1973. But if we were as efficient as Western Europe and Japan, we would save an additional $200 billion a year. That's enough to wipe out the federal deficit or put an extra $800 a year back in the pockets of every woman, man, and child in the United States. Indeed, by the year 2000, just by choosing the best energy buys, we could save several trillion of today's dollars—more than enough to pay off the entire national debt!

Consumer Guide to Home Energy Savings

Alex Wilson and John Morrill
1992; 220 pp.
$6.95 postpaid from:
ACEEE
1001 Connecticut Ave. NW, Suite 535
Washington DC 20036
(202)429-8873

This is truly the book we've all been waiting for. Now, finally, we have a comprehensive listing of energy efficient-products, with ample text to guide us through a selection process. The practical guidelines in the *Consumer Guide to Home Energy Savings* do not beg readers to turn off the lights, put on sweaters, and shiver in the dark. Instead, they outline a positive approach to saving the earth while saving money in realistic, clearly described steps that include plenty of detailed product information. The book lists virtually every superefficient appliance model by brand name and model number in easy-to-read tables that accompany the descriptive text. Readers are respectfully given plenty of information, and are then objectively left to make their own choices. While the text is a bit technical, the charts are easy to follow. This book is clearly a "must" for anyone interested either in helping the environment or in just saving money.

Excerpts:

> If your furnace or boiler is old, worn out, inefficient, or significantly oversized, the simplest solution is to replace it with a modern high-efficiency model. Old coal burners that were switched over to oil or gas are prime candidates for replacement, as are gas furnaces without electronic (pilotless) ignition or a way to limit the flow of heated air up the chimney when the heating system is off (vent dampers or induced draft fan).

> A typical heating system will last about 25 years, though some boilers can last twice that long. Your heating system technician or energy auditor may be able to help you evaluate your existing system and decide whether replacement is a good idea. If you're not going to replace it, see the sections on Maintenance and Modifications for ways to boost its efficiency and performance.

> Before you actually start shopping for a new furnace or boiler it pays to figure out how large a system you need. A system that is too large wastes fuel and money because it keeps cycling on and off. It only runs at peak efficiency for short periods of time and spends most of the time either warming up or cooling down. Many existing systems that were installed in the 1950s and 60s are way too large. It is not uncommon for a heating system to be two or three times as large as necessary.

> If you live in a cold climate, it usually makes sense to invest an extra few hundred dollars for the highest efficiency system available. In milder climates with lower annual heating costs, the extra investment required to go from 80% to 90-95% efficiency will be hard to justify.

Retrofit Right: How to Make Your Old House Energy Efficient
Sedway Cooke Associates
1983; 180 pp.
$9.30 postpaid from:
City of Oakland
Planning Department
1330 Broadway, Suite 310
Oakland CA 94612
(415) 238-3941

This graphically pleasing volume is unique in that it identifies specific retrofits for 14 pre-1950 Bay Area architecture styles, from Italianate and Queen Anne (late 1800s) to California Bungalow (1920s) and Wartime Tract (1945). Sketches of each style are accompanied by summaries of the insulating values of the building materials common to that style and the relative ease or difficulty of insulating, weatherstripping, and otherwise modifying the attics, crawlspaces, windows, doors, and other features common to each design. Eighteen detailed retrofit strategies are presented in tabular form, listing 10-20 separate measures, with initial cost, first year and lifetime savings as well as the payback-period-to-cost ratio for each measure. The tables even differentiate the costs and benefits for different family types (depending mostly on whether the occupants are home all day or off at work with the thermostat turned down), and for homeowner- or contractor-installed jobs. While the book is targeted at the San Francisco Bay Area, many of these building types are found in other parts of the country, and the final chapter presents the savings table calculated for each of California's 16 diverse climate zones, which also are applicable to other parts of the country as they range from mild coastline to harsh desert and high mountain. The chapter on solar energy and some of the discussion of appliances and heating or cooling equipment are out of date, and the book pre-dates widespread awareness of the ozone-damaging properties of CFC-blown foam insulation or the common availability of high performance superwindows. On balance, however, it is a very useful resource for those who want to tighten up an older home while preserving it's historic integrity.

Excerpts:

➤ *This book sets out a strategy that is tailored to the architectural style of your house, the make-up of your household, and to your inclination to tackle building projects yourself.*

➤ *Rather than incurring the considerable economic and aesthetic costs of a new low ceiling, the better approach is to insulate the attic. In the Italianate and Queen Anne, with their large, walk around attics, this is a relatively simple task. Even if the attic has been floored it is better to lift up the floorboards in order to install insulation than to construct a dropped ceiling.*

➤ *Victorian, Colonial Revival, Brown Shingle houses, and occasional examples of other styles may have pocket doors—doors practically the size of walls which slide into recessed pockets between the rooms. In one story houses and two story houses with second floor pocket doors, the sliding mechanism at the top of the door opens into the attic. This is a major source of infiltration. Also, unless the sliding mechanism is properly sealed, loosefill insulation blown into the attic will enter the pocket and prevent the door from closing fully. Cover the pocket door opening into the attic with polyethylene sheeting stapled to the framing and affixed on its edges with duct tape.*

The Super Insulated Retrofit Book: A Home Owner's Guide To Energy-Efficient Renovation

Brian Marshall and Robert Argue
1981; 208 pp.
$12.95 postpaid from:
Firefly Books Ltd.
250 Sparks Avenue
Willowdale, Ontario M2H 2S4, Canada
(416)499-8412

As much as many people would love to design and build a new energy-efficient home, few will ever get the opportunity to do so. Most homeowners and would-be homeowners are stuck with the existing housing stock. In fact, 80 percent of the houses currently standing will still be here at the turn of the century. Unfortunately, the majority of these homes are underinsulated energy-gobblers. *The Super Insulated Retrofit Book* takes you far beyond basic energy conserving band-aid measures and shows you how to transform an existing sieve-like home into a superinsulated, tightly sealed one. This information is relevant primarily to homes situated in Canada and the northern U.S. Though the measures outlined are drastic—the total conversion of either the inside or exterior of a home—they can result in up to a 90 percent reduction in heating bills. This comprehensive guide examines the "whys" and "whats" of the super-retrofit; details step-by-step instructions for performing the work, from the initial preparation to the finishing touches; and presents case histories of a variety of super-insulated retrofits carried out on homes throughout Canada. Both interior and exterior renovation are discussed, with an emphasis on continuous air-vapor barriers, superinsulation, and the upgrading of windows, doors, and heating systems.

The authors acknowledge that superinsulation retrofits are major undertakings which will likely be cost-effective only when combined with other significant renovation work. Ideal times to do such work, they say, would be while re-siding a home's exterior, adding a new roof, building an addition, or gutting a home's interior to upgrade its wiring, plumbing, or walls. Though a number of new superinsulated retrofit techniques and materials have been introduced since the book's publication, the bulk of its content still provides timely advice.

Excerpts:

➤ *During the super-retrofit an air-vapor barrier is put in place. This usually consists of a continuous, overlapped and caulked 6 mil polyethylene sheet. By wrapping the entire house in plastic uncontrolled air change is kept to a minimum. Some of the characteristics of a well installed air-vapor barrier include: continuous between floors and around partitions wherever possible; continuous bead of caulking (non-hardening such as acoustical sealant) between sheets overlapped on top of a stud for support; tied-in and caulked to window and door frames, as well as any holes for vents, chimneys, etc.; some means of maintaining continuity around electrical boxes, wires, plumbing and other potential holes; and minimum number of holes and tears.*

➤ *When considering the super-insulated retrofit, the factor of the heat loss through windows is of primary importance. As a house is made super-insulated and air-tight, windows become the largest single source of heat loss. Some homeowners perform more radical surgery on their homes than others. The operation can entail the purchase and installation of new higher efficiency windows, the re-orientation of existing windows, and the incorporation of shuttering devices to reduce night-time heat losses. On the other hand, significant fuel savings can result from the judicious use of caulking, weatherstripping and affordable movable insulation techniques in conjunction with the addition of extra layers of glass to the existing windows.*

How To Weatherize Your Home Or Apartment
Massachusetts Audubon Society
1986; 37 pp.
$3.50 postpaid from:
Massachusetts Audubon Society
Educational Resources Office
South Great Road
Lincoln MA 01773
(617)259-9500

This booklet provides a good overview of simple, mostly low cost ways homeowners and apartment dwellers—particularly those living in smaller and older multi-unit structures—can reduce heating bills while increasing household warmth and comfort. All the weatherization basics are covered: sealing hidden heat leaks; weatherstripping windows and doors; adding insulation and storm windows; improving heating systems; and practicing energy-saving habits. In addition, the most common household weatherization materials, their costs and potential savings, and ways to finance the work are discussed. There's also some advice to help tenants and landlords work together on weatherization projects.

Excerpts:

➤ *Electrical receptacles penetrate into wall cavities. Even when the wall is insulated, the insulation is often pushed away, leaving a gap for cold air to come in and for warm air to escape. A leaky wall outlet can cost $1 per year in wasted heat. If you have ten outlets on exterior walls, that's $10 in lost heat every winter. You can seal up these leaks by installing outlets and switchplate insulators (small foam pads that fit behind the cover plate). The insulators only cost about a dime each and take one or two minutes to install.*

➤ *Caulk is your best friend in sealing most small cracks (less than 1/4 inch) around your house. There are many types of caulk available. Take some time to choose the right type for your particular needs. Pay particular attention to their expected lifetime, ease of clean-up, paintability, and long-term flexibility (important since cracks expand and contract with the seasons and as your house settles).*

➤ *Occupants may have different ideas about what to insulate depending on what part of the building they live in. For example, tenants who pay for their own heat in the third floor apartment in a triple decker would naturally want to have the roof insulated first. Those on the second floor would want to insulate the walls, while the tenants on the first floor might get the greatest savings by insulating the basement ceiling. It is important to plan the project so that the costs of the insulation are shared fairly, according to who benefits from it. For example, the third floor tenants might accept an increase in rent to help pay for roof insulation—as long as the rent increase is less than their monthly fuel savings—but the other tenants should not be expected to do so.*

Your Mobile Home Energy and Repair Guide

John T. Krigger
1991; 120 pp.
$12.50 postpaid from:
Saturn Resource Management
324 Fuller Avenue S-8
Helena MT 59601
(406)443-3433

Mobile homes comprise approximately 5% to 10% of all the single family housing in the United States. Few publications address the specific problems of their upkeep and weatherization. This book is a fairly technical guide for weatherizing and increasing the energy efficiency of mobile homes, covering the effective use of landscaping to repairing mechanical ventilation systems. Repair of mobile homes is an important part of retrofitting, as much of the energy wasted in these structures is due to damage and deterioration.

Excerpts:

➤ *Orientation of your mobile home is one of the most important factors determining energy costs. If you are looking at sites on which to locate your mobile home, make sure the site allows you to orient your home for maximum access to the sun, protection from wind, or access to cooling breezes. If you own a mobile home on an existing site and it is oriented poorly, for example with a long window wall facing west, you might consider reorienting it to take full advantage of the sun or shade available to you. The cost of rotating a mobile home may be relatively low, especially if your heating and cooling costs are extremely high. You can still realize a payback very shortly because of the energy saved.*

➤ *Most oil and gas mobile home furnaces are sealed combustion furnaces. Sealed combustion means that all the combustion air comes from the outside and that the firebox and flue have no openings to the interior of the mobile home. Most mobile home furnaces are downflow furnaces. Downflow furnaces take the return air in at the top of the furnace, heat the air, and force it into duct-work below the furnace in the floor. Return air from the rooms is pulled back to the furnace through the hallway by the blower, which creates a large suction at its inlet. The blower inlet is close to the flue so it could suck flue gases into the home if the flue or the firebox were open.*

Mechanical Systems Retrofit Manual: A Guide for Residential Design

Paul A. Knight
1987; 264 pp.
$41.95 plus postage from:
Van Nostrand Reinhold Company, Inc.
7625 Empire Drive
Florence KY 41042
Customer Service (606)525-6600

Contrary to its title, this comprehensive, not-too-technical reference manual and consumer guide addresses energy efficiency in existing residential space- and water-heating systems. Written for both the homeowner and contractor, it's liberally (often humorously) illustrated text describes how a variety of heating systems work and how they can be adjusted, modified, or replaced for improved efficiency. Step-by-step instructions are provided for a variety of furnace, boiler, and water-heater retrofits, from those a homeowner can perform to more complex jobs best left to professionals. These range from the simple installation of radiator reflectors and water-heater insulation to the more involved retrofits of variable-flow gas valves and vent dampers. Material lists and preparation techniques accompany all installation procedures. Appendices on safety inspections for existing gas- and oil-fired appliances and fuel-bill analysis for sizing or regulating heating systems round out this practical reference.

Excerpts:

➤ *The classic sign of an oversized heating appliance is frequent cycling "on" and "off" during the heating season. Since the heating appliance is oversized, it produces the needed amount of heat to satisfy the thermostat in a short period of time and then cycles off. At first glance, this may seem like an efficient heating system since the heating plant doesn't stay on very long and consequently does not burn much fuel.*

➤ *However, just the opposite is true. Maximum heating appliance efficiency occurs when the burner operates continuously (heat output is matched to building heat loss). As a result of de-rating the heating appliance [reducing the fuel input to its main burner], "on" cycles are lengthened throughout the heating season and the "off" cycles are minimized.*

➤ *All products of combustion must vent to the outdoors for safe operation. If the venting system is not designed or installed properly, or if it becomes blocked, spillage of combustion gases into the home may occur. Spillage will occur at the draft hood or diverter.*

➤ *A simple test for spillage may be performed. After the heating appliance has been operating for about 10 minutes, hold a cigarette or smoking match beneath the draft diverter/hood. If the smoke is drawn into the vent, the system is operating satisfactorily. If the smoke is not drawn into the vent, but rather blows from the vent, spillage is probably occurring. If spillage is suspected, a service person should be contacted for further inspection.*

➤ *The best way to think of efficiently maintaining comfort is to deliver the correct amount of heat, to the correct location, at the correct time. This concept of efficient comfort is the basis for "energy management." A setback thermostat controls the amount of heat to lower temperature at acceptable times....As a general rule, for every 1°F of temperature setback over an eight hour period, 1% of the daily energy usage will be saved.*

Oil And Gas Heating Systems: Maintenance and Improvement

Massachusetts Audubon Society
1990; 38 pp.
Massachusetts Audubon Society
Educational Resources Office
South Great Road
Lincoln MA 01773
(617)259-9500

This booklet provides an excellent introduction to saving energy and money by maintaining, improving, or replacing your present heating system. It explains in simple terms how oil- and gas-fired heating systems work, do-it-yourself methods for improving heating system efficiency, and the potential costs and savings of various heating system modifications and additions. The text is straightforward and nicely illustrated, offering people who know little about the subject a practical starting point for sorting out their options.

Excerpts:

➤ *What To Do First: 1) Get the most out of what you have. Have your existing furnace or boiler cleaned and tuned. Perform do-it-yourself maintenance to get the most heat for your money; 2) Be a good operator. Learn how to control your heating system so that you get the heat you need without waste. Think about installing a clock thermostat; 3) Go halfway. If your furnace or boiler is basically in good shape and will last another five years or more, find out how much you can save by adding modifications such as a new burner, vent damper, etc.; 4) Go all the way. If your furnace or boiler is worn out, very inefficient, or much too large for your building's heating needs, it's time to replace it with a new, efficient heating unit.*

➤ *Sediment builds up in the bottom of boilers and acts like a layer of insulation, keeping heat from getting through the water. You should check your boiler water for sediment build-up regularly. Hold a bucket underneath the faucet on the boiler and drain out water until the water runs clear. If you can't locate this faucet, ask your heating technician to show you when he or she comes to tune the furnace. Some boilers need to be flushed every few weeks, while others require flushing only once or twice a year.*

➤ *There's no point in heating the whole house when you are in bed asleep. Setting the thermostat back 10 degrees for eight hours each night will cut your heating costs by 10%. The amount of energy spent warming up the house in the morning is small compared to what you save during the night.*

Moveable Insulation: A Guide to Reducing Heating and Cooling Losses Through the Windows in Your Home

William K. Langdon
1980; 379 pp.
Rodale Press
(Out of print; check your local library)

This guide concentrates on one of the most troublesome details facing any comprehensive retrofit: insulation of windows, greenhouses, skylights, etc. Geared to the do-it-yourselfer, it is full of good illustrations and pictures as well as clear instructions on how to choose and install a variety of insulating window systems—shutters, shades, curtains, and other moveable types. There's lots of practical advice here you can put to use, in lieu of replacing your existing windows with "superinsulated" ones (these are addressed in the next section), to make your home more comfortable and energy-efficient.

Excerpts:

➤ *As you survey the windows in your home or in the design of a home you are planning to build, assess the amount of time you are willing to spend each day operating the window insulation systems you are considering. Many indoor gardeners have stated that there is an optimum number of house plants an individual can care for. Beyond that number, the plants will suffer from neglect. The same can be said for moveable window insulation, and there is no point in spending time and money on manual window insulation systems that you are not going to take the time to operate. Any windows having only single glazing undoubtedly deserve your initial attention, but, other things being equal, the largest windows are the ones you should focus on.*

➤ *Adding a foil-faced, reflective liner fabric is often the simplest way to increase the thermal effectiveness of an existing curtain or drapery. The radiant heat transfer in the air space behind the drapery is decreased by an added layer of Foylon, Astrolon III, or Mylar on the back side of the curtain. Another air space is created since this lining material usually hangs freely, apart from the folds of the drapery. It can either be pinned to the drapery beneath each hook, or, if a hem is sewn in at the top it can be hung directly from the drapery hooks.*

Thermal Shutters And Shades: Over 100 Schemes for Reducing Heat Loss Through Windows
William Shurcliff
1980; 238 pp.
$19.95 (hardcover) postpaid from:
Brick House Publishing Company, Inc.
P.O. Box 134
Acton MA 01720
(508)635-9800

Windows are the weakest link in most homes' energy-conserving "armor." This reference manual reviews a wide variety of strategies for making existing, low-R-value windows more energy-efficient by covering them at night with insulating shades, shutters, curtains, and other barriers. (If your existing windows are in need of significant repair, consider replacing them with "superinsulated" units rather than installing insulating shades or shutters.) The book is comprehensive and to the point. Shurcliff addresses how heat is lost through windows, the economics of shutters and shades, considerations governing design of shutters and shades, insulating materials, and a host of indoor and outdoor window insulating devices. Although essentially a survey of already-invented window insulating schemes, some innovative new ones are proposed as well.

Excerpts:

➤ *An easy way to reduce heat-loss at windows with little fuss and bother is to use two roll-up shades instead of one. Adding a second shade is easy, and the added saving of heat is moderately large depending on the materials used and the tightness of seal. If one of the shades is aluminized and edge seals are used, the heat-saving may be about 40 to 60% as compared to about 10 to 20% provided by an ordinary, unsealed roll-up shade.*

➤ *Consider on the other hand, a shutter employing a 1/2" sheet of Thermax [rigid insulation board]. A 36" x 36" plate of such material weighs only 1 lb. Lifting such a plate is a cinch for anyone....The significance of this is that the plate may merely be secured against the window: clipped into place in the evening and removed and stored during the day. No hinges are needed. No strength is needed— no perimeter frame—because no strong force will ever be exerted on the plate. Because the plate has no frame, its size is easily adjusted; for example, a 1/2" slice can be trimmed off with a knife or carpenter's saw. Fitting a dozen plates to a dozen windows, each of which is slightly off-square and off-size, is simplicity itself. Throughout the summer the plates may be stored in a closet or basement. The edges of the plates may be taped in any way the homeowner sees fit, and the faces may be painted or otherwise beautified. The entire situation (buying, cutting, fitting, beautifying, removal in the spring) is entirely within his understanding and control.*

5D. Superinsulated Housing

Though virtually unheard of a decade ago, superinsulation is rapidly becoming the most popular way to build an energy-efficient home today. And with good reason: superinsulated homes use little or no energy for heating or cooling, loads that typically use far more energy than any other task in the average household. Numerous building methods have been developed to reduce heating and cooling loads, but none have proven to be as versatile or as cost-effective as superinsulation. According to the authors of the book *Superinsulated Design and Construction*, several reasons for this are:

Earlier energy-efficient strategies such as passive solar or earth sheltering had to be incorporated into the design process at the very beginning. These strategies often dictated the architectural form of the building as well. While this is still true to some extent, the techniques of superinsulation are far less demanding of the architectural style than were earlier energy concepts. A sophisticated simplicity has developed that allows tremendous freedom in the architectural design of energy-efficient homes. The technology is more forgiving and flexible. The details of air/vapor barrier installation or wall construction are now more important than the angle of the windows or the quantity of thermal mass.

Successful superinsulation requires careful consideration be given not only to how much insulation you put in a home's shell, but also to a concert of other design and construction details which affect airtightness, controlled ventilation, and building heat gains and losses. The following references review the fundamentals of superinsulated housing and show you how to incorporate this technology into new or existing dwellings.

The Superinsulated Home Book
J.D. Ned Nisson and Gautam Dutt
1985; 316 pp.
John Wiley & Sons, Inc.
(Out of print; check your local library)

This comprehensive reference book/building guide clearly and thoroughly describes the design and construction of superinsulated homes. The book offers a refreshing mix of theory, technical explanations, and practical information, all reinforced with photographs and drawings. Its first part, Principles, provides a conceptual understanding of the superinsulated house. The fundamentals of the thermal envelope, airtightness, controlled ventilation, insulation heat loss and energy consumption, and designing the superinsulated house are covered. The second section, Practice, presents details of design and construction for walls, foundation, roofs, windows, and air/vapor barriers, and discusses ventilation systems, heating systems, appliances, and methods of evaluating the performance of the superinsulated home. The authors explore the subject in a step-by-step format that will inform both the do-it-yourselfer and the master builder about all the design and construction details which must be considered in order to build a superinsulated home that works well.

Excerpts:

➤ *No amount of design sophistication will work if it is not supported by proper workmanship at the site. If the insulation contractor doesn't completely fill a wall cavity, or if the air/vapor barrier installer leaves out a couple of square feet because "such a little bit won't matter" then the system will not work as it should.*

➤ *Superinsulation does not demand an extraordinary standard of work quality. It simply demands quality in an area where it has never before been stressed. A plumbing system must not have even one leaky pipe; an electrical system must not have even one short circuit; a roofing system must not have even one leak; so an insulation system must not have even one square foot of missed insulation or one hole in the air/vapor barrier.*

➤ *Superinsulated walls differ from conventional walls in several ways. Thick insulation alone does not make a superinsulated wall. Compared to conventional walls, superinsulated walls are much more air-tight, have less thermal bridging, have a higher R-value, and are built more carefully, avoiding in-*

sulation voids and other defects. There is no one best wall design for superinsulated houses. What is right for one builder or homeowner may be wrong for another. Materials and labor costs vary, so do regional styles.

Superinsulated Design and Construction: A Guide To Building Energy-Efficient Homes
Thomas Lenchek, Chris Mattock, and John Raabe
1987; 172 pp.
$30.95 (hardcover) plus shipping from:
Van Nostrand Reinhold Customer Service
7625 Empire Drive
Florence KY 41042-2978
Toll-free for orders: (800)926-2665

This book contains one of the best, most up-to-date, in-depth summaries of current energy-efficient building practices. "What you'll find," according to reviewers at *Progressive Builder* magazine (Feb. 1987), "is careful, unbiased writing—plenty of terrific construction details—summarizing the best techniques for insulating houses well, facing windows south, and reducing air infiltration. Luckily, the approaches are also the easiest ones tested by builders in the field over the past decade. The authors do a remarkable job of simplifying the language of low-energy construction and of organizing construction details, cutaway illustrations, and graphs."

"The basic ingredients of the book are the construction details and the accompanying text that explains the principal problems they aim to solve—air sealing, moisture and vapor control, and adding insulation in tricky places. But the discussions on energy costs and the economics of energy-efficient techniques are worth more than passing mention. The authors have included a sensible approach to analyzing the costs and energy savings achieved by moving from a base-case house representing a code-minimum level of construction or standard practice to successively higher levels of insulation and air tightness. The payoff for conservation measures is charted in five cities—Portland, Boston, Denver, Minneapolis, and Anchorage."

"On top of all its other merits, *Superinsulated Design and Construction* makes a special effort to highlight trends, tips, warnings, and rules of thumb that circulate in informed circles."

Excerpts:

➤ *Before siding over the exterior wall, a wind barrier such as building paper or polyolefin sheeting should be applied, especially if the wall was not sheathed and the insulation is exposed. This will ensure a still air cavity for the insulation and allow the product to provide its full rated R value.*

➤ *Do not seal or tightly caulk the exterior surface of the wall. While you do want to keep wind and water from blowing into the insulation, you do not want to trap moisture in the wall cavity. Let the outside surface breathe moisture out.*

➤ *In most construction a higher insulation level is placed in the ceilings than in the walls, in part because of the belief that more heat is lost through the ceiling and in part because flat ceilings are easier and cheaper to insulate than walls. As we have stated before, the ceilings lose more heat than walls only in poorly sealed older structures where temperature stratification and the stack effect combine to pump out a considerable amount of heat through the ceiling. So the first point is true for older housing, but not for the tighter houses we are considering here. The second point, that ceilings are cheaper to insulate, is only true for flat ceilings. Cathedral ceilings are not cheaper to insulate. Here, as in walls, structure must be purchased to house the insulation. Determining the most cost-effective insulation level for a cathedral ceiling will often give you a different (and lower) value than that for a flat attic ceiling. Depending on costs for the installed insulation, fuel, and the climate, this level will range from R-30 to R-50 or higher.*

Also, see *The Super Insulated Retrofit Book: A Home Owner's Guide To Energy-Efficient Renovation* reviewed in Section 5C.

5E. Solar Housing

Now in houses with a south aspect, the sun's rays penetrate into the porticoes in winter, but in summer the path of the sun is right over our heads and above the roof, so that there is shade. If, then, this is the best arrangement, we should build the south side loftier to get the winter sun and the north side lower to keep out the cold winds.

Socrates, as quoted by Xenophon in *Memorabilia*

Solar power represents our most underutilized home energy resource. At the same time millions of household furnaces and boilers hungrily consume expensive and irreplaceable fuels to heat our homes, enough sunlight often shines right outside the front door to accomplish the same task. There are many ways we can tap into the sun. The most efficient, reliable, and inexpensive techniques are often the simplest. While some early solar houses incorporated large solar collector arrays and complicated mechanical distribution and storage systems, well designed ones currently incorporate "passive" alternatives—high-efficiency south-facing windows, and superinsulated construction. In essence, state-of-the-art solar housing blends ancient building practices— the sensitive siting and layout of one's dwelling—with simple yet high-tech construction materials. The following references can show you how to best take advantage of the solar resources available where you live.

The New Solar Home Book
Bruce Anderson with Michael Riordan
1987; 199 pp.
$16.95 postpaid from:
Brick House Publishing Company
P.O. Box 134
Acton MA 01720
(508)635-9800

This venerable primer provides a comprehensive introduction to solar theory, technology, and application. Written for the novice designer, builder, or alternative energy buff, the book reviews the various ways you can harness the sunlight falling on your house for space heating, water heating, and electricity generation. After covering the fundamentals of solar energy and heat flow calculations, it examines passive solar house design, solar domestic hot water systems, and solar space heating systems in depth, and photovoltaics (electricity from sunlight) in brief. Included are 45 pages of appendices containing climatic and design information such as degree days and design temperatures, insulating values of building materials, and solar radiation maps, which can assist you in calculating the feasibility of solar projects you may be considering.

Excerpts:

➤ *Energy conservation is the first step in good shelter design. Only the house that loses heat begrudgingly can use sunlight to make up most of the loss. Some people might think it rather dull to let sunlight in through the windows and keep it there, but others delight in its simplicity. In fact, conserving the sun's energy can often be more challenging than inventing elaborate systems to capture it.*

➤ *A vital question in a solar-heated house is where to store the heat. When the house is used as the solar collector, it needs a method of "soaking up" or storing heat so it doesn't become too hot when the sun is shining, and retains some of this heat to use when it isn't. Probably the most efficient heat storage container is the material of the house itself—the walls, floors, and roofs. All materials absorb and store heat as they are warmed. For example, water or stone will absorb more heat for a fixed temperature rise than straw or wood. Heavy materials can store large quantities of heat without becoming too hot. When temperatures around them drop, the stored heat is released and the materials themselves cool down.*

➤ *Well-insulated homes with reasonable amounts of south glazing (no more than six percent of the floor area) usually have enough thermal mass in the standard building materials without adding more... Extra thermal mass is now looked at more as an "option" than as a "necessity."*

The Fuel Savers

Bruce N. Anderson
1991; 83 pp.
$6.45 postpaid from:
Morning Sun Press
P.O. Box 413
Lafayette CA 94549
(510) 932-1383

Whether you're a homeowner, builder or architect, this book de-mystifies solar energy while emphasizing its cost-effectiveness. Window treatments, sunrooms, solar hot water heaters and other concepts are explained, and the advantages, disadvantages and economics of each discussed. Written for the novice and easy to understand, this book is a valuable tool for homeowners looking for cost-effective ways to help the environment.

Excerpt:

➤ *Trellises and Vegetation: Fortunately, when Mother Nature gave us the sun, she also gave us plants that can be used to shade our homes in the summer. In the summer, bushes, small trees, and trellises on the east and west sides of the house are the best solution for blocking out the low-angled light of the morning and afternoon sun. And when you want that solar heat in the winter, the leaves have dropped off, letting the sun's rays through. In ideal situations, proper use of vegetation can reduce the summer cooling load to 20-25 percent of what it was. Variations: You can grow vines over porches to shade outdoor spaces and wall areas.*
If you know the prevailing wind patterns at your house, you can plant shrubbery so that it funnels a breeze into the house.
Advantages: Trees, shrubs, vines and plants are alive and beautiful.
Disadvantages: You need a green thumb!

The Passive Solar Energy Book: Expanded Professional Edition

Edward Mazria
1979; 687 pp.
$29.95 postpaid from:
Rodale Press
(Out of print; check your local library)

Despite advanced age in a fast-changing field, Mazria's book remains the single best guide to passive solar house design. Its basic information on solar energy, orientation, and the arrangement of rooms is current. Organization, illustration, assemblage of tools, and use of pattern (based on Christopher Alexander's *A Pattern Language*) are first-rate.

Use the book with confidence but consider these warnings: Mazria works in the sunny Southwest and shows a slight bias toward that climate. For example, the book recommends too much south glass per square foot of floor area given today's tight, well-insulated houses.

The book does leave out some important technologies. For example, high-performance glazings threaten to replace the movable insulation recommended by the book. Similarly, you won't find discussion of such current issues as radiant floors, vapor barriers, back-up heating systems, phase-change materials, and the anomalous heat leaks that can rob insulation of its value.

The professional edition adds several hundred pages of useful climate data and performance calculations for fine-tuning designs.

Reviewed by David Godophin in *The Essential Whole Earth Review*

Excerpts:

➤ *To take advantage of the sun in climates where heating is needed during the winter, find the areas on the site that receive the most sun during the hours of maximum solar radiation—9:00 a.m. to 3:00 p.m. (sun time). Placing the building in the northern portion of this sunny area will (1) insure that the outdoor areas and gardens placed to the south will have adequate winter sun and (2) help minimize the possibility of shading the building in the future by off-site developments.*

➤ *Perhaps the greatest advantage of a passive system is the simplicity of its design, operation and maintenance. A passive system can usually be installed, operated and maintained by people with a limited technical background. These systems are built with common construction materials and usually have a long life, low operating temperature, no fans, pumps, compressors, pipes or ducts and few moving parts. Since there is no mechanical equipment, there is little or no noise associated with passive systems. In addition, most systems are completely invisible from the interior of the building; there are no radiators, convectors or grills to deal with.*

Passive Solar Design Strategies: Guidelines for Home Builders
Passive Solar Industries Council (PSIC), the Solar Energy Research Institute (now the National Renewable Energy Laboratory), and Charles Eley Associates
1989; 80 pages, 224 different versions for separate locations
$50.00 from:
Passive Solar Industries Council
1090 Vermont Ave., NW, Suite 1200
Washington, DC 20005
(202)371-0357

As the title implies, this book is geared toward home builders. The first half of the book is devoted to basic passive solar design principles and strategies for improving energy performance. The second half of the book provides data tables, worksheets, and worksheet instructions. A detailed, worked example using the worksheets is provided. In all there are a total of four worksheets: conservation performance level, auxiliary heat performance level, thermal mass/comfort, and summer cooling performance level. In August 1990 SERI and PSIC published user-friendly software and a manual to be used in conjunction with this book. The software allows the user to fill out the worksheets on a computer. There are different versions of the book and software for 224 locations in the United States, and data from additional locations can be loaded on the software disk. When ordering be sure to specify which location most closely matches your site.

Excerpts:

➤ *The energy performance of passive solar strategies varies significantly, depending on climate, the specific design of the system, and the way it is built and operated. Of course, energy performance is not the only consideration. A system which will give excellent energy performance may not be as marketable in your area or as easily adaptable to your designs as a system which saves less energy but fits your other needs.*

➤ *In the following table several different passive solar systems are presented along with two numbers which indicate their performance. The Percent Solar Savings is a measure of how much the passive solar system is reducing the house's need for purchased energy.*

➤ *The Yield is the annual net heating energy benefit of adding the passive solar system measured in Btu saved per year per square foot of additional south glazing.*

Also see Chapter 10 for more information on solar technology.

5F. Earth-Sheltered Housing

Every creature except man builds unobtrusive or hidden homes. In contrast, it is rare to see new human dwellings that blend with or enhance their surroundings. Earth-sheltered housing offers an alternative to what many people view as this blighting of the American landscape. Far from being glorified basements, well-designed and built earth-sheltered homes can be beautiful, light, airy, dry, and cozy.

Building into the earth is an ancient idea that has re-emerged as a popular alternative housing form. These modern structures, buffered from environmental extremes by the earth's mass, have been touted as great energy savers. While this has proven true (where proper insulation detailing was tended to), progress in superinsulated construction techniques has made it possible to accomplish the same results more cost-effectively above the ground. What an above ground house can't do nearly so well, however, is to preserve open views and habitats for plants and animals. Once construction "wounds" have healed, earth-sheltered housing can provide a habitat for not only people inside, but also the natural world all about its outside.

The books and organizations listed below can help you decide whether building into the earth is right for you and if so, how to do a good job of it.

Underground Space Center
790 Civil and Mineral Engineering Building
500 Pillsbury Drive, SE
University of Minnesota
Minneapolis MN 55455
(612)624-0066

The Underground Space Center at the University of Minnesota is one of the leading earth sheltered housing resource centers in this country. Its staff has published a number of outstanding books and fact sheets on the subject. In addition, it has a small research staff which can assist the general public by giving information and advice on earth sheltered housing matters. The following publication is an example of the center's work. For more information, order its publications list.

Earth Sheltered Housing Design: Second Edition
John Carmody and Raymond Sterling
1985; 350 pp.
$19.95 postpaid from:
Underground Space Center (address cited above)

This is an excellent introduction to the state of-the-art in earth sheltered housing design. The authors acknowledge that advances and new technologies for earth-sheltered homes are appearing very rapidly. They have managed to incorporate most of them into this book. It is extensively illustrated and packed with useful information on the history of earth sheltered housing, site and building design, energy use and costs, and public policy issues. The work concludes with 18 diverse case studies of earth-sheltered homes located in various parts of the country. Though the book provides comprehensive coverage on the subject, the authors suggest that experienced professionals, engineers, or architects be consulted before you start digging.

Excerpts:

➤ *The most fundamental characteristic of any waterproofing material is its ability to resist water penetration without deteriorating in a below-grade environment. Since replacement of products below grade is extremely costly if not impossible, materials should last the life of the structure. This means that waterproofing materials and their adhesive or bonding agents must be compatible with soils and other materials used in construction.*

➤ *A truly successful design requires the resolution of structural, waterproofing, thermal, landscaping, cost, and aesthetic concerns simultaneously.*

➤ *In order to develop effective construction details, it is necessary to understand all of the technical issues and problems and then attempt to resolve them. There is no standard or ideal way to design most details—design will depend on the climate, the availability of materials and skilled workers locally, relative costs, and the objectives or priorities of the designer. It is important to remember that, unlike conventional buildings, earth sheltered structures represent a relatively new and emerging technology. In the building industry, the use of new products and details tend to evolve over a period of years, not overnight.*

Passive Annual Heat Storage: Improving the Design of Earth Shelters
John Hait and the Rocky Mountain Research Center
1983; 152 pp.
$25.00 postpaid from:
Box 4694
Missoula MT 59806
(406)728-5951

Passive Annual Heat Storage advances the state-of-the-art in energy efficient housing by blending new alternative building technologies with many of the best features of passive solar and earth-sheltered buildings. This easy to read, nicely illustrated book is a complete exposition of the principle and practice of storing summer heat for winter use while, as you'd hope, keeping things cool during the warmer months. Hait clearly shows how, by installing an insulating-watershed umbrella in the earth above an underground structure, you can simply and inexpensively protect an earth-sheltered home from chilling cold and seeping water. Combined with passive solar heat gain and passive ventilation (provided by open-loop convection-powered earth tubes), this technique works by altering the temperature in the earth around an underground home. The result is a building capable of providing a comfortable indoor climate year around (with plenty of fresh air circulation) without, according to the author, requiring any auxiliary heating, cooling, or ventilating systems!

Excerpts:

➤ *There is a dramatic difference between a Passive Annual Heat Storage home environment and the conventional or super-insulated above-ground house. All year long the above ground one has precisely the same outside surface area exposed to the harsh environment, regardless of the time of year. This surface is designed to lose heat all winter, only at a slow rate because of the heavy amount of insulation. The new subterranean environment, on the other hand, operates more like a south facing window. Although windows are known for their large heat losses, when the sun shines through them, even on a cold winter's day, they present a net HEAT GAIN to the inside. All winter long the subterranean surfaces of the improved earth shelter design are conducting heat BACK INTO into the house...out of the storage mass. The walls, ceiling and floor provide a "heat gain" rather than a "heat loss." Therefore, they act like that south facing window when the sun is shining. All but the exposed, above-grade walls (which naturally should be designed using good energy conservation methods) are effectively REMOVED from the list of heat losers.*

➤ *Unlike above-ground shingles, the underground shingle in the insulation/watershed umbrella must contend with some new problems. The earth over which it is put will settle. This settling will be uneven. If you do not watch closely during installation, to see that a steep enough slope is provided, the earth may settle enough to back water up under the overlap of the adjacent uphill shingle, or maybe even create a lake.*

Underground Houses: How To Build A Low-Cost Home
Robert L. Roy
128 pp.
$13.00 (includes update) postpaid from:
Earthwood
RR I, Box 105
West Chazy NY 12992
(518)493-7744

This book details the saga of one man's successful efforts to build an underground home for less than $8,000. The result was Log End Cave. This book is as close as you're ever going to get to building your own underground home without actually taking shovel and hammer in hand and doing it. Roy outlines the entire project in a very readable and instructive format which addresses the significant issues he dealt with in choosing a site for this home, designing it, and building it. His effort stands as a ray of hope for those without, they think, enough money to build their own home. No raging egoist, Roy also includes a whole section on what he did wrong, what he should have done better, and what he learned during the construction of his home. This is a good introduction to building your own low-cost earth-sheltered or underground home. It is full of pictures illustrating every step of the construction from pouring the concrete footers to planting the landscaping.

Excerpts:

➤ *If this were purely an instruction manual on how to build a particular house, it would be unforgivable to stop halfway through a discussion of plank and beam roofing for any reason whatsoever. But it is not simply an instruction manual; it is also the story of an owner builder wrestling with a little known style of building. The reality is that we were interrupted by unforeseen circumstances, and the reader might as well expect that he, too, will be confronted with such circumstances, though unforeseen as ours.*

5G. Adobe Construction

Constructing homes with indigenous building materials rather than importing timber, for example, from halfway across the country can sometimes significantly reduce the resource-intensiveness of new construction. Adobe and rammed earth construction work with what is probably the oldest and most widely available building material known to man: earth. The strength, durability, and availability of earth make it an attractive building material, particularly when other resources are in short supply. Contrary to popular belief, earth can be effectively used as a building material not only in the hot, arid Southwest, but also in wetter Northern and Eastern climates. Soils suitable for earth construction, ideally a 70%-sand-and-aggregate 30%-clay mix, can be found nearly everywhere in the world. This section reviews several excellent references that show you how to build with earth.

The Earthbuilders' Encyclopedia
Joseph M. Tibbets
1989; 196 pp.
$20.35 postpaid from:
Southwest Solaradobe School
P.O. Box 153
Bosque NM 87006
(505)252-1382

The Earthbuilders' Encyclopedia is the most thorough and practical book available for adobe and rammed earth construction. It is an alphabetically arranged reference manual which explains and illustrates the terms, tools, materials, and techniques of earthbuilding. Written with the insight and sense of humor that come from practical experience, the encyclopedia covers everything from making adobes and plasters to solar building design. In addition to the necessary details of foundation and roof construction and electrical and plumbing systems for earth buildings, the encyclopedia incorporates such unusual entries as passive radon elimination systems, non-toxic wood-preservatives, and energy-efficient "Count Rumford" style fireplaces. Also included is a current "who's who" and display section for tradespeople, suppliers, and professionals in the adobe and rammed earth trades. The book is the text used in the Southwest Solaradobe School's owner-builder classes, and is an absolute must for anyone building with earth.

Excerpts:

➤ *The Solaradobe [house] will "coast" through the day. Remember that the adobe flywheel also works for you. The coolest time on the interior wall face will hit about the time that it is hottest out-side. Winter ventilation in the low desert is much like summer ventilation on the higher plateaus—the house can often be opened up to extend living onto patios, portales, etc.*

➤ *A variety of finishes are possible for exposed adobe walls. If the owner wishes to maintain the natu-ral color, he first works the wall over with a large brush and bucket of water which will tend to create a "slip" of the same mud the adobes are made of. Holes must be filled to taste, and once the wall has attained the desired look, it is left to dry out for a few days.*

➤ *Throwing the Shovel: The art of loading a full-sized, round-pointed shovel with mud mortar, then tossing it up to an adobero on the scaffold. Workers who have never learned this technique may consider it folly—until they have tried bucketing the mud up. They will soon find that the shovel toss is fluid, fairly fast, and much less dangerous than other methods. The trick is a sort of underslung pendulum arc, ...*

Reviewed by Susan Hassol

Manual For Building A Rammed Earth Wall
Lydia A. and David Miller
1980; 50 pp.
$8.00 from:
Lydia and David Miller
2319 21st Avenue
Greely CO 80631
(303)352-4775

Homes made with rammed-earth walls don't have to resemble mud huts. They can be attractive, energy-efficient, economical, and well within the capabilities of a determined owner-builder. The Millers have put their experience with rammed earth construction into this manual, which is one of the first of its kind geared specifically to do-it-yourselfers. The manual contains good first-hand, field-tested information about the positive and negative qualities of rammed earth. The illustrations used to depict the various stages in rammed-earth construction are ample and instructive. The designs used are generally on the standard suburban side, but that doesn't mean the techniques and principles of rammed-earth construction in the manual cannot be transferred to a design of your choice. Rammed earth presents the owner builder with some intriguing possibilities, and this little primer can introduce you to the modern version of this ancient building technique. Also available is *Rammed Earth Bibliography: A World Overview*, a reference and source book which reflects the authors' research of 40 years in 27 nations ($11.00 plus shipping).

Reviewed by Tom Enos

Excerpt:

➤ *Rammed Earth (Pisé de Terre) is a building material resulting from the application of compaction to selected soils. Of all the forms of earth building, rammed earth is the most durable. It has been suc-cessfully used in most parts of the world for hundreds of years. After World War II, it was used as an economic technique for under-developed regions. Its use is limited to soils with high sand and low clay content, 70% to 30% being the usual proportions, with sand graded to various particle sizes. The mix, with about 10% water added, is compacted in form panels by ironheaded rammers weighing from 5 to 20 pounds each.*

Adobe: Build It Yourself (2nd Edition)

Paul Graham McHenry, Jr.
1985; 158 pp.
$22.95 from:
University of Arizona Press
1230 N. Park Avenue, #102
Tucson AZ 85719
(602)621-1441

This has become a standard construction guide for adobe builders. It's probably the best one-volume treatment of all the aspects of designing and building your own adobe home. McHenry provides thorough information on adobe construction from foundations to decorations. Included are concise and very useful techniques and tips about making adobe bricks, foundations and roofs, plumbing and wiring adobe structures, and other common concerns. McHenry also includes numerous construction diagrams and drawings which address the structural aspects of construction, including how to build solid floors, lintels, and bondbeams. Adobe is a very flexible and practical building material and this book does it justice by outlining how to take advantage of everything adobe can offer an owner-builder.

Reviewed by Tom Enos

Excerpt:

➤ *Adobe is the ideal material for the beginner. It is a warm, kind material that is forgiving of mistakes, and amenable to change. If you don't like what you have wrought, it is a simple matter to take it down and try again. The adobe bricks may get a little battered in the process, but it won't matter a bit. Adobe is a tough plastic material that will stand almost any sort of misuse.*

5H. Log and Timber-Frame Construction

Combining the rustic aesthetic appeal of traditional log and timber construction with modern building materials and technology can yield dramatic results: homes which blend yesterday's pioneering spirit with today's demands for energy efficiency and comfort. Like many alternative building approaches, designs for log and timber homes can incorporate super-insulation, passive solar, and numerous other resource-conserving features. The following references provide a good starting point from which to explore these opportunities.

Log Home Living: 1992 Annual Buyer's Guide

320 pp.
$11.95 postpaid from:
Home Buyer Publications, Inc.
P.O. Box 220039
Chantilly VA 22022
(800)826-3893

This slick, magazine-style yearly publication provides a comprehensive, unbiased source of information on the log home industry. It is packed with consumer advice, fact-filled articles, product information, design ideas, and contacts for hundreds of additional sources of log home information. Among its highlights are a consumer checklist of 25 questions to ask before you buy any log home, a series of primer articles on wood for the log home, designing the log home, log home living, the Log Home Bookstore (which offers numerous log home catalogs and how-to-build books), and presentations of many of the industry's most attractive floorplans. Clearly and concisely written text makes for easy and enjoyable reading. The publishers are so confident they've done a thorough job covering all the subjects prospective log home buyers will want to know that they invite readers to call them for further elaboration on any issues which are not amply addressed. Please note, however, that this guide is not billed as a construction manual. The publishers cover those subjects in detail in Log Homes: *Construction & Finance Guide* (1988; 184 pp. available from the address cited above for $10.95 postpaid). In 1989, they launched a quarterly magazine called *Log Home Living*, $21.95 bimonthly.

Excerpts:

➤ Super-insulated log walls are typically constructed with half logs or log siding on the exterior, affixed to a conventionally stud framed insulated interior wall. The interior walls are then covered with either half logs or some form of paneling. When completed the homes look as if they were built with solid log walls. When using this system, the added four to six inches of insulation increases the home's thermal efficiency while retaining at least some of the benefits of the thermal mass of the exterior wall.

➤ A company's construction manual can tell you a great deal about their product; don't overlook them as a comparison tool. A well-prepared construction manual could tell you that a company wants to help you and your builder do the best job possible of building your home. Conversely, if a company offers a poorly written and illustrated construction guide, you may find it very difficult to properly construct your log home on your building site.

➤ Remember that while rain water usually drains too fast to be a concern, it may collect in cracks or splash on the lower logs in your house, along with dirt. Logs affected by this water may retain enough of it to cause problems. Dry wood won't rot if it's kept dry. To help do so, you may apply a good water repellent treatment to your house once it's built. One exception: if your logs have a moisture content of 25 percent or more, some builders advise you to apply a wood preservative without a water repellent at first. Re-treat your home with a water-repellent wood preservative once every several years after that.

Complete Guide to Building Log Homes
Monte Burch
1990; 406 pp.
$16.95 from:
Sterling Publishing Co.
387 Park Avenue South
New York NY 10016

Not just for the committed log home builder, this book gives a thorough, step-by-step explanation of home building. Over 40 pages are devoted to practical explanations of plumbing, water systems and lighting. Of course, issues specific to log building are addressed, starting with a chapter entitled "Is log building for you?" Detailed explanations of the many different log building techniques are accompanied by pictures and diagrams of every concept and construction step. The energy efficiency of high mass log homes, different types of renewable energy systems, and energy and water independence for remote sites are also addressed. A great resource for those considering building a log home.

Excerpts:

➤ Chain saws get rough use by the nature of the work they do. At first thought, saw maintenance might seem complicated. But it is actually quite simple. A bit of time spent on proper care and repair can mean the difference between an easy-to-use and long-lived tool and a prematurely worn-out and wasted one. Chain saw maintenance can be divided into three operations: (1) chain sharpening, (2) guide bar and chain maintenance, and (3) powerhead maintenance.

➤ The interior design of your log home can follow almost any style. In fact, the interior doesn't even have to suggest that it's part of a log home. But the beauty of polished and hand crafted logs on the interior is what endears log homes to many. One of the minor benefits of a log interior is that almost anything can be hung on the walls by simply driving a nail. If you want to move the item, just pull out the nail and patch the hole. Most of the damage simply disappears into the rough-hewn look of the logs.

The Timber-Frame Home: Design, Construction, Finishing
Tedd Benson
1988 225 pp.
$24.95 from:
The Taunton Press
63 South Main St.
Newtown, CT 06470

The 2000 year old craft of building homes with massive posts and beams is undergoing a late 20th century revival. With 97 color photos and 140 technical drawings, this exquisitely produced, hard-bound book is both a coffee table beauty and a practical guide to the theory, engineering, design, and finishing of timber frame construction. While it doesn't cover all the front-end details of selecting chisels and wood, and cutting and assembling joints, it does a beautiful job on all the rest, with chapters on frame design, home design, skins and frames, foundations, wiring and lighting, plumbing, frame and finish details, including cases studies and sources of supply.

Excerpts:

➤ *There are two important challenges for those who build timber-frame homes today. The first challenge is to cherish and nurture the values and standards set centuries ago, to understand in both spirit and substance the legacy of durable, classic timber-frame building that we have inherited from our forefathers. The second challenge is to bring the timber-frame house into the 20th century.*

➤ *The problem with plumbing a timber-frame house is not so much how to do it, for the standards and techniques are essentially the same as those used in conventional construction, but how to hide it.*

Timber Frame Construction: All About Post-and-Beam Building
Jack Sobon and Roger Schroeder
1984; 204 pp.
$12.95 from:
Storey Communications
Schoolhouse Road
RD #1 Box 105
Pownal VT 05261-9988
(802)823-5811

This soft-cover volume is an excellent complement to Tedd Benson's *The Timber-Frame Home*. It does a better job of explaining the details of the frame itself—wood selection, joint types, hand tools, and how to use them. It isn't as strong on roofing, wiring, plumbing, sheathing, and finish details. There are abundant black and white photos and line drawings and a detailed how-to chapter on a good beginner's project—a 12'x16' Shaker design garden toolshed. We recommend both books to anyone seriously considering a timber frame project.

Excerpts:

➤ *A timber frame of today has distinct advantages over a log home. First, a timber frame does not require the walls to hold it up, so expanses of glass, even, can be used without weakening the frame. Also, the timber frame uses less wood, even though it may be more labor intensive. As for insulating value, the log is one of nature's best insulators, but compared to man-made insulations, its R-value is low. An 8-inch log gives you an R of about 10, not even as high as a 3-1/2 inch common stud wall with fiberglass insulation. With a timber frame and rigid insulating panels, you can have as much as R-26 for a panel with 3-1/2 inches of urethane laminated to gypsum board and particle board.*

➤ *There is a misconception that early housewrights, if they had the chance, let their timbers season before working them with tools. . . Actually, wood is easier to work when green, though it will be heavier because of the water in it. This can be considerable. An 8-foot 2x4 can hold up to three quarts of water.*

5I. Cool Houses For Hot Climates

Energy-efficient strategies for keeping houses cool in hot climates are not as well known or widely practiced as those used for keeping houses warm in cold climates. Though many of the same basic energy efficiency measures should be incorporated into new or existing homes in either climate, those situated in southern regions must be equipped to treat the sun as a major liability (during all but the short heating season) rather than as a benefit. This requires that homes be systematically designed, constructed, and outfitted to prevent excess solar heat from penetrating their shells and to exhaust or cool warm air that does build up inside. There are many ways to accomplish these tasks using little or no energy. You can use, for example, radiant barriers, low-emissivity reflective glass, and shading devices to protect a house's interior from the sun's radiation and thermal mass, natural ventilation, fans, and evaporative coolers to help keep it comfortably cool. The particular measures that would best serve you, however, will depend not only on your climate's average daily and seasonal temperature swings, but also on its relative humidity. Different cooling strategies will be dictated for a hot, dry climate than for a hot, humid one. The following resources can help you explore a variety of passive and active techniques for providing maximum comfort at minimum expense.

Cool Houses for Desert Suburbs: Optimizing Heating & Cooling For Arizona's Builders

Jeffrey Cook, AIA
1979; 124 pp.
$11 postpaid from:
Arizona Dept. of Commerce
Energy Dept.
3800 N Central Ave. Suite 1200
Phoenix AZ 85012
(602)280-1440

Although this book focuses on helping Arizona architects, builders, and contractors optimize the design of standard, production houses for energy-efficient cooling and heating, it contains much valuable, straightforward information useful to anyone building or renovating homes in hot, dry climates. Numerous active and passive energy-conserving measures are addressed. The building and landscape design techniques detailed show you how to control heat gain and heat loss through desert homes' foundations, walls, windows, and roofs, and cool them with natural ventilation and energy-efficient mechanical systems. Perhaps most valuable is the book's "Typical House" case study series, which demonstrates how conventional production houses can be designed to optimize cooling and heating performance in desert climates. A multitude of high-quality architectural drawings—construction details, site and floor plans, and perspectives—illustrate all the key points covered. Though a number of technical innovations have appeared since this book was published, particularly in energy-efficient window options, the book still serves as an excellent general reference on the subject.

Excerpts:

➤ *Roofs on desert houses should always be either vented or totally shaded. This means that trussed roof construction such as is typical in Phoenix is ideal for this climate. Either sloped roofs with shingles or tiles, or flat roofs with built-up roofing are compatible with trussed construction. Such trussed attics provide enough clearance for blown insulation as well as batts. Attic or roof joist cavities should be vented at both the top and bottom. It is recommended that the net venting area of each be at least 1/150 that of the attic area.*

➤ *In hot, arid regions a house may be cooled by evaporation at a fraction of the energy costs of refrigerated air conditioning. Conventional evaporative cooling is a well-developed technique for summer space conditioning in the Southwest. Generally shading the cooler cabinet may produce only up to a 5% increase in efficiency. Thus, other factors are important. Air circulation around the cooler must not be impeded. When placed on the ground, plants should not be near the cooler if they interrupt air circulation. An ideal location for evaporative cooling equipment is a cool, shaded, but open place.*

➤ Generally the goals of residential landscaping in the desert should be two-fold: (1) absorb solar radiation (with the use of vegetative ground cover) to avoid both heat build-up and reflection; (2) shield both houses and the adjacent earth with the use of trees and shading devices but allow heat to be ventilated away. Typically the kinds of vegetation native to deserts do the best job and are also light water users. Light airy trees such as the Palo Verde provide good shade and ventilate continuously.

Design Notes and Energy Notes
Florida Solar Energy Center
Public Information Office
300 State Road 401
Cape Canaveral FL 32920
(407)783-0300

The Florida Solar Energy Center prepares many excellent publications on a wide variety of energy-efficient cooling techniques for new and existing houses. Applicable to homes situated in hot, humid climates, each four-page report in the FSEC's Design Note and Energy Note series concisely explains and illustrates a specific approach to energy-efficient cooling. Some examples of the topics covered include: passive cooling and human comfort, designing and installing radiant barrier systems, fans to reduce cooling costs in the southeast, techniques for shading residential walls and windows, and dealing with heat and humidity in Florida homes. Write the FSEC for a complete publications list and ordering information.

Cooling With Ventilation
Subrato Chandra, Philip W. Fairey, and Michael Houston
1986; 84 pp.
publication #061-000-00688-5
(out of print; available from the "Government documents" section of main libraries
or from The Department of Energy (202)556-8372)

Cooling With Ventilation examines ways to design houses which integrate passive low-energy technologies with air-conditioning to meet cooling needs efficiently in climates with both high temperatures and high humidity. While this detailed, practical report primarily addresses new construction, there is much valuable information applicable to existing homes. Energy-efficient options discussed include: strategies for reducing cooling loads through window shading and radiant barrier roof and wall systems; guidelines for selection and use of ceiling and whole-house fans; and building and landscape designs which enhance natural ventilation. The work is profusely illustrated and effectively communicates to both individuals and professional homebuilders.

Excerpts:

➤ A roof radiant barrier, placed in the airspace between a sun-heated roof and the cooler attic floor, eliminates most radiant heat transfer across the attic airspace. A roof barrier system with R-19 ceiling insulation is more effective than R-30 ceiling insulation as far north as Baltimore. Roof barrier systems should be installed in an attic in a manner to avoid dust accumulation on the reflective surface since dust reduces performance. Cooling needs can be reduced by up to 10%, with payback in less than five years.

➤ For every Fahrenheit degree a house thermostat is raised, air-conditioning costs are reduced by 7-10%. Since an air-circulation fan (ceiling, paddle, or portable) allows a thermostat increase of about 4°F with no decrease in human comfort, it can provide up to 40% savings in cooling costs.

5J. Greenhouse/Sunspace Additions

Imagine a simple greenhouse, attached to a living room, turned to the winter sun, and filled with shelves for flowers and vegetables. It has an entrance from the house—so you can go into it and use it in the winter without going outdoors, and it has an entrance from the garden—so you can use it as a workshop while you are out in the garden and not have to walk through the house. This greenhouse then becomes a wonderful place: a source of life, a place where flowers can be grown as part of the life of the house. For someone who has not experienced a greenhouse as an extension of the house, it may be hard to recognize how fundamental it becomes. It is a world unto itself, as definite and wonderful as fire or water, and it provides an experience which can hardly be matched by any other pattern.

Christopher Alexander, *A Pattern Language*

Besides greatly enhancing a home's livability, a sunspace or greenhouse (the former is designed primarily as a living space, the latter to grow plants) can also supply a substantial portion of its heating needs. Realizing the most benefits from either style addition, however, requires careful design and construction so that it performs well as a living space, growing space, or solar heat collector, and requires low maintenance. The books in this section will help you decide what type of sunspace or greenhouse will best accommodate your needs, site, and budget, show you how to go about designing, building, and/or purchasing it, and give you advice about ways to equip and maintain your completed structure.

Residential and Commercial Sunspaces
1990 edition; 80 pp.
$4.95 postpaid from:
Home Buyer Publications
P.O. Box 220039
Chantilly VA 22022
(800)826-3893

This glossy annual magazine answers many of the most frequently asked questions about sunspaces and greenhouses. It offers valuable information and advice on adding a sunspace/greenhouse to your home or upgrading an existing one (the coverage, in general, emphasizes the purchase of manufactured components). Ten beautifully illustrated articles address a broad range of relevant topics, including: selecting the best sunspace for your home, planning sunspaces for the healthy coexistence of plants and people, designing your greenhouse for maximum heating, installing spas or hot tubs in sunspaces, the greenhouse as an investment, sunspaces for low-rise condominiums and townhouses, and preventative care and general maintenance of sunspaces. In addition, *Residential and Commercial Sunspaces* provides a complete listing of greenhouse/sunspace manufacturers and a state-by-state list of greenhouse builders/dealers.

Excerpts:

➤ *It is important to take into consideration shadows cast by trees or buildings. The winter sun is low in the sky and any obstacle over 10 feet tall that is within 15 feet of the south glass is likely to block the sun. If your greenhouse falls in the shade only in the early morning or late afternoon there is no major cause for concern. The period of the day when direct sunlight is most important is between 10 AM and 3 PM. It's during this time that the majority of heat energy from the sun is there for the taking. Be particularly wary of big trees. A well formed deciduous (winter leaf shedding) tree will screen over 40% of the winter sunlight as it passes through its branch structure. A big evergreen can be as effective as the neighbor's garage at shading sunlight from your greenhouse. When you find such conditions you don't necessarily have to discard the idea of a greenhouse...just don't plan on substantial solar heating to come out of it.*

➤ *In addition to creating a structurally sound enclosure, the glass in a sunspace must also transmit light and view while controlling the the flow of heat, keeping it in during the winter and out during the summer. Fortunately, there is a variety of glazing products on the market today that cut down on heat loss, minimize heat gain and reduce air infiltration. These new glazing systems may "look" like typical windows but they "act" like completely self contained energy saving systems.*

The Homeowner's Complete Handbook For Add-On Solar Greenhouses & Sunspaces
Andrew M. Shapiro
Rodale Press
1985; 355 pp.
(Out of print; borrow from your local library)

Very thorough, this book is the best and most up-to-date reference we know of on designing and building energy-efficient sunspace or greenhouse additions. Whether the goal of the project is to provide solar heat, fresh vegetables and flowers, or an enjoyable living space, Shapiro authoritatively presents the critical planning, design, and building information needed at each step in the process to get the job done right. The book can help both the do-it-yourselfer and the professional builder answer such essential questions as: what design options are best suited for a given site, climate, and budget; how much solar heat will a sunspace contribute to a house; should you buy a manufactured greenhouse or build from scratch; and the best type of building material/product—caulk, glazing, insulation, etc.—and construction detailing for a particular application. Lots of photographs and illustrations reinforce the clearly written text. In addition, the appendices list sources for many hard-to-find greenhouse products.

Excerpts:

➤ *Of the four factors necessary for plant growth—air, water, light and nutrients—light and ventilation (air) are the most often neglected elements in solar greenhouse design. But they are, in fact, the elements that must be the most thoroughly planned before construction begins. Problems of inadequate light and ventilation are difficult and expensive to remedy after the greenhouse is built.*

➤ *Whatever style you use, be sure that the interior sheathing is moisture resistant. It should be as moisture resistant as outside sheathing, to withstand the high humidity you'll have if you grow many plants. If you use plywood, use an exterior grade or MDO board (medium-density-overlay plywood). MDO has a paper covered surface that looks like drywall but is actually much more durable than exterior grade plywood. If you use drywall, use the moisture-resistant type that is used in bathrooms. After the sheathing is up, paint on a vapor-resistant primer, such as alkyd resin primer or latex vapor-barrier primer. The resin primer is preferred for wood sheathing, since it has greater adhesion. Pay attention to painting any exposed edges of sheathings, since they are particularly susceptible to water. All caulking should be done after the sheathing is primed. Caulk all joints and edges, let the caulk cure and then put on the finish coats of paint. Use only galvanized nails or screws.*

The Food and Heat Producing Solar Greenhouse
Bill Yanda and Rick Fisher
1980; 208 pp.
$8.00 plus shipping from:
John Muir Publications
P.O. Box 613
Santa Fe NM 87504
(505)982-4078

Written by two of the pioneers in the field, this book offers an excellent introduction to building and operating greenhouses that will contribute solar heat to your home and put fresh, nutritious vegetables on your table. The basics of designing and constructing a simple attached or free standing greenhouse are covered, as are the procedures for planting, maintaining, and harvesting crops for optimal food production. Lots of practical "how and why" explanations are given and reinforced with numerous photos and illustrations. Diverse and interesting examples of greenhouses built across the U.S. are also shown, running the design gamut from small, inexpensive plastic ones tacked onto existing homes to deluxe, newly built, "greenhomes"—structures which incorporate the house and greenhouse as integral elements. Though new building materials and design techniques have been developed since this book was published, most of its content still offers good fundamental advice and ideas to prospective greenhouse builders or buyers.

Excerpts:

➤ *When you build your greenhouse, you will be creating a very special space, an earth in microcosm. You will control the character of the space to a great extent. Your imagination and design will determine how well the natural life force sustains itself and what you derive from it in return. You are, in effect, producing a living place that will grow and evolve with a life force of its own. The special environment that you will create is a biosphere. Webster's definition of a biosphere is: "A part of the world in which life can exist...living beings being together with their environment." As a living being, you are an essential element in maintaining your biosphere. Sowing seeds, nurturing the earth, watering, fertilizing plants and soil, and controlling the temperature and humidity will be your contribution to the biosphere. The greenhouse will reward you with the personal fulfillment of living within the cycle of growth.*

➤ *An important aspect of solar greenhouses is that the principles of design can be applied at any economic level. The $7.00 recycled lumber and polyethylene greenhouse slapped to the south side of a dilapidated dwelling can be just as important and valid a solar application as a $200,000 new solar greenhome under construction in a nearby resort community.*

➤ *Together with sunlight and water, carbon dioxide [CO_2] is essential for photosynthesis. Minimum CO_2 for plant growth is 3%; doubling CO_2 in a greenhouse can approximately double photosynthesis. Increasing carbon dioxide levels in a greenhouse can partially offset the reduction of light in winter. An attached greenhouse has a CO_2 advantage over an independent one in that the air from the home circulating through the greenhouse on winter days is naturally higher in CO_2 than outside air. This is another example of the symbiotic relationship between house and greenhouse.*

➤ *A well-designed solar greenhouse has a passive convection cycle established by proper venting to the adjoining structure. Heated air in the greenhouse rises and flows through a high opening into the home. A low opening in the shared wall allows cool air from the house to enter the greenhouse for heating. Without any mechanical devices this natural cycle will function continuously on any relatively sunny day.*

The Bountiful Solar Greenhouse: A Guide To Year-Round Food Production
Shane Smith
1982; 221 pp.
John Muir Publications
(Out of print; borrow from your local library)

Raising food crops in a solar greenhouse requires very different growing methods than those used in backyard gardens. This book clearly explains the fundamentals and specific techniques which indoor gardeners will need to know to grow healthy and productive crops in the unique environment of a solar greenhouse. For example, greenhouse plants must adapt to lower light levels, higher humidity, limited air circulation, and often greater vulnerability to pests and disease. The comprehensive text is friendly and understandable. The topics addressed include the solar greenhouse environment, interior layout design, crop layout, selecting solar greenhouse crops and varieties, plant propagation, fertilization techniques, flowering and pollination, greenhouse food crop scheduling, and pest and disease control. Organic gardening techniques and integrated biological pest controls are stressed. With this straightforward reference in hand, you can confidently start growing a variety of tasty, nutritious crops through the winter, including sweet, flavorful tomatoes and, with some luck and plenty of tender loving care, even such warm weather exotics as figs and citrus fruits.

Excerpts:

➤ *It's when your first plant dies or becomes sickly that you fully realize your greenhouse is a miniature ecological environment that won't always do as you wish. You can fight it with a war-like extermination attitude. You can let it go to hell with pests and diseases running rampant, or you can manage it ecologically, trying to create new balances and microenvironments to produce the desired result...food. All new greenhouses go through a "honeymoon" period. It usually takes 2-8 months before the first pest or disease attacks. The first pest usually shows up just when people begin to get cocky about how pest-free things are. After that, watch out. It will be constant excitement, with a few new pests or diseases regularly finding a way to prevent boredom in your greenhouse. Some will be easy to deal with, while others will be quite challenging. The first step when things go wrong is to learn to look at your greenhouse. It's so easy to look and not see. Don't even attempt to figure out the problem if you're feeling rushed or nervous. A calm, relaxing time of day is best. When something goes wrong, determining the cause requires looking closely at individual leaves as well as examining the greenhouse for general trends. Looking closely is helped greatly by a magnifying glass. The type used for reading will do. Low cost hand lenses (10x) are also a great tool; usually they can be be found at college book stores because they are often used in labs. When looking closely, don't just look at the top of the leaves near the aisle, but look under the leaves and into the far corners of the beds. Try to do this regularly. I like to do it before my day gets going, walking around the greenhouse with my coffee cup in one hand and my hand lens in the other.*

➤ *To best utilize greenhouse space, prune or train your plants. Greenhouse tomatoes can grow as high as 10' plus, and if properly trained can yield all the way up the vine. Pruning should be done only to "greenhouse variety" tomatoes or those listed as indeterminate or vining. Never prune bush or determinate varieties. As with transplanting and seed sowing, before pruning is begun wash your hands with soap and water to prevent the spread of disease.*

5K. State-Of-The-Art Building Materials and Technology

Deciding to build an energy-efficient home is one thing; finding the best products and materials to do the job is another. The references in this section can help you identify what options are available and where to find them. Since the information in these references can become dated rather quickly, consider borrowing them. You might be able to find these or other sources of information at college libraries, or in the office of an energy-conscious architect, engineer, builder, energy auditor, or alternative energy professional.

Solaplexus Product File
1990 edition
$58 postpaid from:
Solaplexus
21 Tamarack Circle
Fishkill NY 12524
(914)896-4796

Compiled by an experienced crew of energy-efficient house designers and builders at Solaplexus, the Product File is a valuable source-book for products that enhance the energy efficiency of new or existing homes. The 3-inch-thick looseleaf binder contains advertising literature for 150 select products ranging from energy-efficient windows to insulated concrete blocks to whole-house ventilators. Products are organized and indexed by eight major categories: sitework and foundations; framing and insulation; infiltration; windows and window insulation; sunspaces and greenhouses; heat absorption and storage; mechanical/controls; and hot water/water conservation. Advertisers don't pay to get into this product information catalog or they pay a small handling charge if what they submit is large. They are included only if the professionals at Solaplexus think the product is useful, unique, or hard to find. A large number of new and existing products are constantly reviewed and the best of these are ferreted out for inclusion in future editions. They also publish a Solaplexus Radon Product and Service Guide, a unique catalog of manufacturer's literature on more than 100 radon-related products and services ($48.00 postpaid).

Also see the Resource-Efficient Housing Periodicals listed in Section 2, and Catalogs and Source Books listed in Section 4.

5L. Community-Scale Housing/Planning

It is easy to dream about making our society more ecologically sound. Working to make this come about, though, is another matter. If we declare, for example, the village, town, and city are the primary physical building blocks of society, then it quickly becomes clear that any cohesive visions must consider the relationships between such complex and interconnected elements as ecology, technology, politics, and sociology. The references in this section explore these elements from many perspectives. They propose a variety of exciting strategies for making existing communities more sustainable, and they present designs for new communities which incorporate, from the ground up, resource efficiency into their infrastructure.

Cohousing: A Contemporary Approach to Housing Ourselves
Katherine McCamant & Charles Durrett
1988; 208 pp.
$22.80 postpaid from:
Habitat Press
1250 Addison St., #113
Berkeley CA 94702
(415)549-9980

Cohousing is a new approach to participatory human settlement that combines privately owned housing with communally owned amenities. The book is written by two American architects who spent 2 years studying cohousing projects in Denmark. Cohousing is based primarily on four ideas: 1) participatory process—residents organize and participate in the planning and design process for the housing development and are responsible for all final decisions; 2) intentional neighborhood design—the physical design encourages a strong sense of community; 3) extensive common facilities—an integral part of the community, common areas are designed for daily use, to supplement private living areas; 4) complete resident management—residents manage the development making decisions of common concern at community meetings.

Because residents share facilities that would otherwise be replicated in each household, the communities are more resource efficient by their very nature. The automobile is typically relegated to the periphery to allow for safe play areas and quiet zones for the residents. Buildings are clustered to allow the remaining land to be used for community gardens, play fields, or woodland. In short, cohousing creates pleasant, neighborly places to live. The book offers a thorough explanation of these concepts and describes several examples of Danish cohousing communities. It concludes with chapters on the development process, community legal structures, and design considerations.

The authors have started a development company to bring the idea to the American housing market. Several cohousing communities are in various planning stages throughout the country. Davis, California, will likely become the first city with a cohousing community conceived and built by its intended residents.

Reviewed by Eric Anderson

Excerpts:

➤ *Traditional forms of housing no longer address the needs of many people. Dramatic demographic and economic changes are taking place in our society and most of us feel the effects of these trends in our own lives. Things that people once took for granted—family, community, a sense of belonging—must now be actively sought out. Many people are mis-housed, ill-housed or unhoused because of the lack of appropriate options.*

> In many respects, cohousing is not a new concept. In the past, most people lived in villages or tightly knit urban neighborhoods. Even today, people in less industrialized regions typically live in small communities linked by multiple interdependencies. Members of such communities know each other over many years; they are familiar with each other's families and histories, talents and weaknesses. This kind of relationship demands accountability, but in return provides security and a sense of belonging.

Organizations offering information and referrals on cohousing:

Innovative Housing
2169 E. Francisco Blvd.,
Suite E
San Rafael CA 94901
(415)457-4593

**Cooperative Resources
and Services Project (CRSP)**
Los Angeles CA
(213)738-1254

Cohousing Company
Berkeley CA
(415)549-9980

Resettling America: Energy, Ecology and Community:
The Movement Toward Local Self-Reliance
Gary Coates, editor
1981; 555 pp.
$27.50 hardback and $17.95 paperback postpaid from:
Brick House Publishing Co.
P.O. Box 134
Acton MA 01720
(603)487-3718

According to its publishers, "*Resettling America* provides practical, people-oriented solutions to the complex community problems of food, energy and shelter. Rooted in the theories of Mumford, From, Schumacher, Bateson and others, the twenty-two articles in this book contain the best ideas about ways of living more harmoniously with nature and with each other. Coates is concerned not with the current emphasis on self-sufficiency but on the interdependencies that can enhance a community or...if neglected...destroy it."

"*Resettling America* is written in the belief that human environments must grow out of the collective efforts of their inhabitants and be integrated gracefully and intelligently with the natural systems upon which all life is based. Its joyful, holistic approach, the optimistic view of the future and its excellent illustrations make *Resettling America* a major contribution to the broad implementation of that belief."

We agree. This excellent compendium is among the best introductions to community.

Excerpts:

> If a significant reduction in energy consumption is to be achieved, the energy use inside a building cannot be separated from the energy use dictated by its location and its interrelationships with other buildings. A building is tied to energy use not only by its structural and mechanical design, but by its implicit infrastructure (the amount of pipes, roads, and utility wires it demands), and by its connections to employment areas and community services.

> Over the long run (the next 50 years and beyond) these changes must be complemented by and coordinated with a bioregionally based shift in the location of population and the allocation of employment. We must repopulate our rural areas as we restructure our urban habitat, if we are to achieve the overall goal of meeting basic human needs from renewable resources. This implies the development of policies for the conversion of nonviable megalopolitan areas to productive uses (e.g., urban agriculture), the construction of rural new towns and the reconstruction of more viable communities in existing regional cities and small towns.

➤ *Similarly, programs aimed at energy conservation and solar retrofitting of existing commercial and residential areas would not only rehabilitate existing building stock, but would also increase local employment, thereby decreasing welfare and unemployment costs, while simultaneously reducing the outflow of local capital for increasingly costly and expensive fossil fuels.*

➤ *Central to the rural new town idea is the concept of the community land trust. A community land trust (CLT) is a legal entity that serves to hold land in stewardship for perpetuity. Land which is either purchased by or donated to the trust is "decommoditized" by being taken permanently off the market. The trust is permitted only to lease land, never to sell it. Land leases, at nominal cost, are made available only to actual or potential direct users. Thus usership rights, rather than the rights of ownership, become paramount. Subleases are not permitted and the possibility of absentee land-lordism is permanently avoided.*

Sustainable Communities: A New Design Synthesis for Cities, Suburbs and Towns
Sim Van der Ryn & Peter Calthorpe
1986; 238 pp.
$23.00 postpaid from:
Sierra Club Bookstore
730 Polk Street
San Francisco CA 94109
(415)923-5600

Sustainability implies that the use of energy and materials in an urban area can be in balance with what the region can supply continuously through natural processes such as photosynthesis, biological decomposition, and the biochemical processes that support life. The immediate implications of this principle are a vastly reduced energy budget for cities, and a smaller, more compact urban pattern interspersed with productive areas to collect energy, grow crops for food, fiber and energy, and recycle wastes.

How this concept is to be implemented is what this book is about. It isn't just talk; there are case studies and lots of eminently practical ideas here, complete with the economics. The call to action is backed philosophically by seven essays from such authors as Paul Hawken and John Todd. Solid and timely, the book is a recipe for what we can and probably must do.

Reviewed by J. Baldwin in *The Essential Whole Earth Catalog*

Excerpts:

➤ *In older cities and towns, the framework and traditions for compact and efficient communities are already in place. Not to reuse them not only wastes the material, energy, and ingenuity that created them in the first place, it squanders our history and depth. By reuse, we are forced to relearn many of the traditions and disciplines lost to modern architecture and planning. These lessons range from how to daylight a building, to how a street becomes a neighborhood; from how to shelter the pedestrian and make common areas that work, to how certain building forms respond to the local climate. Many of these older urban patterns were born of climate and community as well as technologies and style. While respecting these traditions, we must modify them according to our current needs and knowledge. We know more about passive solar heating and cooling, we have different requirements for housing types and workplaces, and we have new techniques for transportation, utilities, and services. The challenge is to synthesize the relevant pieces of the past with the progressive ideas of the present.*

➤ *Buildings have a responsibility beyond their walls. Their location and density control the kind of transportation mix that is viable; their climatic intelligence controls the number of power plants we build and the amount of energy we import; their configuration affects the health of the community; and their sensitivity either raises our spirits or dulls our exuberance.*

Also, see *Permaculture (A Design Manual)*, reviewed in Section 8.

5M. Alternative Construction

Alternative Housebuilding
Mike McClintock
1989; 367 pp.
$18.95 from:
Sterling Publishing Co.
387 Park Avenue South
New York NY 10016

Why alternative housebuilding? To "enjoy the trip as much as the destination" says owner-builder Mike McClintock. If you're looking into the alternatives, this book is an excellent, practical reference. Log, timber-frame, pole, cordwood, stone, earth and earth-sheltered houses are discussed. The design decisions and pre-construction needs precede discussions of the techniques of each method, including energy efficiency considerations. A good book for comparing between building methods and deciding on the style that best suits your needs.

Excerpts:

➤ *If you work without professional help you will undoubtedly make some mistakes. Expect them. Learn from them. And press on. Alternative housebuildng won't stump you with high-tech engineering trickery. Alternative materials make sense. They will be familiar and comfortable from the start, even though you may need some time to use them with great skill.*

➤ *Pole house bracing: Properly embedded poles are strong enough to stand on their own. You can think of the depth of embedment as compensating for the root system on a tree in the forest. And those trees stand very well without brackets and concrete and steel pins and soil cement. But on less-than-ideal sites (and there are more and more of them compared to excellent natural sites), bracing between poles can reduce embedding requirements.*

Plastered Straw Bale Construction: Super Efficient and Economical Buildings
David Bainbridge, Athena and Bill Steen
1991
$10 postpaid from:
The Canelo Project
HCR Box 324
Canelo AZ 85611

The story of the Three Little Pigs was a lie. Straw is an excellent construction material and has been used to build permanent structures for over 100 years. Throughout midwestern United States and Canada, plastered straw bales have been used to construct homes, churches, barns, schools, hotels, airplane hangers, government buildings, and commercial buildings up to 25,000 square feet. *Plastered Straw Bale Construction* is the everything-you-always-wanted-to-know book on straw bale construction. Documented details are provided on the structural integrity, energy efficiency, fire safety, environmental benefits, and potential problems of this type of construction. Also available from this address for $5 is *Straw Bale Buildings: A Bibliography in Progress*, which lists over 80 articles that have been written on straw bale construction in journals ranging from *Agricultural Engineering*, *Paper Trade Journal*, and *Fine Homebuilding* to *Mother Earth News* and *The Permaculture Activist*.

Excerpts:

➤ Building walls from straw is much less labor intensive than using either adobe, brick or stone, less damaging to the forests than using wood framing, easier to work with than wood, steel, brick or concrete, and provides much better insulation than any of the above.

➤ Material costs represent less than a fifth of the cost of the wall system so owner-builders can realize even greater savings by providing the labor. Bale houses recently constructed in New Mexico and California have been owner-built for less than $10 per square foot.

➤ Straw bale buildings are thermally efficient and energy conserving, with R-values of 26-160 depending on the straw and the wall thickness. They can provide improved comfort and substantial energy savings compared to much more expensive, conventional building systems.

➤ The National Research Council of Canada carried out fire safety tests of plastered straw bales and found them to be better than most conventional building materials. The mortar-encased bales passed the small scale fire test with a maximum temperature rise of only 110°F over four hours, double the required time.

A Straw Bale Primer
S. O. MacDonald and Orien MacDonald
November 1991; 25pp.
$10 postpaid from:
S. O. MacDonald
P.O. Box 58
Gila NM 88038

This is the how-to book for do-it-yourselfers, complete with detailed high quality hand drawings and step-by-step instructions. This publication is a must for anyone building with bales for the first time. Details are provided on using bales as structural material and as infill with a post-and-beam frame, wiring with AC and 12 volt photovoltaic systems, and stucco recipes and techniques. If a picture is worth a thousand words, then this book is the bible of straw bale construction. Contains over 2 dozen drawings and an easy-to-follow 10-step plan.

Excerpts:

➤ Nebraska-style (i.e., roof resting directly on bale walls without post-and-beam support) straw bale houses are still being inhabited after almost 90 years. Matts Myhrman tells of one 92 year old Nebraska woman who had lived in a house made of straw for 50 years and raised 5 children in it. When asked what she remembered about it, she said, "It was cool in the summer and warm in the winter."

➤ Recent local 2-wire straw bale prices ranged from $1.50 per bale to $2.50 delivered. Three-wire models cost a little over $4.00 each. Our 20 x 32-ft house required about 175 bales (fiberglass insulation went in the ceiling). A 20 x 36-ft studio with high footings required 155 bales for the walls. A 12 x 16-ft cabin needed 76 bales, including 13 bales of straw spread loose to a depth of 20 inches in the ceiling space.

➤ Better to put effort (and money) into conservation (i.e., superinsulation and no infiltration) than into large amounts of added glass and mass.

The Complete Book of Cordwood Masonry Housebuilding:
The Earthwood Method

Robert L. Roy
1992; 264 pp.
$16.95 from:
Earthwood
RR 1, Box 105
West Chazy NY 12992
(518)493-7744

This practical do-it-yourself guide updates an age old building technique, cordwood masonry construction. Cordwood masonry houses incorporate walls made from stacked short logs—called log ends—laid up widthwise and bound together within a strong mortar matrix. There are several benefits to this type of construction. First, it's fairly inexpensive, especially if you cut the wood yourself. Secondly, it doesn't take great technical skill. And third, the resulting home can be visually striking and, if proper attention is paid to insulating details, quite energy-efficient. Roy highlights the three different ways to employ cordwood masonry in building: within a post-and-beam framework; within a log or log-end framework of built-up corners; and as a load-supporting curved wall. With the help of numerous clear construction drawings and photos of work in progress, he then takes you step-by-step through the process of designing and building a cordwood home. All the major aspects involved are tackled as well as many finish details. Included are up-to-date case-histories of houses whose owners—many of them first-time builders—created unique, handsome, low-cost, and energy-efficient dwellings.

The second part of the book documents the construction of one particular round, earthsheltered, cordwood home, the author's own Earthwood house. It takes you from foundation to finished roof and includes the construction of cordwood outbuildings: sauna, office, shed, etc.

Excerpts:

➤ *It is very important, when laying up the first course, to get away from the flat plate and into a random pattern as quickly as possible. If the first course is laid with log-ends of the same diameter, there is a danger of getting stuck in a pattern which is hard to break and, paradoxically, hard to maintain. Aesthetically, masonry looks good if it is totally random or if it is very carefully laid up to a pattern. It looks bad if someone tried to incorporate a pattern and failed; and it looks bad if a seemingly random wall becomes patterned.*

➤ *A constant part of design is—or should be—costing analyses. No sense designing the unaffordable. The materials we had were right for a 38'8" diameter round house. A rough estimate of the materials' cost of the one-story design was approximately $12,000. A good method of stimulating the imagination in house design—or in writing science fiction, as John Wyndham was fond of saying— is to ask, "What if...?? I asked myself, "What if the house had two stories? How much would this cost?" I totaled it up. To add a second story of the same size would require about five extra cords of wood for the log ends, a few extra posts, floor joists and 1,000 square feet of flooring, a stairway, and some extra internal wall framing and covering, including a few more doors and windows. The foundation and earth-roof structure would remain constant, as well as all the ancillary systems, such as the septic tank, driveway, and wind plant. I figured the cost of the second story to be about $4,000, just $4 per square foot, compared with $12 for the first floor. It seemed too cheap to turn down, and provided scope for such integrative design features as a hot tub, a pool table, and a reasonably large office. Here would be a house we could grow into.*

Illustration by David Gross, Public Image, Boulder CO

6. Owner-Builder Design and Construction

One of the greatest pleasures of life is to build a house for one's self. . . . I notice how eager all men are in building their houses, how they linger about them or even about their proposed sites. When the cellar is being dug, they went to take a hand in it; the earth evidently looks a little different, a little more friendly and congenial than other earth. When the foundations walls are up and the first floor is rudely sketched by rough timbers, I see them walking pensively from one imaginary room to another, or sitting long and long, wrapped in sweet reverie, upon the naked joist.

John Burroughs, *Signs and Seasons*

There is some of the same fitness in a man's building his own house that there is in a bird's building its own nest. Who knows but if men constructed their dwellings, with their own hands, and provided food for themselves and families simply and honestly enough, the poetic faculty would be universally developed, as birds universally sing when they are so engaged? But alas! We do like cowbirds and cuckoos, which lay their eggs in nest which other birds have built.

Henry David Thoreau, *Walden*

Building your own home is the ultimate do-it-yourself project, one which requires great forethought, planning, and hard work.

Nearly one out of every five new houses built in this country is constructed, wholly or in part, by owner-builders. Such efforts can not only save money, but also create custom dwellings which uniquely reflect the occupants' tastes, values, and lifestyles.

Building your own home is the ultimate do-it-yourself project, one which requires great forethought, planning, and hard work. All that time and work is rewarded, however, when the end result—your home—enriches your life with a sense of accomplishment and beauty that simply can't be bought.

There are many ways to get involved in the construction of your own home. You can take a full-fledged, I'm-gonna-do-it-all approach: designing the house, drafting building plans, pouring the foundation, raising the frame, closing it in, finishing the interior, and landscaping the site. Another option, well advised for the novice builder, is to get some help. Hiring skilled professionals, whether architects, masons, carpenters, electricians, or jack-of-all-trades-builders, to work with you can help you get the job done most smoothly and cost-effectively. And besides, you'll probably enjoy the whole process more while working with a pro at your side who can guide you through the crises that typically crop up on the job site.

Before seriously considering building your own home, it is critical that you understand the magnitude of the project and are aware of all the issues, details, and logistics involved. This section highlights several outstanding resources which can help equip the "ultimate do-it-yourselfer" with the knowledge and skills required to quit dreaming about a dream house and start building it.

6A. Owner-Builder References

Designing Houses: An Illustrated Guide to Building Your Own Home
Les Walker and Jeff Milstein
1976; 152 pp.
$12.40 postpaid from:
The Overlook Press
RR 1, Box 496
Woodstock NY 12498
(914)679-6838

So you want to be an architect, eh? This book will show you how, right down to dressing like a real-life member of the profession. The authors seize on a fictional couple named Fred and Lois who decide to design their own home. Fred and Lois then walk you through all the steps that go into that process, beginning with the aforementioned wardrobe selections and how to set up a fully-equipped architect's office. Once that is done, you are shown how to think, dream, see, and draw like an architect. Next come site planning principles and the use of simple, basic design concepts. Light, movement, climate, and shape are all addressed. You are shown how to make cardboard models of your design and there is an excellent checklist of details that can help you personalize your house. All of these exercises lead up to the final payoff: the ability to draw your own construction plans. The book's only notable drawback is that it isn't quite up to date regarding the latest energy-efficient design strategies and hardware, and tends to lead one towards more traditional types of home design. On the other hand, the funky, and informative cartoon-like illustrations which are liberally scattered throughout make the whole volume enjoyable. In general, this book is a marvelous introduction to the world of do-it-yourself architecture and can help you get your vague architectural notions and goals down in black and white.

Reviewed by Joe Eddy Brown in *The Essential Whole Earth Catalog,*
and Brian Kent of *Maine Tomorrow*

Excerpt:

➤ *Looking: How you see and what you observe is very important. You can teach yourself to be more visually observant. Look at inside and outside spaces you like. Ask yourself why you like them. Study what is going on in the space. How does that light enter? What does it bounce off of? How are color and texture used? What is the feeling—open? intimate? Try asking yourself these questions as you look. One way to develop your visual comprehension is to look at a building for a while; then, without looking, try to draw it. Then compare what you've drawn to the building.*

Building Your Own House
Robert Roskind
1984; 438 pp.
$19.95 postpaid for Part 1
$8.00 postpaid for Part 2 from:
Owner Builder Center
1250 Addison Street, Suite 209
Berkeley CA 94702
(415)848-6860

This companion volume to *Before You Build* (reviewed above) picks up where the latter left off, addressing such matters as when to hire or contract, purchasing tips on lumber, and work habits and attitudes. It then guides the novice owner-builder step-by-step through the technical process of building a house, from getting a foundation in and framing the structure to sheathing the roof and walls and installing the windows. The information is complete and well illustrated, with special attention given to the "tricky" parts—the details inexperienced builders commonly get into trouble with. In addition to the expected instruction, each chapter includes features such as What You'll Be Doing, What To Expect, and What You'll Need for each task, which include specific elements describing The Margin of Error, The Most Common Mistakes, and Safety and Awareness. The book is nicely rounded out with a set of Worksheets and Daily Checklists for every aspect of the job, invaluable tools to help you manage building your own house from start to finish.

➤ *Design is by far the most important single process of the entire project. Along with good workmanship and sound engineering, design is a keynote in the building of a successful house. If it is designed poorly to begin with, no amount of expert craftsmanship can correct the mistakes that are written into the design. Before you ever start to build, consider this point well. A successful design is one that is the most supportive of the lives of you and your family, a place that feels like a loving home, a basis from which to grow and confidently confront the rest of the world. This is the basic function of a home.*

➤ *I think every owner builder should couple themselves with a local professional to act as their mentor and advisor during the construction process. A construction guru if you will. Pay them by the hour to advise you on key points. They can inspect the forms before the pour, inspect the framing, help with complicated roof framing, solve problems, correct mistakes, etc. The money will be well spent.*

➤ *More than in almost any other area of housebuilding, you want to constantly strive for an efficient system in roofing materials with the least amount of effort in the least amount of time. Go watch a few professionals at work. Note the way they sit, where the materials are in relation to where they are working, what their assistants do, what tools they have and what tricks they use. Often observing a professional for half an hour can save you many hours on your own roof. Speed and efficiency of energy use are essential here.*

The Owner-Builder Experience: How to Design and Build Your Own Home
Dennis Holloway and Maureen McIntyre
1986; 188 pp.
$19.95 hardback postpaid from:
Rodale Press
33 East Minor Street
Emmaus PA 18098
(800)441-7761

The *Owner-Builder Experience* is an excellent primer for anyone considering building their own house. It will pull you out of the world of dream houses and "what ifs" and land you solidly in the middle of the real hammers-and-nails world of opportunities, choices, and pitfalls that await any owner-builder. Fluidly written and packed with practical, up-to-date information, the book takes you step by step through each of the significant details you have to consider when designing and building a home. Among the topics discussed are: the levels of involvement an owner-builder can undertake; ways to acquire necessary skills; finding and hiring professional assistance; designing your own home; choosing building techniques and materials; shopping for land; arranging financing; dealing with building codes; and last but certainly not least, invaluable advice on ways to carry out the project so you can enjoy the extraordinary experience of building your own home. Most importantly, the authors alert prospective owner-builders to pitfalls which, if overlooked, can potentially set them back at numerous points in the design/build process. Nice photos, charts, and drawings are featured throughout the book. The lengthy construction sequence flow chart shown in Appendix A is a particularly valuable tool to help organize the whole project—people, materials, equipment, and money.

Excerpts:

➤ *No matter how long you think it's going to take to build your house, it will take longer. Many owner-builders wish they had spent more time on planning and design. The amount of money you'll save on your project and the ease with which you'll accomplish it are more dependent on planning than any other factor. The time you spend designing and redesigning, exploring alternatives, estimating costs, shopping for "deals," and studying other owner-builders' experiences is the most valuable time you can spend. We find again and again that the people who ran into major problems and made expensive mistakes are the ones who didn't do the necessary planning or didn't want to spend the money to take a housebuilding class or consult with professionals.*

Owner Builder Center

1250 Addison Street, Suite 209
Berkeley CA 94702
(415)848-6860

The Owner Builder Center in Berkeley, California, is one of the first, and certainly the biggest of such enterprises—they've taught more than 10,000 people how to build. What the OBC staff has learned from all that teaching has been gathered into a series of workbooks and information kits. The following three publications are available from OBC. Write for a complete publications list.

Before You Build: A Preconstruction Guide

Robert Roskind
1983; 197 pp.
$11.95 postpaid from:
Owner Builder Center (address cited above)

Building your own home represents the largest single investment of money and time most people will make in their life. Without thorough preparation, owner-builders may encounter great frustration, delays, and even squander their money. *Before You Build* can help you avoid these pitfalls. This comprehensive guidebook/workbook addresses the critical issues which prospective owner-builders should consider to determine the feasibility of taking on such a project. Roskind has created an easy-to-use reference which will enable prospective owner-builders to asses confidently their desires and needs against the reality and constraints of their skills, budget, time, and attitude. The book fully outlines the planning, scheduling, and execution of all the significant tasks required to build a house efficiently. The narrative, worksheets, and checklists lead you one step at a time through the entire preconstruction process, including buying land, choosing a building site, identifying solar heating and passive cooling potential, examining water supply, waste disposal, and utility hookup options, designing the access road/driveway, meeting requirements for building permits, codes, and inspections, estimating building costs, and insuring and financing new home construction. Equally important is the Inner Resources section, which explores the often overlooked psychological effects a housebuilding project may have on owner-builders. Answering all the questions in this book before going ahead with any housebuilding project will ensure that, once underway, owner-builders encounter few if any costly monetary, labor, and/or emotional surprises.

Excerpts:

➤ *The impact of the property that you choose on the success of the entire project and especially on your life in the house once it is completed cannot be emphasized enough. There are three main considerations at this stage. First, be sure that the property you buy is suitable and workable for the project that you have in mind. With today's energy costs sometimes being greater than monthly mortgage payments, a second vital consideration for the potential land buyer concerns the solar and natural ventilation qualities of the land. Any house built today that does not use these design elements is obsolete before it is built. The third consideration is that once you find the property that has all the features you need, you are certain that it is really the piece you want and feel good about. If the land does not feel welcoming and appealing to you, it will not enhance the quality of your home life. Too often owners have chosen property by its price, solar orientation, location or some other physical feature of the property, or out of weariness of the search for the right piece, only to later realize that they never really feel quite at peace with the land and home.*

➤ *The house which actually costs less than its estimate is so rare that it ascends into the realm of miracles. Houses go over their estimate so commonly that it seems inevitable. The consequences of projected costs exceeding the amount planned can be ruinous—an additional several hundred dollars a month in loan or mortgage payments, for as long as thirty years. Such a long-term burden can seriously limit your ability to realize the other fantasies, like vacation, a new car or boat, or travel, for twenty to thirty years.*

6B. Owner-Builder Schools

Owner-builder products, publications, and organizations are more numerous than ever before. One of the best places to go for more information is your local owner-builder organization or school. The schools offer varying services, but they all share an orientation toward energy-efficient, intelligent housing that meets the needs of the occupants. Most offer classes, seminars, and workshops in all phases of the building process, as well as consultants who can help you work through the snags that you run into during the project. Many also act as informal "networking" centers, putting owner-builders in touch with each other, guiding them to useful government agencies and receptive lenders and helping them find well-qualified architects, realtors, tradespeople, and other sources of expertise and information. Following is a list of organizations around the United States and Canada which offer instruction in various types and phases of housebuilding to prospective owner-builders. Contact those that interest you for more information and ask in your area for other sources of instruction.

Dennis Holloway and Maureen McIntyre, *The Owner-Builder Experience*

Do-It-Yourself Building & Remodeling Classes

The addresses and a brief program description for each organization noted here follows this topically organized list.

Adobe/Earth Building
Rammed Earth Works
Southwest Solaradobe School

Conventional Framing
Durango Owner Builder Center
The Southface Energy Institute
Owner Builder Center at Houston
  Community College
Owner Builder Center at Berkeley
Owner Builder Center at Miami Dade
  Community College
Sacramento Owner Builder Center
Red Rocks Community College
University of California/Santa Barbara Extension
Yestermorrow Design/Build School

Cordwood/Underground
Earthwood Building School

Design/Architectural
Yestermorrow Design/Build School

Dome Building
Natural Spaces

Historic Preservation/Renovation
Eastfield Village

Building Skills for Women
Bear Mountain Outdoor School

Log Building
B. Allan Mackie School of Log Building
Bear Mountain Outdoor School
Great Lakes School of Log Building
Pat Wolfe Log Building School

Remodeling
The Southface Energy Institute
Owner Builder Center at Berkeley
Owner Builder Center at Miami Dade
  Community College
Sacramento Owner Builder Center
University of California/Santa Barbara Extension

Solar/Alternative Energy/Energy Efficiency
Solar Technology Institute
Florida Solar Energy Center
The Southface Energy Institute

Timber Framing/Post & Beam
Bear Mountain Outdoor School
Eastfield Village
Heartwood Owner-Builder School
Riverbend Timber Framing School
Shelter Institute
Timber Framers Guild of North America

Directory:

Alaska Craftsman Home Program
PO Box 876130, Wasill AK 99687, (907) 373-2247. Conducts a mandatory 2 day course for Alaskan residential contractors, as well as a semester program through state colleges.

B. Allan Mackie School of Log Building
P.O. Box 1925, Prince George, British Columbia V2L 4V3, Canada, (604)563-8738. Offers instruction in log building for novices and professionals. All sessions cover the same basic material, ranging from foundation and log selection through roofing and finishing.

Bear Mountain Outdoor School, Inc.
Hightown VA 24444, (703)468-2700. Offers practical building skills workshops, included log cabin construction, stone masonry, building skills for women, and timber frame construction.

Durango Owner-Builder Center
502 Ludwig Drive, Bayfield CO 81122, (303)884-9021 or 884-2226. Offers classes designed for novice and experienced builders who want to improve their design and construction skills.

Earthwood Building School
RR 1, Box 105, West Chazy NY 12992, (518)493-7744. Conducts workshops on earth sheltered and cordwood masonry at its northern New York state headquarters.

Eastfield Village
P.O. Box 143 RD, East Nassau NY 12062, (518)766-2422. Emphasizes historic preservation. The student can learn how to build a stone foundation, cut and shape frame timbers, make trim and moldings, and fabricate kitchen tinware or door hardware.

Florida Solar Energy Center, Continuing Education Office
300 State Road 401, Cape Canaveral FL 32920, (407)783-0300. Offers workshops on energy-efficient construction techniques, photovoltaic system design, and visions of quality developments.

Great Lakes School of Log Building
570 County Road #2, Isabella MN 55607, (612)822-5955 or (218)365-2126. Offers programs which can give participants the knowledge, experience, and skills required to build their own log house, cabin, or outbuilding.

Heartwood Owner Builder School
Johnson Road, Washington MA 01235 (413)623-6677. Offers workshops in timber framing, contracting, renovation, basic and finish carpentry, cabinetmaking, and energy-efficient housebuilding.

Owner Builder Center of Berkeley
1250 Addison St., Suite 209, Berkeley CA 94702, (415)848-6860. Offers a variety of classes that cover the nuts and bolts of building or remodeling a home from beginning to end.

Owner Builder Center at Houston Community College,
Community Service Programs
4141 Costa Rica, Houston TX 77092, (713)956-1178. dedicated to helping people improve the quality of their lives. It offers classes that teach everything from how to build a house to how to hang a ceiling fan.

Owner Builder Center
Miami Dade Community College
11011 S.W 104th Street, Miami FL 33176, (305)237-2600. Teaches people how to build or remodel their homes. Its goal is to encourage energy efficient and affordable housing by teaching skills that can save homeowners 10-50% of the cost of comparable contractor-built homes.

Natural Spaces
37955 Bridge Road, North Branch MN 55056, (612)674-4292. Offers hands-on owner builder dome construction workshops. Energy-efficient construction techniques are stressed.

Pat Wolfe Log Building School

R.R. 3, Ashton, Ontario K0A 1B0, Canada, (613)253-0631. Has 15 years of log building experience and offers hands-on courses, as well as a video on log building.

Rammed Earth Works

1350 Elm St. Napa CA 95257, (209)293-4924. Specializes in offering plans, workshops, and consultations to assist architects, contractors, and owner-builders design and build earthen homes.

Red Rocks Community College

13300 W. 6th Avenue, Lakewood CO 80401, (303)988-6160, Ext. 369 or 380. Offers courses on all aspects of house design and construction, such as drafting, carpentry, electrical, plumbing, masonry, passive solar house design and active solar system installation

Riverbend Timber Framing School

P.O. Box 26, Blissfield MI 48228, (517)486-4355. Conducts Timber Framing Classes at actual building sites throughout the country. Students receive instruction in blueprint reading, layout skills, and cutting procedures, and then are given the opportunity to develop hands-on log-construction building skills.

Sacramento Owner Builder Center, Inc.

4777 Sunrise, Fair Oaks CA 95628, (916)961-2453. offers house design and housebuilding courses which are designed for novices, but are sophisticated enough for the semi-professional. It also offers building consulting services, a computerized path of clients' projects, and a building inspection program for homebuyers.

Shelter Institute

38 Center Street, Bath ME 04530, (207)442-7938. Now in its seventeenth season, teaches people how to design and build their own post and beam houses.

Solar Technology Institute

P.O. Box 1115, Carbondale CO 81623-1115, (303) 963-0715. Hands-on education specializing in renewable energy technologies. Intensive workshops for practitioners include. Photovoltaics, passive solar design and micro-hydro electric systems. A comprehensive solar home program workshop series teaches participants how to design and build state-of-the-art energy-efficient solar homes.

The Southface Energy Institute

P.O. Box 5506, Atlanta GA 30307, (404)525-7657. Runs the Southface Home Builder School, which offers several workshops for homebuilding enthusiasts who want to learn the essentials required to build or contract the construction of their own house.

Southwest Solaradobe School

P.O. Box 153, Bosque NM 87006, (505)252-1382. Offers intensive workshops on building with earth at several locations in the Southwest and West. Students' individual needs and interests are taken into account, stressing passive heating and cooling techniques.

Timber Framers Guild of North America

P.O. Box 1046, Keene, NH 03431. A not-for-profit educational organization of over 700 members founded by and for timber framers, professional and amateur. They publish a quarterly journal, the *Timber Framers News*, and annually conduct national and regional conferences.

University of California/Santa Barbara Extension

Santa Barbara CA 93106, (805)893-4200. Offers a series of owner-builder classes that address subjects such as house-building, tile setting, finish house carpentry, and design or remodeling your own home.

Yestermorrow Design/Build School

P.O. Box 76A, Warren VT 05674, (802)496-5545. Courses are intensive programs of hands-on instruction. Students' time is divided between the studio, where they learn the skills and technical information involved in architectural design; and the building site, where they learn how to turn a blueprint into reality.

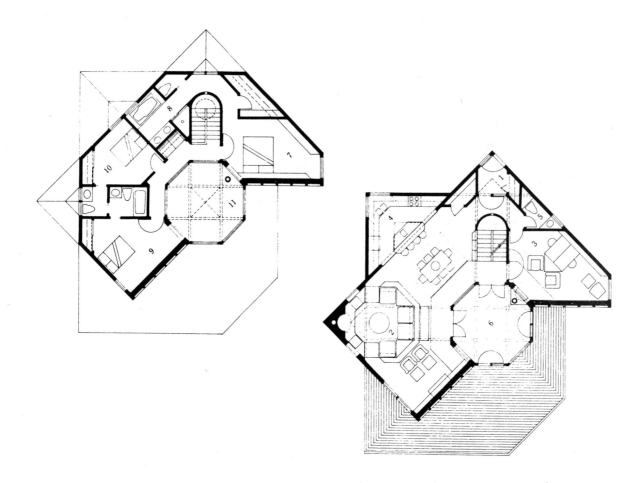

7. Energy-Efficient House Plans

House plan books and stock house plan packages can provide owner-builders (as well as people looking to contract out the construction of a new home) with invaluable sources of information, ranging from simple design and construction ideas to full sets of working drawings and construction documents. Numerous organizations produce or distribute these, including magazines, owner-builder schools, architecture firms, utility companies, and state energy offices, to name a few. One excellent way to track down many such resources is to contact the National Appropriate Technology Assistance Service or the Conservation And Renewable Energy Inquiry And Referral Service (both organizations are cited in Section 3B) and request that they send you their most up-to-date source lists for energy-efficient house plans. Make the most of any such inquiries by specifying the type of plans you're looking for: passive solar, superinsulated, earth-sheltered, log construction, attached greenhouse, etc. The following house plan sources represents a sampling of those cited by NATAS and CAREIRS.

House plan books and stock house plan packages can provide owner-builders with invaluable sources of information, ranging from simple design and construction ideas to full sets of working drawings and construction documents.

Illustration courtesy of *The Owner-Builder Experience*, Rodale Press, Emmaus, PA

7A. House Plan Sources

American Ingenuity, Inc.
**3500 Harlock Road, Melbourne FL 32934-7707,
(407)254-4220.** Offers energy-efficient, superinsulated dome kits using non-CFC foam and a patented prefabricated, panelized building system. For those homeowners who do not select one of the standard house plans, they can design a custom floor plan to fit individual lifestyles.

Architectural Designs,
Davis Publications, Inc.
380 Lexington Ave., New York NY 10017. Five issues per year, available at newsstands. Each issue contains approximately 200 plans for traditional and contemporary homes, including energy-efficient, solar and vacation home designs.

Best-Selling Home Plans
Hachette Magazines, 1633 Broadway, New York NY 10019, (800)526-4667. Bi-monthly. Features over 150 plans of various architects and designers. Each issue includes plans for about 30 solar homes incorporating passive solar features such as greenhouses, clerestories, and masonry storage walls. Some include earthberming, superinsulation, and active solar systems.

Better Homes & Gardens Home Plan Ideas,
Special Interest Publications
1716 Locust Street, Des Moines IA 50336. Quarterly (available at newstands). Includes plans for a wide variety of passive, earth-sheltered, and superinsulated homes.

The Bloodgood Plan Service
**3001 Grand Avenue, Des Moines IA 50312,
(800)752-6728.** Provides plans for energy-conserving houses of traditional and contemporary styling, ranging in size from 800 to 5000 square feet.

Energy Saving Homes, Vol. 1 No. 1
**Home Building Plan Services, Inc., 2235 NE
Sandy Blvd., Portland OR 97232, (503)234-9337.**
Contains plans for 57 energy-efficient homes.

Integrated Energy House Design Book
**Passive Solar Environments, 821 W. Main
Street, Kent OH 44240, (216)673-7449.** Lists 23 solar house plans available from PSE.

NU Solar Homes Planbook
**Northeast Utilities, P.O. Box 270, Hartford, CT
06141, (203)721-2715.** Discusses considerations in energy-conserving house construction and lists eight plans for traditional-in-appearance New England-style homes that are passive solar by design.

Passive Home Designs
**Florida Power & Light, P.O. Box 029100, Miami
FL 33102, (305)227-4332.** Brochure presents two homes designed for each of the three climatic regions of Florida.

Small Home Plans
**The Garlinghouse Company, Inc., 34 Industrial
Park Place, P.O. Box 1717, Middletown, CT
06457, (800)235-5700.** Features 185 plans for passive and energy-conserving homes with under 2000 square feet of floor area.

Solplan 5: Energy Conserving Passive Solar Houses
**The Drawing-Room Graphic Services, Ltd., Box
88627, North Vancouver, BC V7L 4L2, Canada,
(604)689-1841.** Presents plans for 21 energy-efficient homes.

8. Resource-Efficient Landscaping and Site Design

Perhaps for millions of years your land has been untouched by humans and it is beautiful and pure. For 30 to 60 years you will live on your land, so consider well what kind of impact your brief stay will have on that land. It is not really "your land" for we can never really own that land. We only have the privilege to use it as we will for a period of time. Before us and after us will come many other caretakers. It is possible for one man in his lifetime to destroy the aesthetic quality and useability of a piece of land for many generations to come. We are seeing this done all around us and for many of us, it is one of the many reasons we want to retreat into the shelter of our own home. Treat your land with love and respect, and appreciate the gift it is giving you, with its beauty, its quiet, and its love. Design and build with this in mind, and your land will reward you a hundredfold.

Robert Roskind, *Building Your Own Home*

Our treatment of the land around our homes makes a powerful statement about our feelings and commitment to the earth itself. The following books provide an insightful look at the connections between people, land, water, buildings, wildlife, and food production. They will help you weave together these elements to create beautiful and productive landscapes which respect your little piece of the planet.

Illustration from proceedings of *The Village As Solar Ecology,* courtesy of John and Nancy Todd, New Alchemy Institute.

8A. Landscaping/Site Design Primers

The Chemical Free Lawn
Warren Schultz
1989; 194 pp.
$14.95 paper, $21.95 hardcover postpaid from:
Rodale Press
33 Minor Street
Emmaus PA 18049

The cover of this book proclaims, "The Newest Varieties and Techniques to Grow Lush, Hardy Grass. No Pesticides, No Herbicides, No Chemical Fertilizers." The text thoroughly fills that promise with a simple guide to mowing, feeding, watering, and insect/disease control that is easier than conventional chemical approaches, better for the lawn, and does not have the undesirable effects of chemical use. The book provides an attractive solution to those who still want a lawn—for their children to play on, to dine on, etc—but who also want to be ecologically responsible. For example, Schultz details dozens of varieties of weeds, and recommends several varieties—including clover—that promote a healthy lawn, in a density of up to 20%. Clearly written chapters help the "grass gardener" select the best grass for the area and situation, feed the grass organically (coffee grounds, bonemeal, and wood ashes are good for many lawns), and control pests by inviting beneficial insects and birds. This is an outstanding book for all who want to have a lawn.

Excerpts:

➤ *Americans spend $6 billion a year to keep [lawns] looking good and apply an estimated 5 to 10 pounds of pesticide per acre of lawn each year. Of the dozen or so most popular over-the-counter pesticides, nearly all are suspected of causing serious long-term health problems.*

➤ *Keep in mind that your lawn problem may not be caused by disease, but by environmental stress or an injury. The problem could be drought; scalping from a lawnmower; herbicide or fertilizer burn; or even dog damage.*

➤ *Fortunately, the tide has begun to turn against chemical lawn treatment. Legislation that restricts the use of lawn chemicals is on the books in counties and states across the country. And lawn service companies report that business began tailing off in the mid-1980s. At universities and research laboratories, scientists have turned their attention to low-maintenance, low-chemical techniques. Breeders are bringing out new grass varieties that resist both diseases and insects. New research confirms that organic fertilizers are better for the lawn, and that cultural practices like mowing and watering can beat weeds. And researchers are learning that common pesticides actually harm the lawn.*

Permaculture (A Designer's Manual)
Bill Mollison
1988; 576 pp.
$39.95 postpaid from:
agAccess
P.O. Box 2008
Davis CA 95617
(916)756-7177

This is that book everybody was looking for 20 years ago. The one that explains how to grow food, fix broken land, and devise a better society—anywhere you happen to live. Couldn't find it then because the only folks doing decentralized, ecologically sustainable agriculture systems in those days were scattered around the Third World, and they didn't publish. Well, here it is—a treasure-house of keen observation, responsive design, patience, and hope.

Reviewed by Richard Nilsen, *Whole Earth Review*, Spring 1989

Bill Mollison has taught permaculture design courses all over the world, so it's no surprise his new book is organized as a training manual for use by an individual or groups. Topics covered include affordable housing, clean water and air, decent neighborhoods, landscape restoration, sustainable agriculture, ethical investments, economic development, unpolluted food and sane organizations. The chapter on patterns in nature—detailing what he calls "pattern understanding"—is a sparkling gem of a read (with beautiful illustrations) unlike anything I've seen anywhere else. *Permaculture* is so full of information that if information had mass, the book would surely be a black hole—yet a generous dose of sketches and color photos, lucid prose and lively anecdotes make it easy reading in spite of its size (8-1/2" by 11", nearly 600 pages) and technical depth. Fifty cents from the sale of each copy goes to plant trees to replace those cut for pulp for the paper for this book. Even the paper is a special formulation, expected to outlast normal hardbound book papers by over 500 years. All profits from sales go into a Permaculture Institute Third World Fund to assist permaculture education in poor areas of the world. If the price is too expensive for you, get your library to order it. An extraordinary book.

Reviewed by James Kalin, *Whole Earth Review*, Spring 1989

Excerpts:

➤ *Permaculture [permanent agriculture] is the conscious design and maintenance of agriculturally productive ecosystems which have the diversity, stability, and resilience of natural ecosystems. It is the harmonious integration of landscape and people providing their food, energy, shelter, and other material and non-material needs in a sustainable way. Without permanent agriculture there is no possibility of a stable social order.*

➤ *Mollisonian Permaculture Principles:*
1. *Work with nature, rather than against the natural elements, forces, pressures, processes, agencies, and evolutions, so that we assist rather than impede natural developments.*
2. *The problem is the solution; everything works both ways. It is only how we see things that makes them advantageous or not (if the wind blows cold, let us use both its strength and its coolness to advantage). A corollary of this principle is that everything is a positive resource; it is just up to us to work out how we may use it as such.*
3. *Make the least change for the greatest possible effect.*
4. *The yield of a system is theoretically unlimited. The only limit on the number of uses of a resource possible within a system is in the limit of the information and the imagination of the designer.*

Permaculture Activist
$13/year (4 issues) from:
P.O. Box 3630
Kailua Kona HI 96745
(808)322-3294

This quarterly newsletter reports on innovative ideas for creating self-sustaining agricultural systems which are adaptable to both backyard and large scale rural and urban sites. These permaculture systems integrate trees, plants, animals, buildings, and human activities in the design of energy-efficient, low-maintenance landscapes, with the ultimate goal being ecological diversity and stability. Besides covering the latest in permaculture research and field experiences, each *Permaculture Activist* includes updates from regional and international permaculture groups.

Nature's Design

Carol A. Smyser
1982; 390 pp.
Rodale Press
(Out of print; check your local library)

Nature's Design is an invaluable resource for any homeowner wanting to plant a natural landscape. "Natural landscaping" means more than simply "letting the weeds run wild." This book leads you through a fascinating design process in the creation of a customized landscape plan which serves your needs and is an extension of the local ecosystem. Close study of your site's micro-environment and selection of indigenous plants to fit it are emphasized. Smyser carefully guides you through site analysis, functional analysis, site planning, plant selection, drawing, phasing, and construction detailing. Each step is accompanied by helpful examples and beautiful illustrations. *Nature's Design* is a very practical and accessible guide filled with a wealth of information which can help you work with nature in establishing a rich, evolving landscape that requires less water, energy, and money to maintain than conventional landscapes.

Reviewed by Jane Sorensen

Excerpts:

➤ *The best way to decide on individual plants is to look at natural environments that have ecological conditions similar to your own. This may sound like a lot of work, and it is. But the amount of time invested in planning your landscape will result in time and expense saved later. Once you've designed and planted an ecological landscape, you can relax. If it is truly ecological, you can sit back and watch the slow but spectacular process of succession.*

➤ *If you want to have healthy plants that eliminate the need for extensive sprinkling or drainage systems, you must understand the hydrologic conditions of your property and use only those plants that are adapted to those conditions. For example, plants found naturally along streams or in wetlands, like willows or spicebrush, will thrive in a poorly drained yard. If your yard is dry, plants suited to well-drained soils or dry areas will flourish with no need for watering.*

➤ *In natural landscaping, the ecology of the site speaks, the constructed features speak and the plants speak. A harmonious chorus results. All elements must have a say, so all elements must interact on your paper plans.*

➤ *Ground-cover plants are abundant. There's one for every situation and every climate, roughly 450 of them if you survey the literature. A true ground cover is a plant that is low and self-spreading, forming a dense colony that resists invasion by weedy plants.*

➤ *The key to a successful wildlife planting plan is variety. Offer a wide selection of vegetative species that will give your yard a good blend of closed and open spaces and will create a practical combination of plant sizes. Choose your species carefully and look for multipurpose types that can provide both food and cover. By doing this, you will be creating a vast number of animal niches, the special combination of physical requirements that are unique to every creature.*

Plants, People and Environmental Quality

G. O. Robinette
1972; 129 pp.
U.S. Government Printing Office
(Out of Print; borrow it through inter-library loan.)

This classic book presents one of the best overviews of the incredibly varied uses of plants in human settlement. Although written for practicing landscape architects, Robinette's work is extremely useful for anyone planning a home, designing a small homestead, or using plants to control a building's environment to promote natural heating, cooling, and ventilation. For design work, it presents excellent guidelines for using plants as screens and walls, for noise reduction and air purification, to give green rather than glare to the eye, and for controlling such microclimatic variables as solar radiation, wind and air temperature. With its wide scope, depth of treatment, and excellent use of graphics, the book is unique in its field. You can practically skip from one chart to the next collecting good ideas on how to use plants for landscaping needs. Much of the material comes from hard-to-get scientific papers, foreign sources, and university research reports. Robinette has done a great service by presenting all this information in such a readable, usable, and visually pleasing manner.

Reviewed by Jerry Yudelson, *Energy Primer*

Excerpts:

➤ *The functions of plants should be the basis for their use in environmental design. We are selling plants short when we use them for beautification only.*

➤ *30 to 40 square meters of plants supply the oxygen requirements for one man.*

➤ *Functions performed by plants can be categorized and evaluated to help man solve environmental problems. Plants are among the most effective air-conditioners. They remove carbon dioxide and other pollutants from the air and release oxygen for man's use. Plants trap dust. They release moisture into the atmosphere. Scientists have found that a peach tree, each year, consumes and transforms carbon dioxide from the air in an amount equivalent to that found within the space of 800 single family homes. The leaves, branches, roots, and litter of the plants deter the erosion of soil into creeks, rivers, and streams, thus reducing the pollution of waterways.*

➤ *Plants control snow by intercepting snowflakes, by directing wind to scour a clean area or control snowdrift location, by determining confirmation and depth, by providing shade areas for snow retention and controlled melt, and by causing variations in frost depth to slow down melting.*

The Complete Book of Edible Landscaping

Rosalind Creasy
1982; 400 pp.
$19.95, postpaid from:
Sierra Club Store Orders
730 Polk Street
San Francisco CA 94109
(415)923-5600

Here's another excellent reference for people interested in ecological and productive yards. This book tells you how to create beautiful home landscapes with food-bearing plants, using less money and natural resources than conventional landscapes require. The book is divided into three parts. Part One is a how-to-do-it guide which takes you through the basic groundwork of site analysis, layout, and design. An example, complete with base maps, analysis, and final design, illustrates the process. Part Two provides an outstanding encyclopedia of edible plants, describing each plant's maintenance needs, hardiness, and general characteristics. The last part contains much valuable information on edible landscaping "Resources and References," including a coveted list of nurseries that supply edible plant stock (especially ornamental edibles), and helpful organizations working in the field.

Reviewed by Jane Sorensen

Designing and Maintaining Your Edible Landscape Naturally

Robert Kourik
1986; 370 pp.
$18.95 postpaid from:
The Edible Landscape Book Project
P.O. Box 1841
Santa Rosa CA 95402

Edible landscaping is a new term for an old idea. It is a reaction to the lawns and shrubs that make many suburban yards look so boring. Its goal is to integrate food plants into the landscape by liberating fruits and vegetables from rectangular prisons often hidden at the back of the lot. Bring those salad herbs up and put them right outside the kitchen door where they will be tended and used. And put the peaches (dwarf) under a south-facing eave of the roof where they can enjoy maximum frost protection and warmth. Kourik has produced a classic homemade book in the best sense of the term. His mind works referentially. As a self-publisher, he didn't have to conform to a linear-minded editor eager to streamline his work. The book is massive, detailed, and totally indexed. It is full of charts and graphs that allow the kind of comparing and decision-making that landscape design is all about. There is extensive information on selecting fruit tree varieties and appropriate rootstocks. Best of all, he is not dogmatic. If there are two schools of thought, such as till versus no-till gardening, he will explain the advantages and disadvantages of each in different situations. Like all gardening books, this one is written with a sense of place in mind (northern California), but Kourik is aware that your garden, right down to its microclimates, is unique.

Reviewed by Richard Nilsen in *The Essential Whole Earth Catalog*

Excerpts:

> ➤ *Instead of designing a landscape just after moving into your new home, wait and observe the yard through a complete cycle of seasons. For at least a year, grow edibles in a number of spots that seem to have beneficial sunlight and climate. You will probably get a very good feel for the nuances of sunshine patterns, frost pockets, windy spots, wet soils, rocky soils, and other important information before designing your edible landscape.*

> ➤ *The amount of effort needed to sustain a landscape or garden is, perhaps, the single most important design consideration. Planting happens quickly, at the peak of the gardener's enthusiasm. Maintenance usually ends up being crammed into busy, everyday life.*

Water Conservation in Landscape Design and Management

Environmental Design Press
1984; 256 pp.
(out of print; check your local library)

Watering our landscapes typically represents one of the most inefficient uses of water at home. This book can show you how to change that. Three approaches to conserving water are thoroughly explored: using water more carefully; applying it more precisely; and designing landscapes so less is required. These principles underlie a host of strategies, which the book discusses at length, using clear graphics to illustrate each point. Some examples of water-conserving strategies discussed are: using drought-resistant vegetation, erecting wind barriers, altering cultivation practices, expanding the use of mulch, re-using water, and establishing water priorities. This book is packed full of often overlooked common ideas vital to efficient use of water in designing and managing landscapes, whether by a homeowner, grounds keeper, landscape contractor, or landscape architect. Information is presented for most of the climatic regions found in the U. S.

Reviewed by Jane Sorensen

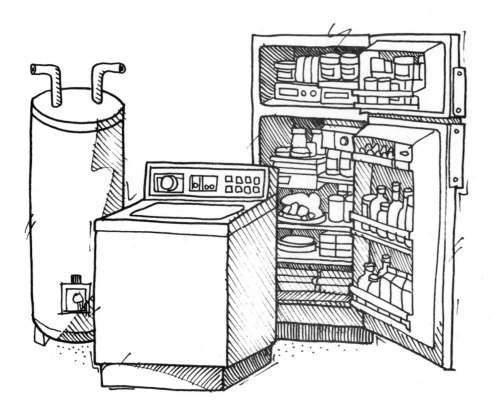

9. Energy-Efficient Appliances

American homes are full of energy-guzzling appliances. For example, water heaters with inadequate insulation, refrigerators with skimpy insulation and inefficient compressors, and ranges with pilot lights consume far more energy than necessary. These design deficiencies are frequently compounded by the ways we use and maintain such equipment: when was the last time you stood in front of an opened refrigerator debating between grabbing the leftover lasagna or lamb chops, set your clotheswasher's water temperature to "hot" when "warm" would have done just fine, or put off yet again giving your furnace a complete tune-up? It all adds up. The lifetime energy bills for household appliances, in fact, often far exceed their initial purchase price!

Prudent operation and care of existing appliances can help counter this waste. Installing new energy-efficient appliances can do even more. Though they usually cost more to purchase, the dramatic energy savings made possible by many new appliances can offset such premiums many times over. And since high-quality, energy-efficient appliances don't have to work as hard to do their job as less efficient ones, they will probably last longer and require less maintenance.

The books and trade organizations listed in this section can show you how to get the most work out of your existing appliances for the least energy cost and can help you identify the most energy efficient appliances presently available. None of these resources, however, offers specific product buying recommendations; you'll have to look in Consumer Reports for such advice (reviewed in section 2D). Also remember that while energy-efficiency is an important criterion in new appliances, you should also look at overall quality, performance and durability. Unfortunately, we know of some energy-efficient products whose utility savings are offset by repair bills.

Illustration by David Gross, Public Image, Boulder, CO.

9A. Energy-Efficient Appliance Resources

The Smart Kitchen: How to Design a Comfortable, Safe, Energy-Efficient, and Environment-Friendly Workspace
David Goldbeck
1989; 140 pp.
$17.95 postpaid from:
Ceres Press
Box 87
Woodstock NY 12498

This innovative guide explores all facets of design, appliances, fixtures, and materials for the resource-efficient kitchen. It is written from a cook's point of view (not an architect's), and gives a plethora of practical suggestions about topics such as air and noise quality, recycling, energy-efficiency, water purity, appliance maintenance, and kitchen comfort.

The sections on kitchen appliances and on recycling are particularly strong. For example, Goldbeck thoughtfully evaluates many gas and electric appliances from an environmental perspective. The author even tells his audience how to make old appliances more efficient. The information on microwaves far surpasses any material supplied with the product. In regard to recycling, Goldbeck transforms the topic of "garbage" into "kitchen composting," with a system of scraping food scraps directly into a hole in the kitchen counter, which are then stored in a bin and accessed as compost outside the home.

The Smart Kitchen will be of interest to anyone with a kitchen, regardless of whether your home is rented or owned. The text, which is technical but easy to follow, covers many important issues normally outside the scope of "kitchen" books.

Excerpts:

➤ *According to all the experts, refrigerators can account for as much as one third of household energy expenditures. They also account for about 7 percent of the United States' total electric usage.*

➤ *Modern eating habits have made the kitchen the center of nationwide efforts to recycle. The careful disposal of garbage and the saving of materials to be recycled is a responsibility that can be made easier with some forethought.*

➤ *More than seven hundred different chemicals have been found in America's drinking water, and at this writing at least thirty-four states have serious water quality problems. Contaminant levels in public water are regulated by the U.S. Environmental Protection Agency (EPA). No matter where you get your water today—whether well, spring, or public water works—it's most likely to have some sort of contamination.*

Cooking Under Pressure

Lorna J. Sass
1989; 268 pp.
$18.95 from:
William Morrow
105 Madison Avenue
New York NY 10016
(212)261-6500

Pressure cooking saves time and energy in the kitchen. This rediscovered method works by boiling food and liquids in a sealed pot, so that pressure increases and the boiling point rises. By raising the boiling-point temperature, food cooks in about a third the usual time and therefore uses less energy. Flavors are forced to blend under the high pressure, so taste is not compromised and less salt is needed. It's also especially useful for cooking foods that normally require long soaking or stewing periods, like beans and soups. This book has a wide variety of recipes, from elegant to ethnic. Simple explanations for using a pressure cooker make the whole process unintimidating and enjoyable.

Excerpts:

➤ *Cookers based on the traditional design have a removable pressure regulator that sits on the vent pipe and rocks gently, emitting a chug-chug sound when the pressure is up. Newer appliances with a more contemporary look regulate pressure with stationary valves and use indicator rods to reveal when the pressure is up. They make little or no noise. I worked with both types while testing the recipes for this book and found all of them simple and entirely safe to use, eliminating the pitfalls that beset our mothers and grandmothers.*

Gas Appliance Manufacturers Association

1901 N. Moore Street
Arlington VA 22209
(703)525-9565

GAMA publishes the consumers' *Directory of Certified Water Heater Efficiency Ratings*, which contains listings of nearly all gas, oil, and electric water heaters on the market, including heat-pump water heaters. This directory also tells you how to choose the correct size of water heater for your home. It only describes, however, the efficiency of these appliances in isolation—not how to downsize them and use them less, by using hot water more efficiently. Write GAMA for a publications list and ordering information.

Excerpt:

➤ *The various measures of water heater efficiency listed in this Directory are: Energy Factor—A measure of the overall efficiency of a water heater based on the model's recovery efficiency, standby loss and energy input. First Hour Rating—The amount of hot water that the water heater can supply in the first hour of operation. It is a combination of how much water is stored in the water heater and how quickly the water heater can heat cold water to the desired temperature. Recovery Efficiency—The percentage of energy put into the water compared to the total energy used by the water heater. Standby Loss—The percentage of heat lost from the stored water per hour compared to heat content of the stored water.*

Association of Home Appliance Manufacturers

20 North Wacker Drive
Suite 1500
Chicago IL 60606
(312)984-5800

This industry trade group publishes several consumer guides, including: *Directory of Certified Room Air Conditioners* and *Directory of Certified Refrigerators and Freezers*. These publications list nearly all models on the market, ranking them by energy costs. AHAM also publishes a guide to room air-conditioner sizing and a series of fact sheets and booklets on saving energy. Write for a publications list and ordering information.

Excerpts: (from the AHAM booklet, *Saving Energy With Your Home Laundry Equipment*):

➤ *Heating water accounts for 90% of the energy used in washing clothes automatically. The remaining 10% is used to operate the clothes washer's motor and other parts. So the best way to save energy with an automatic clothes washer is to: Avoid wasting hot water. Use hot water only for washing heavily soiled loads and for sanitation purposes. Most laundry loads can be washed in warm water. Some lightly soiled loads can be washed in cold water. Use cold water rinses for all loads. The temperature of the rinse water does not affect cleaning. Match the water level to the size of the load. Permanent press and synthetic loads are the exception since extra water is needed so wrinkling is reduced and clothes can move freely. Use low water settings for small loads.*

➤ *The most important way to save energy and money with all three drying systems is to: Do not mix heavy and light articles, synthetics and permanent press with cottons, or lint "givers" (towels) with lint collectors (corduroy) in the same load. If you do the dryer will run longer than necessary and waste energy. Don't overload the dryer. Articles must be able to tumble freely. Overcrowding causes wrinkling and uneven drying. It also increases the drying time. Dry only full loads. Drying small loads wastes energy. Don't overdry. Most people do when they use the "timed" setting. This not only wastes energy, but it also shortens fabric life, causes shrinkage and generates static electricity. Try to reduce your regular drying time by about five minutes or more. Remember, most fabrics have some natural moisture and should not be "bone dry." Seams and waistbands should still have a hint of moisture when taken out of the dryer. If possible, dry loads one right after another. In this way you can use the heat remaining from the previous load. Check the lint trap screen before each load. A buildup of lint on the screen can lengthen drying time. Use the automatic cycle if your dryer has one. This helps prevent overdrying. Be sure your dryer is exhausted properly to the outside. Use the straightest, shortest duct for venting. Keep the outside vent clean. Check it at least monthly. Also check the flapper on the outside hood to make sure it opens and closes freely. A flapper that remains open allows heated air to escape and cold drafts to enter the house. Remove articles to be ironed while still damp. Some fabrics such as corduroy, quilted items and knits keep shape better if not dried completely. Remove items as soon as the dryer stops. This helps prevent wrinkling and can cut down on ironing. Avoid restarting the dryer to fluff out wrinkles. Try to run your automatic clothes dryer during off-peak utility hours so you won't contribute to power overload in your area. These hours are usually in the early morning or late evening, but check your local utility. (Note: Some utilities offer reduced rates for off-peak hours.)*

COMPETITEK

Rocky Mountain Institute
1739 Snowmass Creek Road
Snowmass CO 81654-9199
(303)927-3851

Rocky Mountain Institute's COMPETITEK update service offers extremely detailed guides to advanced techniques for saving electricity in appliances, water-heating, space-conditioning, lighting, and motor systems, as well as policy strategies for getting such technologies implemented. These publications are the most current and thorough available, thus are correspondingly expensive. They are designed mainly for utilities, major architect/engineering firms, energy agencies and regulatory commissions, and large electricity users. For more information on COMPETITEK's publications and services, contact Rocky Mountain Institute.

Air Conditioning and Refrigeration Institute

1501 Wilson Boulevard, Suite 600
Arlington VA 22209
(703)524-8800

ARI publishes the *Directory of Certified Unitary Equipment* which lists the specifications—cooling capacity and energy efficiency rating—for nearly all air conditioners and air-source heat pumps on the market. Note: this publication only describes the efficiency of these appliances in isolation—not how to downsize them and use them less by keeping your house cool in the first place. ARI also distributes several informative consumer publications, such as *How to Keep Your Cool and Save Cold Cash*, *Consumer Guide to Efficient Central Climate Control Systems*, and *Heat, Cool, Save Energy with a Heat Pump*. Write for a publications list and ordering information.

Excerpts: (from ARI booklet, *How To Keep Your Cool and Save Cold Cash*)

➤ *Should I turn my thermostat up when I leave for work in the morning? If your house is going to be empty for more than about four hours, it's a good idea to turn your thermostat up to about 82 degrees or so instead of the 78 usually recommended. Keep the house closed to minimize heat build-up. When you come home, don't set the thermostat any lower than the temperature you actually want—your air conditioning system wouldn't cool any faster, and might easily waste money by cooling your home more than needed.*

➤ *How do I go about shopping for a new system? Ask friends and neighbors about the types of systems they have, how much they cost, how long they've had them, and how satisfied they are with them. Then ask for recommendations as to brands and local contractors, or ask several different contractors to take a thorough look at your home, evaluate your overall comfort needs, and recommend the best system for you. Look at all indoor climate control options—the entire spectrum of heating, cooling, air filtration, and humidification equipment.*

Also, see *Cut Your Electric Bills In Half***, and** *Consumer Guide to Home Energy Savings***, reviewed in Section 5C.**

Illustration courtesy of *The Village As Solar Ecology*, 1979, courtesy of John and Nancy Todd, New Alchemy Institute.

10. Using Renewable Energy

What are the fastest-growing sources of energy in the U.S.? If you answered nuclear, oil, or coal, try again. Energy efficiency improvements and renewable energy top the list! Renewable energy sources—water, biomass, geothermal, wind, solar-thermal, and photovoltaics—already deliver more than twice as much energy as nuclear power plants. More new renewable energy generating capacity has been ordered in recent years than coal and nuclear combined. These renewable energy gains, though, have been made through many hard-learned and expensive lessons. As a result, we now know much about what does and doesn't work, both on the centralized and the home scales. What is clear is that there is plenty of "free" renewable energy out there for the taking. But it's going to cost you money, sometimes big money, to harness it. The resources in this section can help you identify and wisely tap those renewable energy sources available to you which can save you money and make you more energy self-sufficient.

10A. Renewable Energy Organizations

Florida Solar Energy Center
Public Information Office
300 State Road 401
Cape Canaveral FL 32920
(407)783-0300

The Florida Solar Energy Center prepares many excellent publications on a wide variety of energy-efficient cooling techniques for new and existing houses. Applicable to homes situated in hot, humid climates, each four-page report in the FSEC's Design Note and Energy Note series concisely explains and illustrates a specific approach to energy-efficient cooling. Some examples of the topics covered include: passive cooling and human comfort, designing and installing radiant barrier systems, fans to reduce cooling costs in the southeast, techniques for shading residential walls and windows, and dealing with heat and humidity in Florida homes. Write the FSEC for a complete publications list and ordering information.

American Solar Energy Society
2400 Central Avenue, Unit G-1
Boulder CO 80301
(303)443-3130

ASES is a non-profit, professional organization involved in transferring and disseminating technical information on practical uses of solar energy, wind power, photovoltaics, etc. They publish *Solar Today*, $25.00/year for 6 issues. Write for a publications catalog and sample of the magazine.

Solar Energy Industries Association
777 N. Capitol Street, Suite 805
Washington DC 20002
(202)408-0660

This is the national trade association for photovoltaic and solar thermal manufacturers in the U.S. They do the political work for solar energy. Their quarterly publication, the *Solar Industry Journal* (25.00/year) features industry news, events announcements, and legislative updates on solar issues.

American Wind Energy Association
777 N. Capitol Street, Suite 805
Washington DC 20002
(202)408-8988

AWEA is the trade association for the wind industry, but is also open to individuals with an interest in wind energy. It distributes several informative publications on residential-scale windpower, and can refer individuals to wind system manufacturers and dealers. Write for publications list and membership information.

10B. Photovoltaic and Solar Resources

Photovoltaic References

Photovoltaic power—the direct conversion of sunlight into electricity—will profoundly affect both how and where we generate power. This miraculous technology uses solid-state solar cells—specially treated semiconductor materials—to generate electricity simply, quietly, and reliably. This can be done on any scale wherever the sun shines. No fuel is burned or turbines spun. At present, however, photovoltaics' main drawback is price. They typically cost ~2-8 times more to install per kilowatt of average output than do conventional fossil-fueled power plants and their associated grids and fuel sources. In remote residential applications, though, where power lines have to be extended more than half a mile (a number that is steadily shrinking) or where photovoltaics are competing with fossil-fueled stand-alone generators, they are cost-effective today. Their price has been steadily dropping and will drop further as production rises. Dramatic price decreases, however, will require new technical developments still being worked out in the laboratory. The oft-cited projections for great price breaks will likely come, but no one knows quite when. In the meantime, the references in this section can show folks living away from the utility grid how to cost-effectively plug their homes into the sun, and teach those now hooked into the grid ways in which they can start preparing to make the transition to photovoltaics.

One of the best sources for up-to-date information are the catalogs selling photovoltaic and other solar equipment, listed in Section 4.

The New Solar Electric Home: The Photovoltaics How-To Handbook
Joel Davidson
1987; 408 pp.
$18.95 postpaid from:
The Davidson Company
Box 4126
Culver City CA 90231

This greatly improved and expanded edition of *The Solar Electric Home* provides practically all the information most people will need to "plug their homes into the sun." Davidson, one of this country's most experienced, hands-on PV pioneers, takes a comprehensive look at the design of complete household photovoltaic systems, nicely blending theory, practice, philosophy, and nut-and-bolts information. In the first part of the book, he shares his and others', first-hand experiences living with solar electric systems, discusses the critical importance of energy efficiency in PV-powered homes, and examines the practical matters which you must consider before deciding whether it is feasible to use PV to power your home. He goes on to review the state-of-the-art in PV system hardware—modules, mounting structures, regulators, batteries, and inverters. He then guides you through PV system sizing, installation, testing, and maintenance. Emphasis is placed on the practical application of photovoltaics and inverters—electronic devices which "invert" low-voltage DC power into the 110-volt AC power you and your appliances are used to—and larger homes, equipped with all the "basic" creature comforts. Plenty of interesting case studies and illustrative photos show how people throughout the country are doing just this. Useful appendices and a short course in electricity, PV sizing data, and the National Electrical Code's PV requirements, wrap up the book.

➤ *If you are in the process of making the decision of whether to use PV to power your home, you need to know both sides of the story. Advantages: 1. There is a one-time cash outlay to purchase solar cells, 2. There is no monthly utility bill, 3. Users are not affected by electricity price increases or inflation, 4. Modules are reliable, sturdy, and lightweight, 5. They can be used wherever the sun shines, 6. There are no moving parts to wear out or break, 7. Modular system design can be augmented as money permits and needs require, 8. DC appliances are compatible with recreational equipment, 9. New solid-state high-efficiency inverters make the use of AC appliances practical, 10. Battery technology has long been proven reliable, 11. Modules can be used in conjunction with commercial electricity, generators, wind, or hydropower, 12. Users are not affected by commercial power outages, and 13. Autonomous systems do not pollute at point of production or use. Disadvantages: 1. The initial system cost is high, 2. Electricity is not produced at night, 3. Very cloudy weather significantly reduces power production, 4. Storage batteries must be serviced, 5. An inverter must be used to power standard AC appliances, 6. The power output per dollar invested is low, 7. A back-up generator or other power source may be needed to maintain batteries if the system is undersized, 8. The manufacture of solar cells may produce some environmental pollution, and 9. Small arrays need seasonal adjustment to maximize production.*

➤ *Practical use of solar power is a blend of science and art. Sizing a PV system can be reduced to numbers. However, before attempting the math, it's a good idea to examine the general principles behind a properly sized system. The variations of climate, the unique characteristics of the equipment selected, and the different ways people use electricity combine to produce a range of system possibilities. The most appropriate system is the one specifically designed for your applications.*

The Solar Electric Independent Home Book

Paul Fowler
1991; 200 pp.
$16.95 plus shipping from:
Fowler Solar Electric, Inc.
P.O. Box 435
Worthington MA 01098
(413)238-5974

The *Solar Electric Independent Home Book* is an excellent reference written specifically for owners and potential owners of solar electric systems for remote home sites. It is filled with how-to information about designing, installing, and living with photovoltaic systems. Valuable for both do-it-yourselfers and electricians alike, the book is clear, concise, and illustrated with numerous helpful system and wiring diagrams. Basic electrical theory, individual system component selection and sizing, energy-efficient appliances, and lighting protection are covered in the body while the extensive appendix provides much useful supporting data and information.

Excerpts:

➤ *After ten years of research into the components and design of alternative energy systems, we've come to believe that not everyone should engage in the same cumbersome process. This book is designed to be used by the owner or potential owner of a PV system.*

➤ *Owning and installing a PV system is a significant commitment. You will need to understand its use just as you had to learn to drive a car. You will also need to troubleshoot the basics of the system to be able to call your dealer or the manufacturer. Hopefully this book will give a greater understanding of a PV system in the remote site home.*

The Solar Electric House: A Design Manual for Home-Scale Photovoltaic Power Systems

Steven J. Strong with William G. Scheller
1987; 276 pp.
$19.95 postpaid from:
Rodale Press
33 Minor Street
Emmaus PA 18098
(800)441-7761

This book tells you almost everything you will need to know to decide whether photovoltaics are for you, and if so, how to decide what type of system will work best. One of this country's most experienced designers of independent-powered homes, Strong authoritatively and clearly addresses the design, installation, and maintenance of residential PV systems for both remote and grid-connected homes. All facets of the subject are covered in practical detail, including: the economics of stand-alone and utility-interactive PV systems, PV system sizing and design, PV system components and assembly, and the importance of energy efficiency and load management. Many valuable design and installation pointers are given which can help you design and install a PV system to operate as efficiently, safely, and economically as is possible. Where important, useful background theory, nitty-gritty hardware specifications, and technical how-to details are given. At present, this is the best reference text we know on the subject; it is comprehensive and easy to use.

Excerpts:

➤ *You can power anything you want with photovoltaics. However, when financial considerations become the dominant factor in the system design equation, it quickly becomes clear that it is easier and far more cost-effective to conserve electricity than it is to produce it. This does not necessarily mean doing without. What it does mean is doing more with less, by using intelligent design and careful equipment selection to deliver an equal or better living environment and lifestyle while consuming less energy.*

➤ *The most basic scenario for the application of photovoltaic electricity to a load is a DC stand-alone (SA) system, a remote electrical system designed and dedicated for a single purpose, where the DC output of the PV array is delivered directly to the load with no storage and no control or regulation. This type of system will typically power a load that requires power only when light is available. Most PV-powered consumer products, such as calculators, use this approach.*

➤ *Thus, with photovoltaics as an option, the homeowner has more freedom in choosing where he wants to live. Often a site that is much more desirable than land served by the grid can be found at what would be considered bargain-basement prices. Money saved on the purchase of land can be applied to the installation of a photovoltaic system and may justifiably be deducted from the cost of that system when the figures for projected payback time are laid out and analyzed. This concept has even more appeal when more than one house is being considered. There is the possibility of sharing the costs of the power system, especially when careful load management is part of the system design. In years to come, perceptive builders and developers will come to understand the value of photovoltaics as a development tool, and entire energy-independent villages will be built that have no connection to the utility grid.*

Photovoltaics: A Manual for Design and Installation of Stand-Alone Systems

Steve McCarney, Ken Olson, and Johnny Weiss
1987; 285 pp.
$35 postpaid from:
Solar Technology Institute
PO Box 1115
Carbondale CO 81623-1115
(303)963-0715

This comprehensive manual was prepared as the basic training guide to accompany intensive short courses in photovoltaics offered by Appropriate Technology Associates. Written by true pioneers in PV education, the authors founded Colorado Mountain College's Solar Retrofit Program in Glenwood Springs, Colorado and have lead intensive workshops on the subject throughout the country. The guide serves the individual or professional who wishes to learn the practical aspects of designing and installing photovoltaic systems. The best of the author's extensive experience as vocational educators and hands-on practitioners are incorporated into the book; it shows in their easy to understand and complete written and illustrated presentation.

The manual begins with the basic fundamentals, assuming no prior knowledge, and guides the reader through the theory and nuts-and-bolts workings of designing and installing stand-alone PV systems. Detailed information is presented on PV system components, electrical loads, system sizing, installation, wiring, etc. Worksheets are provided to aide in determination of electrical load requirements as well as sizing and specification of each of the system components. Appendices cover solar radiation data, maintenance scheduling, troubleshooting, photovoltaic suppliers, and more.

Excerpt:

➤ *Solar-electric system designers should maximize energy efficiency to provide high performance cost-effective solar-powered systems. A thorough understanding and analysis of electric end-use requirements is critically essential to photovoltaic system designers. Likewise, PV system installers should pay close attention to detail to ensure long-term system reliability. This practical manual of design and installation is for people interested in the "nuts and bolts" of stand-alone solar-electric systems.*

Also, see Home Power magazine, reviewed in Section 2A., and the section on Catalogs and Sourcebooks which Provide access to Resource-Efficient Housing Information and Tools, Section 4.

Solar References

Consumer Guide to Solar Energy

Scott Sklar & Kenneth Sheinkopf
1991; 181 pp.
$9.95 from:
Bonus Books
260 East Illinois Street
Chicago IL 60611

An excellent introduction to solar energy, this book relates the history of the industry while describing easy and inexpensive applications of solar technology. Chapters on pool and water heating, electricity, water purification, solar cooking, and space cooling and heating give overviews and answer important questions about the systems. To pave the way to implementing solar ideas, the issues of financing and economics are addressed, and a list of solar organizations show you "where to go from here." An interesting read, this book will give the curious browser a good idea of what's out there and the more knowledgeable reader an idea of how to use it.

Excerpts:

➤ *As a general rule of thumb, you can figure that for outside uses like walk/driveway lights, solar electric lighting products are cost-effective when compared with electric alternatives if an electrician must be used for the installation and wire needs to be run more than fifteen feet from the electric source. If you're a do-it-yourselfer and don't need to hire someone to do the work, you ought to figure in the value of your time and effort to get a better idea of what the true cost of installation is for the product. Economists use estimates like these to do life-cycle calculations, in which the total cost of a product, including purchase price, installation costs, and energy use, are figured to make accurate comparisons of energy alternatives.*

➤ *What are solar cells? Solar cells are materials that absorb sunlight and convert it into electricity. Today's photovoltaics industry is a product of 1950s solid-state electronics, and was greatly stimulated by the need to find power sources for America's space satellites...Solar cells are very thin (about 1/100 of an inch thick) rectangular or circular wafers typically made of silicon, the same basic material that makes up sand at the beach and is used in most of the electronic components in your stereo and other electronic appliances. The silicon can be "grown" in crystals that are interconnected and layered under glass or plastic, or the silicon can be gasified and layered under glass or plastic as a thin film.*

Home Energy: Your Best Options for Solar Heating and Cooling, Wood, Wind, and Photovoltaics
Dan Halacy
1984; 288 pp.
Rodale Press
(Out of print; check your local library)

This book provides a good overview of the range of alternative energy options available to homeowners. It addresses all aspects of household energy conservation, solar domestic water heating, passive solar space heating and cooling, active solar heating and cooling, heating with wood, wind energy, and photovoltaics. Halacy leads you through the practical and economic considerations—performance, convenience, reliability, aesthetics, and cost-effectiveness—which need tending to in order to sort out what alternatives will, and will not, work for your particular situation. Lots of clear, instructive illustrations are sprinkled throughout the text and a set of unique, very informative "decision trees" makes it easy to get right to the information which is most applicable to your home. The energy marketplace and renewable energy tax credits have changed since this book was written, so many of its economic analyses are dated, but don't let that stop you from using this fine resource.

Excerpts:

➤ *The unfortunate thing regarding misconceptions about which conservation measures do the most good is that we tend to follow through with those that are least effective and not give proper attention to the real energy savers. For a rough approximation, assume that an average household uses 60% of its energy dollars for space heating and cooling, 15% for water heating, another 15% for running appliances, and 5% each for cooking and refrigeration.*

➤ *It makes no sense to spend a lot of time, planning, and money on lighting improvements to save $20 a year when a faulty furnace, poor insulation, and cracks and other openings are wasting almost 10 times that much.*

➤ *At first thought it seems logical to install air collectors rather than water collectors for a space-heating system, since it's air that you want to heat in the house. Furthermore, air collectors won't freeze in cold weather, or leak a liquid in any kind of weather. First impressions can be misleading, however. For example, air collectors can leak air, and air leaks are a lot harder to detect than water leaks. If you do opt for air collectors, you'll have to be very sure they're airtight. Be sure that all ducts are airtight, too.*

> *Solar collectors for pools are usually low-temperature plastic collectors costing much less than conventional solar collectors. Their operation, care, and maintenance are similar to those for solar water heaters, but they probably won't last nearly as long. Here's a Rule Of Thumb: To be effective, collector area should be 50 to 100% of pool area, depending on environmental conditions. For example, in Palm Springs, CA, a 480-square-foot pool can be heated with about 240 sq. ft. of collector. In Denver or Des Moines, however, swimming might be chilly even with 480 square feet. At $5 a square foot, such collectors will cost from $1,200 to $2,400. Remember that a pool cover helps collectors work much better and can reduce the collector area required.*

Passive Solar Water Heaters
Daniel K. Reif
1983; 190 pp.
Brick House Publishing
(Out of print; check your local library)

This is the best book I have seen on batch water heaters. The book begins with a discussion of how batch water heaters work and a look at the different systems. The author is generous with pictures of the different systems, making it easy to understand their features. The chapter on site analysis is applicable for any type of solar installation. Included is information on differentiating true south from magnetic south and determining which surrounding objects are likely to shade the collector. The chapter on plumbing basics helps the do-it-yourselfer install a batch water heater with professional quality plumbing runs. For those who wish to calculate performance or fine tune their design size, the appendices offer information on degree days for dozens of U.S. locations, clear day insolation for several latitudes, and maps showing the average monthly percentage of sunshine in different locations. This is an excellent book for anyone wishing to build a batch water heater system for their home.

Excerpts:

> *If you live in the South or West where the climate is generally mild and there is plenty of sun, the combination of batch water heater and conservation in one household of two to five people can save approximately 18.2 million Btu per year, equivalent to about 5,333 kW-h of electricity, 200 gal. of oil, or 24,300 cu. ft. of natural gas. In colder, cloudier climates, performance is only slightly lower.*

> *For the most cost-effective batch heater, you must carefully balance the three major aspects of the design: water storage capacity, solar collection, and heat retention. These correspond to the solar water tank, glazing and reflector, and collector enclosure.*

> *The next step is to prefabricate the collector sidewalls. Assemble these components on the flat ground. Each of the two sidewalls uses five pieces of 2"x6" and two triangular pieces of 1/2" exterior grade plywood. The two sidewalls can be cut from one 4'x8' sheet of 1/2" CDX plywood. The size of the plywood and 2"x6" pieces are shown in figure 5-15. Label each piece as you cut it to avoid confusion when assembling. Also, label the right and left sidewall.*

10C. Wood Heat Resources

Wood heat went from hick to chic in the '70's, when energy prices inspired many folks to turn from fossil fuels. While it is true that wood heat saves fossil fuel, and the total energy delivered from wood heat is nearly twice the energy delivered from nuclear plants; the drawbacks soon became apparent: there is a lot of work involved, some fire danger, and potential ecological problems. Oregon has led the way with a tough state law that mandates clean-burning designs, thus beginning a strong trend. And remember, please, that if you aren't replacing the trees you burn you are contributing to deforestation, a scourge that has brought down more than one civilization.

J. Baldwin

The resources listed in this section can help you make the most appropriate, efficient, safe, and clean use possible of wood for household heating.

Home Heating With Wood and Coal
Massachusetts Audubon Society
1986; 45 pp.
$3.50 postpaid from:
Mass. Audubon Society
Educational Resources Office
Lincoln MA 01773
(617)259-9500

This practical booklet provides an excellent overview of household wood and coal heating matters—efficiency, safety, economics, and environmental quality—which people thinking about buying a stove, or those already owning one, will find useful. It shows you how to decide if wood or coal heat makes sense for your home situation, determine whether you can save money with wood or coal heat, decide which of these two fuel sources is best for you, choose, install, use, and maintain a stove, distribute heat from your stove into nearby rooms, and upgrade existing stove installations. The explanations are straightforward and cover all important bases—from inspecting the condition of your chimney liner and what details to look for in a well-made stove to how much clearance to allow around a stove and how to shop for and store wood or coal.

Excerpts:

➤ *The basic rule for installing a stove is follow the manufacturer's installation instructions (generally found on a metal tag attached to the back of the stove). These safety guidelines may seem unnecessary, or they may interfere with your plans for the stove, but their importance cannot be overemphasized. There are over 100,000 wood-heat related fires in the U.S. annually; approximately 90% result from faulty installation and upkeep. The guidelines provide reasonable but not extreme margins of safety. Don't guess or compromise where your safety is concerned.*

➤ *Don't burn trash, newspapers, painted wood, chemical chimney cleaners, fire coloring agents, or lighter fluid. Chemicals in these materials can "poison" catalytic combustors so they won't work properly and smoke from many of these materials can be harmful to human health. Smoke from burning colored newspaper and painted wood is particularly harmful to human health; these materials should never be burned.*

➤ *Coal contains a significant amount of sulfur. As a result, sulfuric acid, which is highly corrosive to flue linings, forms in coal smoke. If you burn coal and use an insulated metal chimney it is important to make sure your chimney is rated as an "All Fuel" chimney, capable of withstanding the corrosiveness of coal residue.*

Solid Fuels Encyclopedia
Jay W. Shelton
1983; 268 pp.
Garden Way Publishing
(Out of print; check your local library)

Noted residential heating expert Jay Shelton has condensed his extensive research on wood and coal heating efficiency, safety, installation, pollution control, and economics into this handy consumer reference. It is the best and most comprehensive book that we know on the subject. Shelton covers every aspect of heating your home with solid fuels, ranging from the principles of solid fuel combustion and design of efficient fireplaces to wood storage and the sizing, installation, operation, and maintenance of a wood or coal stove. Whether you are considering using a solid fuel stove, furnace, or fireplace to heat your home or are interested in getting the best performance out of an existing burner, this book can help. Please note, however, that this book is not a shopping guide. No reviews or recommendations are given for specific products.

Excerpts:

➤ *What is the most energy efficient stove? Overall energy efficiency is affected equally by combustion efficiency and heat transfer. The dominant factor affecting combustion efficiency, in most cases, is not stove design, but stove operation, which is not something you can buy. On the other hand, stove design does affect heat transfer efficiency. Therefore, for the average or typical stove user, the most energy efficient stoves are those with high heat transfer efficiency.*

➤ *No stove is literally airtight. Even with the air inlet shut, it is inevitable that some air will leak in—through the air inlet and around the door. Does it matter? No, not as long as the stove is tight enough so that you can control the combustion to any desired rate, including suffocating the fire. In some ways the term "controlled" combustion is more accurately descriptive than "air-tight." However, airtight is more commonly used, and it serves the purpose of distinguishing between air-limited and fuel-limited modes for controlling combustion. So do not worry if your stove has some leakage—as long as you can always keep the heat output down to a comfortable level.*

Wood Heat Safety
Jay W. Shelton
1979; 165 pp.
Garden Way Publishing
(Out of print; borrow it through interlibrary loan.)

Fire inspectors, code writers, and insurance companies are all getting tougher about standards for wood heating appliances. They have good reason to; the statistics show the sad results of inexpert or careless wood heating practices. This book probably has your exact situation and what to do about it, illustrated and discussed down to the last tiny detail. Particular attention is given to problems found in older houses, a subject not often dealt with in other books. Of course, the information you'll need for a new place is there, too, equally detailed. The calm and competent presentation is mercifully free of horror stories and especially easy to use.

Reviewed by J. Baldwin in *The Essential Whole Earth Review*

Excerpts:

➤ *Safety weaknesses in any of the four areas of installation, operation, maintenance, and equipment design can be compensated for by extra precautions in one of the other areas. It is relatively safe to leave off spark screens if the floor protection is unusually large in extent. Having no floor protection can be relatively safe if the stove has a spark baffle in the air inlet, is used only with its door or doors shut, and is used only in the presence of a very watchful operator. A smoke detector in the room with the stove or fireplace can help prevent loss of lives and serious damage to the building in cases where preventive measures have been inadequate.*

➤ The best location for chimneys is inside buildings, although experience clearly indicates any location will usually function satisfactorily. There are five disadvantages to exterior chimneys. Four of them are a consequence of the colder outdoor environment, resulting in cooler temperatures inside the chimney. Cooler flue gas temperatures result in less draft, more creosote, the possibility of the chimney being non-self-starting, and the possibility of chimney flow reversal. The fifth disadvantage is that the heat given off from the sides of the chimney is wasted, heating the great outdoors.

➤ Exhaust fans in kitchens, bathrooms, and clothes dryers, and operation of any other fuel-burning appliances in a house tend to depressurize the house. This contributes to flow reversal and non-self-starting phenomena. Even interior chimneys can be influenced. The negative effect of these other appliances on chimney draft tends to be especially strong in tightly constructed energy-conservative homes with few air leaks. One preventive is to supply direct outside air.

➤ The principal advantage of airtightness in stoves is the convenience of being able to keep a fire burning for a long time. Experiments in my laboratory do not entirely support the notion that airtight stoves are always more energy-efficient than non-airtight stoves; other features tend to be more important. But another attribute of airtightness is the possibility of suffocating a chimney fire by closing the stove, assuming that is the only major source of air for the chimney fire. However, use of airtight stoves tends to result in more creosote accumulation and hence more chimney fires. Thus the safety of airtightness can be argued both ways. I personally feel airtightness is desirable for the control it gives. It is the operator of the equipment who must always be responsible for and is usually the cause of creosote buildup. Airtight stoves need not be operated with very restricted air, and thus need not generate undue creosote.

The Book Of Masonry Stoves: Rediscovering an Old Way of Warming
David Lyle
1984; 192 pp.
$24.95 plus shipping from:
Heating Research Co.
PO Box 300
Acworth NH 03601
(603)835-6109

More than an introduction to the sensible use of masonry heating stoves today, this book presents a fascinating and handsomely illustrated survey of their use throughout the ages. Lyle explores how the masonry stove, widely incorporated into European and Asian homes for centuries, provides an efficient, safe, and clean heating source, overcoming the serious problems often associated with conventional metal woodburning stoves: chimney fires from creosote, air pollution from poor combustion, and structural fires caused by faulty stove installation. The book best serves as an introduction to the major types of masonry stoves, their operation, and potential applications. Though useful masonry stove design and construction information is given, this is not a how-to book. See the *Finnish Fireplace Construction Manual* (reviewed next) for hands-on advice.

Excerpts:

➤ Masonry stoves can sharply reduce wood-burning safety problems. The iron stove is frequently so hot that it will burn anyone who touches it. The masonry stove is commonly designed in Europe with benches attached, so that you can sit and lean against the stove. There is a world of difference in safety between a stove you can lean on and one that burns at the touch. In eastern and central Europe, people slept on the traditional masonry stove. So did Chinese. The chances of getting a burn from such a stove, or of setting fire to anything close to it, are much diminished if not eliminated.

➤ To the extent that a masonry chimney stores and radiates heat, it can also transfer that heat outdoors at the point where the chimney passes through the roof. Some form of insulating masonry built into the chimney just below the roof can greatly limit this loss. Refractory companies produce concrete block made with light aggregate which has an insulating effect.

Finnish Fireplace Construction Manual 1984

Albert A. Barden, III
1984; 65 pp.
$17 postpaid from:
Maine Wood Heat Co.
RFD 1, Box 640
Norridgewock ME 04957
(207)696-5442

Nice books extolling the virtues of massive masonry woodstoves head you in the right direction, but don't lead you by the hand past potential disasters. Building one of these monsters is tricky business—you must allow for expansion, and must not build pockets that could trap explosive or noxious gases. This book, by an acknowledged master of the art, is a minutely detailed, illustrated and genuine manual. It really does get down to the tiniest moves and that's hard to do when one is psychologically involved with tons of material. I expect this manual will have the desired effect: lots of Finnish fireplaces will be built and they'll be good ones.

Reviewed by J. Baldwin in *The Essential Whole Earth Review*

Excerpts:

➤ *Once the burn is completed, dampers in the chimney flue are shut and the entire mass radiates heat for the next 12-24 hours. While the gas flow in the heater moves in a downdraft past the heat exchange surface of the heater, room air outside the heater moves in an updraft pattern along the vertical faces of the heater setting up a circulating flow of warmed air in the living space. It is from the opposing flows of warming heater gases and warmed room air that the name contraflow heater is derived.*

➤ *Mortar: Modern cement mortars are not appropriate for masonry heater inner core construction and are never used in Europe. Traditionally, European masonry heaters have always been constructed with clay-based mortars. The mortar we have found is a high quality, clay-based mortar called Uunilaasti, made in Finland. With care, we find it possible to build our standard heater in such a way that only a single bag of the special mortar, at an approximate cost of $30, is required. For those working with the mortar for the first time we recommend that they buy two in order not to run out at some critical point and have to delay work while waiting for supply.*

Oregon Department of Environmental Quality

Woodstove Heating Program
811 S.W. Sixth Avenue
Portland OR 97204-1390
(503)229-5177

Concerned about air pollution from increased wood burning, Oregon was the first state to limit woodstove emissions by law and require that all woodstoves sold in Oregon be certified by its Department of Environmental Quality (DEQ). The Department maintains a list of wood stoves—"Oregon DEQ certified wood stoves"—which have passed its stringent emission standards. DEQ also distributes several useful, free consumer pamphlets on wood stove use: *Catalytic Wood Stoves, Sizing Wood Stoves, Certified Wood Stoves, Keeping Wood Dry, Heating with Wood, Burn Smart*, and *Healthy Facts of Wood Smoke*. Before sending out-of-state for these, however, we encourage you to see whether your own state's DEQ or energy office has instituted a similar program or prepared comparable consumer materials.

Wood Heating Alliance
1101 Connecticut Avenue NW, Suite 700
Washington DC 20036
(202)857-1181

WHA is the national trade organization representing over 1400 companies in the hearth products industry. WHA's members range from manufacturers to retailers involved in stove and fireplace heating with wood, gas, and pellets. WHA can supply a list of member retailers and/or chimney sweeps within a specified state. Consumers may also request copies of WHA's educational brochures. Current publications include *Straight Answers to Burning Questions* and *Wood—A Responsible Fuel Choice.* Please send a self-addressed stamped envelope with your request to the address listed.

10D. Windpower Resources

Attempts to harness windpower by homeowners have more often than not ended with disappointing results. The winds can be finicky. They change minute by minute and month by month, blowing at gale force one day and becalmed the next. Windmills must be engineered and built to perform reliably and productively in an extraordinary range of conditions. In many situations, they simply haven't withstood this test. In other situations they were never given the chance, for they were poorly sited. Despite this discouraging report, it still may be worthwhile for you to use windpower, particularly if you live in a windy area, and to use electricity or water efficiently, while carrying out routine maintenance which will be required. But remember, careful siting and selection of a well engineered windmill are critical ingredients for success, and even then Mother Nature will have the final say. The resources in this section can show you how to identify a good wind site and calculate its energy-generating economic potential as well as find the best windmill for your application.

Common Sense Wind Energy
California Office of Appropriate Technology
1983; 83 pp.
$8.95 postpaid from:
Brick House Publishing Co.
P.O. Box 2134
Acton MA 01720
(508)635-9800
(800)446-8642 for orders

"Read up on residential scale wind energy in this remarkably clear, mercifully brief roundup of the basics," says J. Baldwin. "In contrast to most other wind power books, this one is realistic—a very essential ingredient for success in this oft over-hyped field." It's a good starting point for any homeowner considering investing in a small-scale wind energy system, whether you want to pump water, generate electricity, or produce process heat. The book addresses household energy needs, economic, legal, and social issues associated with home-scale windpower production, and the fundamentals of wind system hardware, siting, installation, and maintenance.

Excerpts:

➤ *Before proceeding with planning your wind energy system, you must organize the steps you will take. Here is a convenient approach for planning your wind system: Determine how much wind energy is at your site; Figure out how much of the energy you use can be supplied by wind; Select a suitable wind system that matches the wind resource to your energy needs; Proceed with planning the installation, financing, tax credit applications, and resolution of social and legal issues.*

➤ *Generators that produce alternating current and that connect directly to the utility power lines are rapidly becoming the standard type of system being considered by today's windmill buyers. The arrangement not only lets an energy consumer become an energy producer in parallel with the utility's grid, it also offers the advantage of working directly with existing sources of energy and the appliances that are already in place. For most U.S. installations, this type of system—called a grid-connected or grid-parallel system—may prove to be the most cost-effective choice available after a careful examination of alternatives. By operating in parallel with the grid's electricity, you don't have to consider exactly what load will be powered by wind. Simply determine the percentage of the entire load you hope to power, and select a wind system capable of matching that goal with the wind energy available at your site.*

➤ *The primary social issues you must face may already be folded up neatly in a set of architectural restrictions on your property, or in your local zoning lows. They may not entirely, however, be reflected in those restrictions. Your neighbors, with whom you ordinarily play bridge, may have some powerful feelings about you or anybody owning a wind machine on the block. These feelings are usually based on preconceived notions about problems associated with wind machines. Noise, television interference, and general aesthetics, not to mention overwhelming concern for the village's little folks, are the usual concerns. They may be founded in local experience, or they may come from badly researched newspaper stories. In any event, the best way to maintain a happy bridge club is to investigate your neighbors' feelings before you install your wind machine.*

For more on wind energy, contact the American Wind Energy Association listed in Section 10A.

10E. Hydropower Resources

Where its environmental impact can be minimized, hydropower will likely be the most desirable and cost-effective energy resource available for generating household electricity. Unfortunately, few of us have a stream or river flowing through our yard. If you are one of the fortunate few who does, the reference in this section can show you how to convert the power in that moving water into electricity to run your home.

The Residential Hydro Power Book: The Complete How-To Manual For DC Residential Hydroelectric Systems
Keith Ritter
1986; 150 pp.
$10 postpaid from:
John Hill
Integral Energy Systems
(916)265-8441

You can put that nearby stream to work making electricity—maybe. Individual experimenters have been messing around for years with small hydro generator sets that are well within most budgets. As is common with such enterprises, a body of reliable information together with acceptable hardware has slowly developed—everything learned the hard way. Here's the first good book on the subject. It's informal, subjective, and real: what has worked so far and what hasn't. What isn't known reliably yet is admitted and discussed as far as is possible. (That's called honesty.) Alas, our lawsuit-happy society has necessitated the censoring of certain procedures known to work but at some risk. Too bad. Nonetheless, you'll learn enough to set up a working system from dam to end use. A list of suppliers makes the book commendably useful and complete.

Reviewed by J. Baldwin in *The Essential Whole Earth Review*

Excerpts:

➤ *One of the trickiest things to make for a hydro system is a device to divert water from a creek in a controlled way into a pipeline. This diversion structure (a dam) must withstand flood conditions, silt build-up, and moving debris. It has to screen out trash and any solids that could damage the turbine or pipe, yet not get plugged up. It may have to be installed while the creek waters are high. It may have to be installed in a nearly inaccessible place, in solid rock or mucky stream beds. It has to allow enough water to bypass the pipe to keep the creek from completely drying, yet keep water from leaking through or underneath it. Sounds like you need a degree in civil engineering to build a proper dam, huh?*

➤ *No, it doesn't have to be Boulder Dam. Most dams for residential hydro systems are no more than 18" high, and a few feet wide. I have seen some incredibly crude diversion structures work surprisingly well. The simplest way of diverting water into a pipe is to just drop the pipe in a creek and use a couple of rocks to keep it in place. This is the ultimate execution of KISS (Keep It Simple Stupid!).*

➤ *Solar electric (photovoltaic or "PV") backup systems are very worthwhile. I believe they are the best overall backup system for a hydroelectric system, as usually the reason your creek is dry is due to "excessive" sun! With no moving parts, they may well be the most reliable long-term energy producer ever built! (And you heard it from me, a hydroelectric turbine manufacturer!)*

10F. Renewable Energy for Nomadics

One of the most satisfying things about "getting away from it all" in a recreational vehicle (RV) or boat is the sense of freedom it brings us. That is, until the fuel gauge approaches "E" or we have to fire up a noisy, smelly generator for power. Many RVs and boats are notorious energy-guzzlers. There are, however, ways to enjoy our freedom of mobility and be resource-conserving. The references in this section can help you identify opportunities to use energy as efficiently as possible in your RV or boat and, where feasible, to power them with renewable energy sources.

RVer's Guide To Solar Battery Charging
Noel and Barbara Kirby
1987; 176 pp.
$14.45 postpaid from:
AATEC Publications
Box 7119
Ann Arbor MI 48107
(313)995-1470

After putting up with noisy, high-maintenance generators for years, the Kirbys, serious RVers since 1966, discovered the benefits of solar-powered (photovoltaic) battery charging. Photovoltaics gave them a silent and simple way to charge RV (motorhomes and tow rigs) batteries with solar power. This discovery led to their PV/RV equipment business and to this clear and concise how-to book. Its comprehensive text is filled with practical knowledge on every aspect of using energy efficiently aboard RVs and charging RV batteries with photovoltaics. The Kirbys cover the basic theory and practice of electricity generation and storage in conventional RVs and discuss a variety of ways to minimize RVs' power needs by incorporating energy-efficient lighting, cooling, and refrigeration technologies, to name a few. They then describe how you go about sizing, selecting, and installing a PV system, including solar panels, charge regulators, mounting hardware, batteries, and wiring, to charge your RV's batteries. They also cover choosing and hooking up an inverter (these convert low-voltage DC electricity to 120-volt AC) to operate any conventional household appliances you want to take aboard. The book is finely detailed, offering good information, trouble-shooting instructions, and important maintenance advice which will ensure the best performance and life from your system. The guide will prove helpful not only to those people installing a PV system in a motorhome or trailer, but also to those working with a boat or small cabin.

Excerpts:

➤ *Another important feature of a solar battery charging system is its modular construction. You may start small, to fit within your budget, and expand your system as needs or desires dictate. We recommend, as a matter of fact, that you start with a modest solar system of one or two panels, learn to use energy efficiently, and add on as you gain experience.*

➤ *The primary benefit of an inverter-powered AC system is the convenience of instant, reliable power without the noise, fumes, and vibration of the gasoline or diesel generator. Because RVs are already equipped with a 100-hp plus power plant (the engine) and battery charging via the alternator, an inverter eliminates the need to run the generator most of the time. With a properly sized battery bank and high output alternator or solar panels, small RVs can eliminate the generator entirely.*

Free Energy Afloat

Nan & Kevin Jeffrey
1985; 199 pp.
$27.95 postpaid from:
International Marine Publishing Co.
21 Elm Street
Camden ME 04843
(207)236-4837

Free Energy Afloat shows you how to convert the sun shining on your sailboat and the wind or water running by it into electricity. It is the most comprehensive and practical reference available on using alternative energy systems to supply your onboard energy needs. It is appropriate whether you are a daysailer or captain of a larger boat with extended cruising capabilities. After covering the fundamentals of conventional electricity distribution and storage on boats and reviewing the capabilities and requirements of marine photovoltaic, wind, and water generators, the Jeffreys show you how to assess your boat's electrical needs. They show how, based on boat size, type, kind, and extent of usage, energy requirements, and cruising climate, to select a solar-, wind-, or water-powered system to charge batteries. Lots of practical, hands-on installation, maintenance, and operation details and advice are given, as are specifications, evaluations, and sources for dozens of commercially available renewable generators. The book is well illustrated, organized, and written, providing an invaluable resource to anyone striving for energy independence afloat.

Excerpts:

➤ *While most daysailers (boats without overnight facilities) have no engine or charging system, some do carry a few instruments, such as radio, running lights or an outboard engine with electric start. All these can easily be run by an alternate energy system. A daysailer requires a system that can adapt to limited mounting and stowage space, that is suitable for sporadic use and can be left unattended frequently.*

➤ *Our first choice is a small 7-10 watt solar panel that will take up little space and supply all power for an average daysailer (including battery losses). If the boat is equipped with an outboard engine, the solar panel costs the same as an alternator option, or it can be used as a back-up system for days when the sailing was great and the engine not used. Both wind and water systems are probably either too costly and bulky or their output too high for practical use on a daysailer.*

➤ *Despite the advantage of alternate energy, it can be frustrating at times. People with wind generators suffer through days with no wind and others with too much. People dependent on solar panels still use electricity, even on cloudy days. Or, they find themselves sailing with the sails shading the panels. Those using a water generator can be becalmed or find themselves moving too fast. But it's rare when conditions are not favorable for at least one of these systems to be generating. With a hybrid system [combining two or more alternative energy generators], you can increase your electrical output while protecting yourself against breakdown.*

The Solar Boat Book

Pat Rand Rose
1983; 181 pp.
$8.95 plus shipping from:
Ten Speed Press
Box 7123
Berkeley CA 94707
(510)527-1563

Anyone who wants to equip a sleep-aboard boat to be as energy-self-sufficient as possible will find this easy-to-understand book a good general reference. Rose describes how to evaluate your onboard energy needs, reduce them to a minimum, and then, where feasible, supply them with sun-, wind-, and hydropower. The book covers everything from marine refrigeration and solar hot water heating to water desalination and photovoltaic battery charging. Many of the approaches and techniques described are based on landlubber-proven household energy-efficiency tactics which have been cleverly adapted for seagoing duty. You'll learn that using energy efficiently, just as at home, is the key to energy independence on your boat.

Plans and directions are given for several simple and inexpensive solar projects, such as solar water heaters and solar cookers. Please note, however, that some of the technical information presented on solar, wind, and hydro generators and on energy-efficient battery-powered lights and appliances is now outdated: significantly better products presently are available.

Excerpts:

➤ *If your boat leaks water during heavy rains or heavy seas, then you can be sure it also leaks heat in those same places. This is the time to caulk, rebed stanchions, weatherstrip, and see that all ventilators or air scoops have movable or removable air-tight covers. Ports and windows are especially vulnerable to air and water leakage. If necessary, they should be removed and rebedded, replacing the rubber weather seal in the process. Extra care should be taken in weatherstripping hatch openings and exterior cabin doors.*

➤ *Another power hog can be the pressure water system pump, a totally unnecessary piece of equipment, but the last electrical appliance most people will voluntarily give up. This little pump can make the difference between living aboard ship and camping out in an endurance contest. So, rather than eliminating this piece of equipment, I would favor using it with discretion, and adding a header tank and sink sprayer to reduce its electrical demands. A header tank is simply a hollow air chamber into which a small amount of water is pumped against air pressure. This maintains a reserve, which will reduce the amount of cycling your pump must do. The header tank should be mounted vertically and as close to the pump as possible. Header tanks are available commercially from marine plumbing supply outlets, or can be constructed very easily by the home craftsperson.*

➤ *A galley sink sprayer also helps conserve electricity and water because it provides a fine but forceful spray while using a minimum of water, again reducing pump cycling time. Thoughtful use of an efficiently designed pressure water system can be considered "elegant frugality."*

11. Financing Energy Efficiency

There are many ways to make a new home energy-efficient or to reduce an existing one's energy appetite. However, choosing the "best buys"—the ones which offer you the greatest energy savings for each dollar invested—is critical. This means carefully assessing each energy-saving option's purchase price and installation costs and its probable operation and maintenance costs.

Paying for relatively low-cost energy saving measures, like water-heater insulation wraps, low-flow shower-heads, energy-efficient light bulbs, and weatherstripping, may not be a problem. In contrast, bankrolling large efforts, such as superinsulating a new house or replacing an existing furnace with a high-efficiency model, may seem beyond your budget. That shouldn't, however, stop you from pursuing energy- and money-saving opportunities. Many banks, federal and state agencies, and utility companies will help finance the cost of energy efficiency upgrades. The same investments may also qualify you for a larger home loan than you would normally be eligible for, since many lending institutions realize that homeowners who spend less on energy bills will be able to make higher mortgage payments. It is even possible to finance many energy-saving projects so that average monthly energy savings are greater than the monthly loan payment. Ask your state energy office and local lenders and realtors if there is an "energy-efficient mortgage" program operating in your area.

The following references and organizations will help you identify the best energy saving buys for your home, introduce you to the various ways of financing them, and point you toward potentially responsive lenders.

Illustration courtesy of *Tools For A Change,* 1979, proceedings of the Northeast Regional Appropriate Technology Forum

11A. Resources for Financing

Financing Home Energy Improvements
1986; 120 pp.
$3.50 postpaid from:
Massachusetts Audubon Society
Educational Resources Office
Lincoln MA 01773
(617)259-9500

This booklet clearly and concisely explains how wise homeowners (and small apartment building owners) can overcome one of the greatest hurdles to making energy saving improvements: finding the money to cover the initial expense. Though written for a New England audience, the underlying premises of this guide are applicable anywhere. The booklet leads you through the most important issues to consider in evaluating the cost-effectiveness of various home energy improvements and the options for financing them. Examples illustrate the economics of several energy saving retrofits financed with bank loans. There is also valuable advice on the various types and sources of loans, how to shop for them, and the tax benefits of such investments.

Excerpts:

➤ *Energy improvements are the only home improvements that actually make you money, in addition to increasing comfort. Energy conservation measures also protect you against inflation and unpredictable rises in fuel and electricity costs. Energy conservation reduces the share that energy costs have in your household budget, so that sudden rises in fuel and electricity prices will do less damage. As energy prices go up over the years, the money you spend on weatherization will look like a better and better investment.*

➤ *Finding the money to pay for energy improvements can be difficult, and sometimes the payback time is longer than you want to wait for your investment to start making a profit. A bank loan can help you get around these problems. The idea is simple: plan an energy conservation project so that your average monthly savings are greater than the monthly payment on the loan used to pay for the project. This means more money in your pocket starting right away. No waiting around for a lengthy payback period to pass; no large outlay of cash to pay for the project. Because going into debt for energy conservation can actually make a homeowner or apartment building owner financially better off, many people are discovering that 'energy debt is good debt.'*

➤ *Remember also that the money you save on heating bills as a result of weatherization is saved after taxes. That is, if weatherstripping your windows saves you $200 this year, you keep the full $200. The IRS has no right to touch your energy savings. You may pay taxes on the interest from a savings account, or on the dividends from a money market fund, but an investment in home energy conservation is tax-free!*

The Alliance to Save Energy
1725 K Street, NW, Suite 914
Washington DC 20006-1401
(202)857-0666

The Alliance to Save Energy is a national proponent of home energy-efficiency financing. Founded in 1977, the Alliance promotes energy efficiency in all sectors of the U.S. economy through research, demonstration projects, lobbying, and education. The ultimate goal of all the Alliance's efforts is to increase our nation's quality of life and productivity. The Alliance distributes several low-cost or free educational consumer fact sheets and pamphlets on financing energy efficiency at home. For more information, order its publications list. The following publication is an example of the Alliance's work.

Your Home Energy Portfolio
1984; 20 pp.
Free, one copy per request,
or $1.00 per copy in bulk,
from Alliance To Save Energy
(address cited above)

Helping consumers become wise energy investors is the goal of this excellent primer. It shows homeowners how they can save and even make money by investing in cost-cutting, energy-saving features when they buy, maintain, or sell their homes. The booklet contains practical advice for determining your home's current energy efficiency, identifying what energy-conserving features you should look for when home-shopping, determining the actual energy costs of different homes you may be considering purchasing, and calculating whether financing energy efficient improvements as part of your mortgage will be cost-effective.

Excerpts:

➤ *If the house you are considering has been lived in previously, ask to see the utility bills of the previous owner. Although energy consumption varies by lifestyle, past utility bills can still be a good indicator of how wisely, or wastefully, the house uses energy.*

➤ *Recognizing that owners of efficient homes have lower utility bills and therefore more disposable income, many lenders have instituted practices to make it easier to qualify for a mortgage on a more efficient home. Recent changes in mortgage practices may enable you to afford the home with the extra efficiency features. Seek lenders who will take into account your lower monthly energy costs when determining whether you qualify for a mortgage on an energy efficient home.*

➤ *Under new lending guidelines, buying a less efficient house can also be a good deal—especially if you commit at time of purchase to making energy efficiency improvements and decide to finance them through your mortgage. Energy improvements financed as part of your mortgage can be paid for over a longer period of time and at a lower rate of interest than shorter term home improvement loans. If the home you have selected needs to be made more efficient, shop for a lender who will let you finance energy-saving improvements as part of your mortgage.*

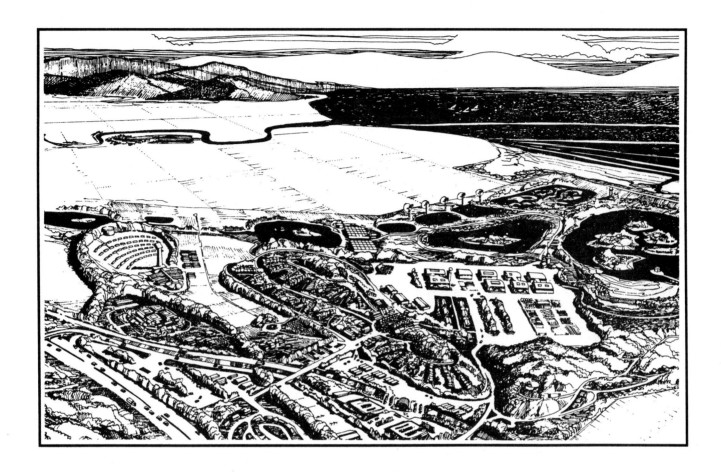

12. Shopping For and Building Resource-Efficient Housing

Buying a home represents the most expensive and resource-intensive investment most people will make in their lifetime. Whether you are shopping for a used house or hiring an architect and builder to create a new dream home, you can demand resource efficiency. Shop for or specify a well designed and constructed building equipped with resource-efficient appliances. This will help ensure that the home you move into is comfortable and costs you as little as possible to operate and maintain.

The references in this section can show you how to get the most value for your money both up front and in the long term.

Illustration from proceedings of *The Village as Solar Ecology*, courtesy of John and Nancy Todd, New Alchemy Institute.

12A. House-Shopping Primers

How To Avoid The 10 Biggest Home-Buying Traps
A.M. Watkins
$12.95 postpaid from:
Dearborn Financial Services
520 N. Dearborn Street
Chicago IL 60610
(800)621-9621

The most common homebuying mistakes fit a pattern which home buyers repeat over and over again. This handy, tell-it-as-it-is consumer book identifies the most frequent of these errors, flaws, and scams, and then tells you how to avoid them. This practical advice is required reading for anyone shopping for a new or used home, lest you fall into the same traps countless others have—some seemingly obvious, some subtle. Among the traps covered are: "The High-Priced House"; "The Unforeseen Expenses of Buying and Owning a House"; "The Vanishing Builder"; "The No-Design House"; "The Garbled Floor Plan"; "The Old-House Lemon"; "The Marginal House"; and "The Gimmick House." Avoiding two of the very biggest traps, "The Tight Mortgage Bind" and "The Energy Guzzler House", is reported in special detail. Watkins offers an 11-point checklist to prevent future mortgage shock for people financing houses with an adjustable-rate mortgage and cites new superinsulation standards that can cut heating and air-conditioning costs in the average U.S. house to less than $100 a year. The book ends with an invaluable "Checklist For Buying A House"—essentially a review of the book's main points—which will remind you what details to be on the lookout for and what questions to ask before signing on the dotted line.

Excerpts:

➤ *It's also important to check on the local zoning rules, assuming you don't want to see those lovely woods across the street invaded by bulldozers someday to make way for a new shopping center or chemical factory. Your best protection is an area that is strictly zoned chiefly for residential use, permitting little or no other kind of development. If there are commercial and industrial zones nearby, watch out.*

➤ *Determining if there's insulation in the walls can be difficult. The older the house, the less likely that wall insulation is present unless the owner had it pumped into the walls. Remove a few electric outlet covers and peer in with a flashlight. Can you see insulation? In cold weather the presence of drafts inside the walls is a tipoff to little or no wall insulation. In cold weather, also try the palm test. Put the palm of your hand flat against the inside surface of the exterior walls in several rooms. The walls should feel almost as warm to the touch as an interior wall in the middle of the house. If the outside wall is cold or downright chilly to the touch, there's little or no insulation. The acid test is what the house heating bills are. Requesting the house seller to produce them is now customary. What is the average total cost to heat the house each year? A request for summer air-conditioning bills is also recommended. Unless you're an expert, hiring a good home inspection consultant is the best way to evaluate the heating system, as well as the insulation and the whole house.*

The Complete Guide to Factory-Made Houses

A.M. Watkins
1988
$12.95 postpaid from:
Dearborn Financial Services
520 N. Dearborn Street
Chicago IL 60610
(800)621-9621

Close to half of all new single-family houses in the U.S. are now made in whole or part in factories. These homes are a far cry from the old "prefabs" of ill repute. In fact, the quality of their design and construction is often higher than that of site-built conventional housing, and they often cost less. Virtually every type and size of home imaginable is available, ranging from "affordable" models costing under $40,000 up to $400,000-plus deluxe custom units. You can even purchase models which incorporate superinsulation, passive solar heating, and attached greenhouses/sunspaces. *The Complete Guide To Factory-Made Houses* gives a comprehensive, non-technical overview of manufactured housing. It's filled with sound consumer advice that will prove invaluable to homebuyers considering factory-made housing. The book covers the different kinds of factory-made housing; whether you wish to build your own home from a factory kit or obtain one completed and ready to move in; the advantages and possible drawbacks of each of these types; the possible savings; how to shop for high-quality manufactured housing; and finally, a list of the names and addresses of more than 25 leading housing manufacturers.

Excerpts:

➤ *As skilled as a carpenter may be, he finds it difficult not to hurry a job on a frigid day in winter. Joints at the corners may show daylight. Window framing, nailed up with a cold hammer held in an icy hand, could easily be more loose than it should. Hastily putting insulation in, he may leave gaps. Other mistakes occur at other times, such as during those dog days in summer when workmen are gasping for air and easily slip up. A house built under a good roof and out of the weather in a factory is another story, as I've mentioned before. Tight joints are par for the assembly line. And workmen, under weather-protected conditions, can take the little extra time necessary to see that things like insulation are snugly installed. The occasional times when not, the slipup is usually caught by the quality-control inspector before the house leaves the plant.*

➤ *The extra cost of high-quality materials is often less than many people think. Paying extra for really good-quality products and materials where it can count can increase the cost of a typical house by a mere 5 to 8 percent, according to a study by* House & Home *magazine. That will mean a relatively small increase in your down payment and monthly mortgage payments, but this will be offset many times over in reduced upkeep and house operating costs. A good example is getting a permanent-finish outside wall surface. This can save the cost of repainting, or a periodic expenditure of up to several thousand dollars.*

House

Tracy Kidder
$9.95 plus shipping from:
Avon Books
Dept. BP
Box 767, Route 2
Dresden TN 38225
(800)238-0658

Pulitzer Prize winning journalist Tracy Kidder thrusts you into the all-encompassing creation of one family's great American dream, the building of its first house. This richly detailed, intriguing story chronicles the building of a home from inception to move-in day. Along the way, Kidder brings you into the lives of the house's owners, builders, and architect. Intense relations and emotions are played out as each party looks after their own best interests and egos. The house's owners, a lawyer and a Ph.D. educator, want to build a dream house at a price they can afford. The builders want to construct a finely crafted home at a price which fairly compensates them for their work. The architect wants to see, most importantly, every last little detail of his design executed. In addition to the complex social dynamics, Kidder embellishes *House* with fascinating information and lore about construction. He takes you deep into the Maine woods where the home's lumber originated, back to the era from which a building term, tool, or tradition came, and much more.

The day-to-day frustrations and crises, the challenges, and ultimately the triumphs are startlingly candid. Besides being captivating reading, this book can give those of you considering contracting out the design and construction of a home extraordinary insights into many of the issues—values, goals, money, communication, aesthetics—that you will have to deal with. This exposure may not only help you in selecting designers and builders, but will thoroughly prepare you to work most effectively with whomever you hire.

Excerpts:

➤ *Adding one nice detail after another can become an addiction. You say, "Oh, it costs a little more and it'll make our lives much nicer." Even sensible people get caught....Jonathan knows that with the kindest intentions in the world, Bill and Apple Corps could arrange his bankruptcy. He wants Bill to be happy with the house, but the house has already been endowed with enough elegance and expense for Jonathan.*

➤ *Jim got the sheetrockers to agree to begin hanging the interior walls and ceilings on July 15. He had to make sure that the lumber arrived soon enough for Apple Corps to frame the walls before the plumber's, electrician's, and insulator's promised arrivals. He remembered to call the building inspector, who would insist on seeing the place before the sheetrock went up. You build a job out of a host of promises, and if the insulator's truck breaks down or the electrician gets the flu, the whole procedure can collapse. You might have to tell the sheetrockers to delay a week and then you might lose them for a month. Timing is everything, and in spite of the vicissitudes of the fast track, the job has not halted or even slowed for the lack of the right materials or the next subcontractor. That is thanks to Jim's fore-thought—both his choices of subs and his scheduling. The house, in this sense, really exists in the meticulously printed notes he carries in his leather case.*

Illustration labels: SHOWER CABINET, STONE WALL, STAIRS, GAS RANGE, HEATING SYSTEM, SUMP, DEEP WELL IN BEDROCK, SOIL, LOOSE FITTING PIPES CRACKS & JOINTS, PHOSPHATE SLAG

13. Household Environmental Quality

According to the Environmental Protection Agency, your greatest exposure to toxic chemicals is probably right in your own home. Vast changes in building materials, building design, construction techniques, energy consumption, and ventilation patterns are harming the environmental quality of many homes. The health consequences of these little-known changes typically appear after a lag time of 15-30 years. Sick building syndrome (SBS) and environmental illness (EI) have been well documented clinically. Unfortunately, as is the case with most new syndromes, those who suffer the effects experience the problem long before it is "discovered" by research scientists and academic physicians. We are just now beginning to realize that SBS and EI are among the maladies of 20th Century civilized living. This section addresses the newly emerging and somewhat scary field of indoor environmental quality. Several excellent references are reviewed which can help you design a healthy new home or rid your existing one of the most threatening and noxious of common indoor pollutants. Debra Lynn Dadd, a pioneer researcher of household toxins, puts this threat into perspective:

These chemicals can cause cancer, birth defects, changes in genetic structure, and malfunctions to the human immune system, as well as a host of annoying symptoms such as headaches, skin rashes, runny noses and depression. Nobody knows the long-term effects of consuming, and being exposed to thousands of different man-made chemicals, day in and day out, year after year. Nor is it clear what the synergistic effects are of the combinations of chemicals we are exposed to daily. It's up to us to protect ourselves and our families from both those obvious and hidden dangers. The problem of exposure to toxic chemicals in thousands of products is enormous and can seem frightening and overwhelming, but we don't have to live with toxic chemicals. We do have a choice—and our choice begins at home.

Illustration courtesy of *Your Home, Your Health, Your Well-Being*, Ten Speed Press

13A. Household Environmental Quality References

The Healthy House
John Bower
1991; 416 pp.
$16.95 from:
Carol Publishing Group
120 Enterprise Ave.
Secaucus NJ 07094
(201) 866-0490

This is one of the most comprehensive books on indoor air pollution prevention, as it addresses building a non-toxic house from the ground up (as well as how to cure a "sick" one). It covers all building materials and construction practices that may have negative health effects, and lists many alternative, less toxic materials and techniques, plus their suppliers. Every step of the building process is discussed, from finding a healthy location to picking the right paint. In each section the hazards are presented, followed by information on avoiding contaminating your home. Organizations and suppliers are highlighted in bold print and are listed in an appendix to facilitate your search for alternatives.

Excerpts:

➤ *Cleaning Up a Mold Problem: When a mold problem is encountered, the first and most important thing to do is locate the source of the moisture and eliminate it. When this is done, the mold can no longer produce spores. It may not be dead, but without moisture it will be dormant and will not produce spores. People often assume that a good, strong disinfectant will kill the mold and there will no longer be a problem, but if the moisture is not eliminated, the mold will simply return again and again. Many sensitive people are bothered by commercial disinfectants. In some cases, "Zephrian" (****Winthrop Pharmaceuticals****) is recommended for these individuals. It is available through pharmacies.*

➤ *Cabinetry: Practically all of the commercially manufactured cabinets, whether for kitchens or bathrooms, utilize plywood or particle board and will out-gas formaldehyde fumes into the house. Even expensive cabinetry will rely on man-made wood products to some degree. The doors and drawer fronts are often solid wood, but the shelves are almost always plywood or particle board. . .*

Clean and Green
Annie Berthold-Bond
1990; 160 pages
$10.95 from:
Ceres Press
P.O. Box 87
Woodstock, NY 12498
(914) 679-8561

Housecleaning isn't most people's idea of a good time, but all too often the chore is compounded by the physical side-effects of handing irritating cleaning products. To make matters worse, many popular cleaning agents cause significant environmental pollution. For everyone concerned about the environment, and the growing population with chemical sensitivities, Annie Berthold-Bond has the solution. This book contains 500 cleaning recipes, including 90 stain removing remedies. It is a practical guide providing innovative alternatives for cleaning literally everything, from the kitchen sink to pesticide-coated food. It even helps you wax the family car. Brand name products are suggested, too, for environmentally safe storebought products that can be readily obtained in natural food stores, supermarkets, and by mail.

Reviewed by David Goldbeck

Excerpts:

➤ *Aesthetics:*
  A commercial package will have images on it to capture your imagination. A company may use a rose to get you to think the cleaning product will make things smell sweetly, even if it doesn't. We are accustomed to seeing packaging that evokes images, and we can make our own to suit ourselves. I happen to love wild roses, so using a container with rose decals brings pleasant thoughts to me when I clean the bathtub.

➤ *Cleaning Agents*
  Decals and gummed labels—rub with vegetable oil
  Grease—sprinkle with salt
  Plastic laminate cabinets—wash with club soda

Windstar Recycling Handbook
Susan Hassol and Beth Richman
1989; 91 pp.
$5.00 postpaid from:
The Windstar Foundation
2317 Snowmass Creek Road
Snowmass CO 81654
(800) 669-4777

Essential to every resource-efficient household are good recycling habits. This handbook contains 101 practical tips for recycling at home and at work, and is full of statistics that will get you thinking about the complete cycle of resource use.

Excerpts:

➤ *Americans throw away enough iron and steel to continuously supply all the nation's automakers.*

➤ *Producing one ton of glass requires: 1330 pounds of sand, 433 pounds of soda ash, 433 pounds of limestone, 151 pounds of feldspar, and 15.2 million BTUs of energy. Pollutants generated include 384 pounds of mining wastes and 27.8 pounds of air pollutants.*

➤ *Bring your own containers for deli-counter foods, and avoid plastic and foam disposables. Store employees are usually happy to weigh your container first and deduct its weight from your purchase (in fact, they do this anyway with the plastic ones they ordinarily use). Besides being a responsible use of resources, this is a good way to educate others—you will often be asked why you are doing this.*

The Healthy Home—An Attic to Basement Guide to Toxin-Free Living

Linda Mason Hunter
1989; 313 pp.
$21.95 hardcover
Rodale Press
Emmaus PA

This practical guide deals with a wide range of health factors in and around the home: water, indoor air quality, household products, furnishings, yards, light, color, sound, pets, safety, and security. The book offers directions for giving your house a "health audit" with a room-by-room checklist of healthy materials, equipment, and practices. It then gives details on how to rid the home of hazards in those areas where it falls short of the recommendations in the audit. In addition to physical health issues, this book addresses creating a healthy emotional atmosphere with light, color, and sound. Appendices list sources for products and services, and resources for more information. Coverage of subjects such as pets and security systems set this book apart from others in this category and make it a good general reference for the safe home.

Reviewed by Susan Hassol

Excerpts:

➤ *Ironically, in the United States today you are far more likely to breathe some of the most debilitating compounds ... at home. Indoor pollution from radon, household chemicals, pesticides, and other products can reach levels five times higher than in the grimiest air outside.*

➤ *Radon is by far the most serious indoor air pollutant...This odorless, colorless, naturally-occurring radioactive gas can accumulate in your home. It is estimated to cause from 5,000 to 20,000 cases of lung cancer each year, second only to cigarette smoking, according to the EPA. The EPA also estimates that as many as one out of five houses has radon levels above the recommended action level of 4 picocuries per liter of air.*

➤ *There are disadvantages to modern methods of thermostat-controlled heating and air conditioning. In addition to being expensive, heating and cooling systems can make air uncomfortably dry—provoking headaches, dry skin, and throat irritation... An alternative is radiant heat—heat from the sun or other hot sources such as a wood stove or radiant heat panels. Instead of heating the air, these raise the radiant temperature of a room's exposed surfaces as well as the contents and make the space feel warmer.*

➤ *Healthy lighting, by definition, is well balanced. That means there is good overall general lighting in the room so you can move about without fear of stumbling, and there is good task lighting, as well, giving you the brightness you need to do a job without straining your eyes. Don't skimp on either one!*

Nontoxic, Natural, & Earthwise

Debra Lynn Dadd
1990; 384 pp.
$12.95 postpaid from:
The Earthwise Consumer
Box 279
Forest Knolls CA 94933

This book raises new standards for evaluating the healthfulness and environmental safety of a wide range of consumer products. A literal "Yellow Pages" of natural and environmentally sound products, this is a comprehensive guidebook for today's health-conscious and environmentally aware consumer. Three hundred different categories of products and mail-order catalogs are evaluated, including appliances, bedding, paint, renewable energy products, personal care products, cleaning products, eyeglasses, water filters, air filters, and kids' toys. Dadd tells you: what harmful substances may be found in a product and the symptoms they cause; what product labels will and won't tell you; questions to ask before you buy; and what to look for in an earthwise counterpart. More than 2000 brand name items, 600 mail-order sources, and 400 inexpensive do-it-yourself formulas are evaluated. The information is presented in an easy-to-use format, complete with icons.

Excerpts:

➤ *The word "nontoxic" appears on many consumer products, but it is misleading. According to the federal regulatory definition, "nontoxic" doesn't necessarily mean "not at all toxic" or "absolutely safe," but can mean, for example, that up to half of the laboratory animals exposed to the product through ingestion or inhalation died within two weeks.*

➤ *Packaging is like a second product that surrounds the product you are buying. It protects the product, holds a label that gives us information, and acts as a potent marketing device. But does a toxic cleaning product become environmentally safe because it is packaged in a recyclable plastic container? No.*

➤ *Beware of 100-percent cotton sheets labeled "Easy Care" or "No Iron," as these owe their convenience to formaldehyde.*

➤ *Avoid plastic wraps or containers. If you believe that plastic is stable and cannot contaminate food, try this: Close an empty plastic container for several days, then open it and sniff. If it has a plastic odor, the plastic polymers can be absorbed by the food. Instead, use glass or ceramic containers, metal tins, or cellophane, a film produced from the cellulose in wood pulp (not to be confused with "plastic wraps").*

➤ *Refrigerators, freezers, dishwashers, washing machines, and clothes dryers should all have interiors of porcelain enamel or stainless steel, not plastic. When purchasing, consider buying reconditioned used appliances; new appliances today all contain significant amounts of plastic, while older appliances have much less plastic, what there is having been outgassed. Also, new appliances with metal interiors are the top of their line and quite expensive; older models provide high-quality non-toxic materials at significant savings.*

Light: Medicine of the Future

Jacob Liberman, O.D., Ph.D.
1991; 255 pp.
Bear & Company
Santa Fe, NM
$22.95 plus shipping from:
Jacob Liberman
P.O. Box 4058
Aspen CO 81612
(800)932-3277

Light: Medicine of the Future presents the story of an ancient, yet newly emerging science, the Science of Light. It bridges the gap between scientific knowledge, intuitive knowledge, health, and personal evolution, thus acting as a foundation for a new paradigm in healing. In an era when we are so concerned about the quality of our environment, it is somewhat amazing that more attention has not been given to light. Energy-efficiency studies have been turning to daylight—primarily as a way to save energy and thereby reduce pollution; the resulting beneficial effects of daylight have been understated. Fortunately, this may change, with the publication of Jacob Liberman's new book. *Light: Medicine of the Future* is both thorough in its detail, and easy to read. It aptly addresses an issue central to our health.

Excerpts:

➤ *Light entering the eyes serves not only vision, but goes directly to the body's biological clock within the hypothalamus. All biological functions in humans are regulated by the combined effects of the nervous system and the endocrine system, which in turn are controlled by the hypothalamus. In addition, the hypothalamus controls most of the body's regulatory functions by monitoring light-related information and sending it to the pineal, which then uses this information to cue our organs about light conditions in the environment. In other words, the hypothalamus acts as a puppet-master who quietly, and out of sight, controls most of the functions which keep the body in balance.*

➤ *In Oriental medicine, the daily life patterns of individuals were always associated with the level of health they maintained. Rhythms, seasons, and their associated cyclic variations were related to special kinds of physical and emotional problems. For them, harmony within one's life process was related to the level of communion between one's body and the environment. Can we experience fluid integration within our mind/body/emotions without creating that same level of harmony in our relationship with nature, or vice-versa? Isn't our internal integration a mirror of our integration with all life (people, animals, nature, work, etc.)?. . . . Within the pineal gland and its interdependence with the rest of the body lie the mysteries of our aging as well as our agelessness.*

➤ *With the development of more sophisticated diagnostic techniques, science and medicine are finding that certain brain regions are not only light sensitive, but actually do respond differently to different wavelengths. It is now believed that specific colors (wavelengths) interact differently with the endocrine system to stimulate or inhibit hormonal production.*

1990 Solaplexus Radon Product & Service Guide
$58 postpaid from:
Solaplexus
21 Tamarack Circle
Fishkill NY 12524
(914)896-4796

Prepared by the organization that developed the EPA's first radon-mitigation training program, this looseleaf binder is divided into five major categories: monitoring/diagnosis, barriers/sealants, mitigation equipment and controls, tools & safety equipment, and information/resources. Solaplexus also conducts workshops on radon-related issues under contract with the New York State Energy Office.

Indoor Air: Risks And Remedies
Richard L. Crowther, FAIA
1989; 264 pp.
$16.95 plus shipping from:
Directions Publisher
P.O. Box 61135
Denver CO 80206
(303)388-1875

This comprehensive book explores the indoor air pollution problem from many interesting perspectives. Although a bit academic, it contains good background information on the gamut of indoor pollution sources, how they affect people, and what you can do to control or eliminate them. It gives an introductory overview of subjects ranging from the physiology of breathing and the breakdown of toxic gases released from indoor gas-fired appliances to the effectiveness of various types of air cleaners and the ventilation requirements for different parts of the house.

Excerpts:

➤ *Humidity plays a critical role in our respiratory encounter with the atmosphere. When airborne humidity exceeds 60% or is less than 40%, exposure to microorganic bacteria and viruses that proliferate more abundantly under such conditions becomes more of an invasive threat.*

➤ *Smoking is a principal offender of indoor air quality. Tobacco smoke contains more than 3,000 constituents, of which some are toxic, carcinogenic, tumorogenic or have adverse radioactive affinities and properties. Smoking one cigarette raises indoor air pollution 10 to 100 times.*

➤ *Most air fresheners and fragrant sprays do nothing to make indoor air more healthful; in fact, they can mask serious sources of air pollution and desensitize the olfactory senses, and can also contribute to air pollution themselves by emitting organic substances.*

Also, see *The Earthwise Consumer*, reviewed in Section 2A.

13B. Organizations Concerned With Household Environmental Quality

Environmental Hazards Management Institute
Box 932
Durham NH 03824
(603)868-1496
(800)446-5256

EHMI serves industry, government, and public groups with hazardous waste materials management consulting, training programs, technology and market evaluation studies, and confidential environmental audits. Individuals will find EHMI's Household Hazardous Waste Wheel, Water Sense Wheel, and Recycling Wheel (each $3.75 postpaid, with bulk discounts available) particularly handy and practical references to tack up on a wall at home where all can see. They also publish the Environmental Manager's Compliance Advisor.

Environmental Health Watch
(formerly Council on Hazardous Materials)
4115 Bridge Ave.
Cleveland OH 44113
(216)961-4646

EHW is a private, non-profit information center on hazardous materials in the home and community. EHW was established to increase public understanding of the health effects of hazardous materials so that people will be aware of significant dangers, yet avoid unreasonable worry. EHW educates people to: 1) adopt prudent practices to safeguard the health and safety of their families and 2) support effective public and private policy on hazardous materials management to protect the community.

Human Ecology Action League (HEAL)
P.O. Box 49126
Atlanta GA 30359-1126
(404)248-1898

The Human Ecology Action League publishes *The Human Ecologist* newsletter ($20/year—4 issues), a central source of information for people who are hypersensitive to the myriad of chemicals common to our everyday life. It reports on "safe" building materials, house designs, construction methods, and household products. New members of HEAL receive a list of HEAL chapters and support groups and a list of nearby physicians specializing in environmental health problems.

The Consumer Federation of America
1424 16th Street NW, Suite 604
Washington DC 20036
(202)387-6121

The Consumer Federation of America is the nation's largest consumer advocacy organization, with 200 member groups representing over 30 million consumers. Its chief role is representing consumer interests before the U.S. Congress and Federal regulatory agencies. The CFA has declared indoor air quality its number one health and safety priority, and has prepared several educational pamphlets for individuals concerned about their home's air quality. Write for a complete publications list.

The American Lung Association
1740 Broadway
New York NY 10019

The American Lung Association cares about your lungs, so it's logical that it is tracking the pollutants that have a good chance of ending up in your respiratory system. The ALA has produced several educational pamphlets on the topic, including: *Toxic Chemicals in the Air: Indoors and Outdoors*; the *Indoor Air Pollution Fact Sheets— Household Products, Ozone Air Pollution, Secondhand Smoke, Asbestos, Biological Pollutants In Your Home*, and provide a brochure on Radon. Contact your local chapter of the American Lung Association to get indoor air pollution publications.

United States Environmental Protection Agency
Information Access Branch
Public Information Center (PIC)
401 M Street SW, PM-211B
Washington DC 20460
(202)260-7751

The EPA, though primarily concerned with the outdoor environment, is another organization which can help answer your household environmental quality questions. Contact your regional EPA office to find out what Indoor air quality information and referral services it offers.

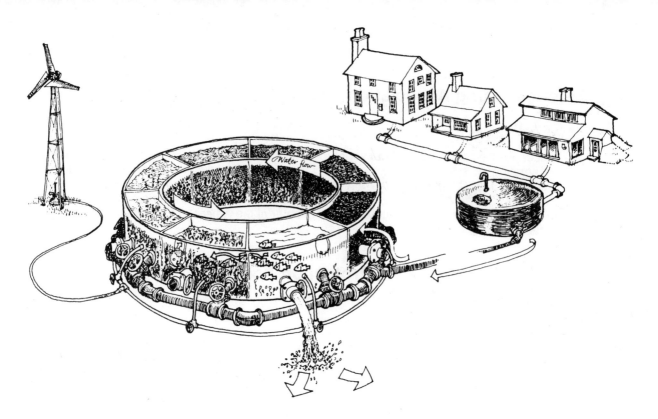

14. Safe and Efficient Water Use/Waste Disposal Resources

Water is the medium of life.

Eighty percent of the weight of a typical living cell is water; 99 out of every 100 molecules in your body are water molecules. We are, through water, intimately connected to each other and to our entire water planet. There is almost nothing that we do that does not affect or rely on water, either directly or indirectly.

Although each of us, on the average, uses about 150 gallons per day directly for cooking, washing, flushing and watering, our indirect use of water amounts to an astounding 1,840 gallons per day. Of this, about 1,660 gallons were used to grow crops and livestock, and 180 gallons were used by industry to create the products we rely on. Approximately 120 gallons were used in the production of one egg, three gallons are used to process one can of corn, ten gallons to make a paperback book, six to flush a toilet.

As we grow more aware of the impact of our daily lives on the streams, rivers, lakes, bays and aquifers that supply our clean water and assimilate our wastes, the wisdom of these words rings ever more true:

"We live in one world and each act of ours affects the whole."

Kim Allsup, excerpted from "We Are the Water" in *New Alchemy Quarterly*, Fall 1984

The following publications and organizations can help you appreciate, protect, and wisely use water, one of our most precious and vital natural resources. Since roughly 95% of the water we use at home each day ends up as sewage, several references are also included here which address alternative ways to conserve water resources while simultaneously disposing of water/human wastes in an environmentally sustainable fashion.

Illustration courtesy of *The Village As Solar Ecology*, 1979, Courtesy of John and Nancy Todd, New Alchemy Institute.

14A. Safe and Efficient Water Use References

We All Live Downstream: For Everyone Who Wants Clean Water. . . A Guide to Waste Treatment That Stops Water Pollution
Pat Costner, Holly Gettings, and Gienna Booth
1990; 92 pp.
$9.95 postpaid from
The Water Center
Route 3 Box 716
Eureka Springs AR 72632
(501)253-9431

We All Live Downstream takes a bold and poetic step toward informing concerned North Americans about both the effects of present waste treatment technologies and some of the ecological alternatives. The book begins with a well-documented description of our country's water crisis. A review of the environmental legislation of the 1970s, such as The Clean Water Act and its companion The Safe Drinking Water Act, is presented. The book points out how legislation has done little more than slow the deterioration of surface and ground waters. Several chapters are devoted to composting toilets and greywater treatment technologies. Thirteen different composters are described by concept, requirements, space, operation, product history, model, cost, and distributor's address. There is also a section on water conservation. It starts with an evaluation of household water use, broken down by device. This is followed by a shopping list of water-efficient devices that range from low-flow shower-heads and toilet tank dams to a thorough critique of the best low-flow toilets commercially available. The latter includes descriptions similar to those given for composting toilets. The poetry and superb illustrations make *We All Live Downstream* one of the best books available on the subject of ecological home waste management. Much more than a technical manual, it is written with the intent of instilling a philosophy of water stewardship.

Reviewed by Tad Montgomery

Excerpts:

➤ *Consider the milk cooler in your grocery store. It may hold as many as 300 one-gallon jugs of milk. Fill all 300 jugs with water; stack them in your living room. You now have a vivid example of the amount of clean, drinkable water that the average U.S. family of four uses every day.*

➤ *Conservation—simply saving water—is the cheapest and easiest form of water protection. If we don't dirty the water, we won't have to clean it up!*

➤ *Since water toilets use 35-45 per cent of a home's water, a composting toilet is the most effective water-conserving device you can use. With feces and urine treated separately, the job of restoring the remaining wastewater, called "greywater" is greatly simplified.*

➤ *Once a household has a composter that treats excreta and food scraps, the volume of wastewater can be reduced even further to as little as 15 gallons per person per day. This is done by using restricting faucets, showerheads, suds savers, etc. In a water-conscious household that conserves water, uses low or no-phosphate detergents (biodegradable, of course), and composts food scraps, this greywater can easily be restored.*

➤ *Most of the low-flush toilets require no special plumbing alterations and work like a regular flush toilet. They use less water because of design changes in the bowl shape, trap pitch and water column height. They are easy to install and results are immediate.*

Troubled Water

Jonathan King
1985; 225 pp.
$8.95 postpaid from:
Rodale Press
(Out of print; check your local library)

We may as well start with the bad news. *Troubled Water* is a well researched and documented work that traces the current problems, and they are legion, with the United States' water supply system. It's not a pretty picture. Rural and urban dwellers alike are routinely subjected to substandard drinking water. Carcinogens from plastic distribution pipes leach into drinking water. The Clean Water Act has been ineffective. Bottled water may be just as polluted as tap water. King dutifully addresses the current messy state of our water affairs and recounts how a technologically sophisticated country allowed such a tragedy to happen. Despite the gloomy picture, this book is one of the best for addressing household water safety and aquatic politics. Its handy listing of all state agencies concerned with groundwater will help you find where to get your water tested. Also included is good advice on steps you can take to purify your home's drinking water. This book will really open your eyes to the sorry state of our water affairs and should prompt a sense of urgency to get out and protect your water supplies and to check the purity of the water you drink.

Excerpts:

➤ *Despite the publicity surrounding chemical poisons in our drinking water, bacterial contamination remains the most common water quality problem in individual or small systems. Nationally, 28 percent of rural households drink water that contains more than the federal limit of one coliform bacterium per 100 milliliters. The presence of coliform, which are found mainly in the intestines of warm-blooded animals, does not necessarily mean that drinking water will cause problems. Rather, because the source of most coliform bacteria is waste, their presence may indicate the presence of other, harmful bacteria and viruses which cause gastrointestinal problems such as diarrhea.*

➤ *Sometimes the color, taste, or odor of your water may indicate problems. If your water smells like rotten eggs, it could be that hydrogen sulfide is indicated. Brown stains on fixtures suggest high levels of iron. Green stains indicate elevated levels of copper. A metallic taste may indicate a variety of problems— deteriorating pipes, leachate from new plumbing, or a chemical contaminant.*

➤ *A filter will remove only certain contaminants. Given this, and the fact that filters may require a fair amount of maintenance, consider whether you really need one. Do the impurities in your water make a filter necessary? Some of them may actually be beneficial. Water is often a significant source of iron, which can prevent anemia, a deficiency of iron in the blood. The calcium in hard water may cause the body to absorb less cadmium and lead, both toxic heavy metals. Iron and zinc also counteract the absorption of cadmium. There is evidence that calcium and magnesium may help prevent heart attacks. Numerous studies have showed lower rates of heart disease in areas with hard water compared to areas with water low in calcium and magnesium.*

Captured Rainfall
1981; 56 pp.
Bulletin 213
$1.00 from:
State of California
DEPARTMENT OF WATER RESOURCES
P.O. Box 942836
Sacramento, CA 94236-0001
Make checks payable to: Dept. of Water Resources
California residents add tax

For anyone interested in using rainfall as a water supply, this book is an excellent resource. It contains the numbers and practical information for designing and building your own rainfall capturing system.

Excerpts:

➤ *A basic rainwater collection system built by the homeowner requires a surface which collects rainfall, channels it, and stores it. In addition, some form of pumping system will be necessary if water is not stored above the point of use and fed by gravity, or if it must be distributed to remote sites. If rain water is used for human consumption, a filtration or purification system may be needed, which could range in complexity from a simple screen or sand filter to one of the modern chemical treatment systems.*

The EPA National Small Flows Clearinghouse
P.O. Box 6064
Morgantown WV 26506-6064
(800)624-8301

This organization was set up in 1977 through the Clean Water Act in order to facilitate the design, planning, and construction of innovative and alternative decentralized wastewater treatment facilities in areas where conventional systems are not economically feasible. Services include a free newsletter, computer bibliographies on topics ranging from composting toilets to failing septic systems, design modules to help evaluate technologies ranging from mound systems to vacuum sewers, septic management and novel alternatives, and case-studies of a number of different decentralized waste systems. The Clearinghouse sponsors annual workshops and seminars, offers a telephone consultation and referral service, and provides books, brochures and videotapes, some free and others at nominal fees.

Water-Efficient Technologies: A Catalog for the Residential/Light Commercial Sector—Second Edition
1991; 200 pp.
$25.00 postpaid from:
Rocky Mountain Institute
1739 Snowmass Creek Road
Snowmass CO 81654-9199
(303)927-3851

RMI's catalog of highly efficient water-saving residential hardware includes price, performance, and where-to-get-it information on ultra-low-flush toilets (1.6 gallons per flush or less), showerheads (2.5 gallons per minute or less), faucet aerators (0.5—2.5 gallons per minute), as well as efficient landscape irrigation equipment and other appliances. Ideal for planners, builders, and architects. A booklet prepared for homeowners entitled *Water Efficiency for Your Home* is also available for $1.00.

Gray Water Use in the Landscape

Robert Kourik
1988; 25 pp.
$6.00 postpaid from:
Metamorphic Press
P.O. Box 1841
Santa Rosa CA 95402

Waste has always been synonymous with the American lifestyle, and our use of water is no exception. Although government policy wastes water it isn't necessary that the individual do the same, so as agribiz empties aquifers it's possible for individuals to conserve their own.

Despite our American lifestyle, middle-class sanitation hangups and archaic health codes, "gray water," anything that's not sewage, is still useful, even though it may have just finished washing your dishes. Robert Kourik, author of the *Edible Landscape* book, gives us some practical ways to convert household plumbing to a gray-water system, diverting water that used to go down the tubes to irrigation instead.

Kourik's pamphlet is based on his experiences during the last California drought, when he struggled with a bureaucracy that briefly relaxed the rules to permit legal experimentation. It's conservative, but will guide the conversion of a home plumbing system into a home irrigation system, a subtle form of un-American behavior that your local aquifer will appreciate.

Reviewed by Dick Fugett in *Whole Earth Review*, Spring 1989

Excerpts:

➤ *Once you've begun to use gray water, you must think more carefully about what goes down the drain. Many common household and bathroom cleaners are potentially rough on plants. Simply put, you must get back to basics, and use only simple soaps, detergents, and "elbow grease." Soaps are safer since they usually have less sodium than detergents. Avoid all modern detergents with claims of softening, whitening, and "enzymatic" powers, as well as bleaches in all forms. Especially harmful are cleansers or detergents with boron, a substance which can quickly build up to toxic levels.*

Residential Water Re-Use

Murray Milne
1980
California Water Resource Center
University of California-Davis
Davis CA 95616
(916)757-8901
(Out of print, but photocopies available from NTIS for $53.00.)
(800)553-6847

The drought of 1977-79 prompted Milne to take pen in hand. He produced what has become a definitive text on home-scale water re-use. Topics covered include: history of water re-use; discussion of rainwater and groundwater; reuse in the garden; extensive coverage of system designs; and a handy index of manufacturers who supply the necessary hardware to get you started re-using your water. The only available copies of *Residential Water Re-Use* are photocopies from National Technical Information Service (NTIS), U.S. Dept. of Commerce, 5285 Port Royal Road, Springfield VA 22161, (703)487-4650, ($53.00). NTIS offers other publications, including *Residential Conservation Program: State-of-the Art Summary of Incentives for Residential Water Conservation* ($15.00) and *Residential Water Conservation Projects Summary Report* ($17.00).

Excerpts:

➤ *The collection and treatment of combined kitchen and toilet wastes in a composter offers a number of significant advantages. The first, and most obvious, is that because the flush toilet and garbage disposal are eliminated, household water consumption is immediately reduced by about 40 percent. The second is that these wastes, which constitute the most troublesome pollution load to water leaving the house in a traditional water-borne sewage system, are instead turned into a beneficial soil amendment. The third is that the separated and relatively clean greywater can be passed through the roughing filter rather than a septic tank, since it is the large size and slow decomposition of fecal material which makes a septic tank necessary in the on-site treatment of combined wastes. This is important because the effluent from the roughing filter is relatively aerobic, whereas the effluent from the septic tank is anaerobic and may promote anaerobic processes in the soil which would be harmful to plant roots.*

➤ *Applications of greywater can be quite significant. For example, the average production of greywater per person in the household is about 40 gallons per day. For a family of four this results in a total annual production of 58,400 gallons. One gallon is equivalent to 2/3 inch of water over one square foot. Assume now, that the family has irrigated. This means that the greywater supplies an additional 58 inches of water for irrigation each year.*

Septic Tank Practices: A Guide to the Conservation & Re-use of Household Wastewater
Peter Warshall
1979; 177 pp.
$6.95 postpaid from:
Whole Earth Access
2990 Seventh St.
Berkeley CA 94710

Septic Tank Practices is a modest title for a book that not only clearly lays out home-site sewage treatment options, but also explores their relationships to soil, water use, and politics. Warshall addresses the subject with lively discourses on the guiding scientific principle behind home sewage systems—the natural purification of water by the soil. He describes how to choose, install, and maintain the best system for a specific site, and techniques for making more efficient use of water and recycling household wastewater ("greywater"). He argues that centralized sewerage pollutes more, costs more, uses more energy resources, and is more of a health hazard than home-site treatment. Many good diagrams and drawings support the theory and practical hands-on information in this book.

Excerpts:

➤ *We are learning: wastes are not wastes. They are misplaced natural resources. We cannot "dispose" of anything on Earth except by sending it to outer space. "Wastes" can only re-enter the Nutrient and Water Cycles on this planet. We cannot avoid our "wastes". Because we exist in the biosphere of Earth and are connected to the Nutrient and Water Cycles of the planet, "wastes" return—usually with a vengeance. But as humans we can encourage "wastes" and "wastewater" to re-enter only certain, specific natural cycles and communities where they can benefit us and other living creatures and plants. By understanding our wastes, by connecting our body's plumbing to Nature's pathways, we can eliminate current practices that damage both our bodies and planet life.*

➤ *The septic-tank system actually has two distinct sections: the septic tank itself and the drainfield. The tank is a box that eliminates at least half the excrement by allowing time for solids to settle and be eaten by microbes. The wastewater then passes into a hole in the ground. The hole can be of almost any shape and depth. The most common shape is a linear trench usually between three and six feet deep. This trench design is called the drainfield (or leachfield, filterfield, absorption bed, disposal or subirrigation field). The wastewater from the septic tank receives further treatment in the drainfield. The soil absorbs viruses, strains out bacteria, filters large wastes, and chemically renovates them into nutrients that can be used by plants. Treatment is reliable for the lifespan of the drainfield.*

15. Transportation

Other than houses, cars are the most resource-intensive purchases most people make. Traveling to and from our homes often consumes more energy each year than we use keeping our homes comfortable and operating our appliances. The reference in this section can help you shop for cars that are energy-efficient, yet don't compromise on safety and long term economical operation.

Illustration courtesy of *Tools For A Change*, proceedings of the Northeast Appropriate Technology Forum.

The Car Book: An Indispensable Guide to the Safest, Most Economical New Cars
Jack Gillis
1992 edition; 160 pp.
$11.00 plus shipping from:
Harper Collins
New York NY
(800)331-3761

The Car Book is the most helpful and easy-to-use guide available on car safety, fuel economy, and maintenance costs. It provides invaluable consumer information—crash test performance, fuel economy, preventive maintenance costs, repair costs, and insurance rates—for all 1991 cars, mini-vans, and light trucks as well as for many 1990 models. Gillis highlights all the critical information prudent shoppers need to know, such as good car choices for 1990, the cars having the best and worst crash worthiness, 1990 fuel economy winners and losers, gas-saving devices that don't work, the best and worst warranties, and which tires last the longest. Child safety seat models are listed, as are state lemon laws. While most other such consumer guides get a good deal of their information straight from the manufacturer' brochures and press releases, *The Car Book* bases its findings on U.S. government tests and independent engineering studies sanctioned by the Center for Auto Safety, the leading automotive consumer group in the country. A number of outright scary auto safety statistics and manufacturers' coverups are revealed which new and used car shoppers have a right to know before they purchase any car. There's also lots of strategic advice for negotiating the best deal in the showroom, finding the best options and buys in insurance coverage, and getting auto repair and warranty complaints resolved. Put simply, *The Car Book* can help guide you through the trade-offs, claims, promises, facts, and myths to the car that will best meet your needs. The Center for Auto Safety can also help consumers who are having trouble getting the dealer or manufacturer to respond to complaints. Send a self-addressed, stamped envelope with 45 cents postage and include the make, model, year, and specific complaint. They also have a publications list available.

Excerpt:

➤ *Here are three tips for getting the best tire buy: 1) Never pay list price for a tire. A good rule of thumb is to pay at least 30 to 40 percent off the suggested price, 2) Remember to inquire about balancing, mounting, and valve stem charges. These may vary considerably among dealers, and 3) The best way to ensure you are getting the best tire value is to divide the price of the tire by its treadwear grade. The tire with the lowest cost per grade point is the best value.*

Manifold Destiny: The One! The Only! Guide to Cooking on Your Car Engine!
Chris Maynard and Bill Scheller
$7.95 postpaid from:
Villard Books (a division of Random House)
Order Services:
Random House
201 E. 50th Street
New York NY 10022
(800)733-3000

How many miles does it take to roast a chicken? Should you use your spark plugs or your radiator for a tenderloin of pork? With easy-to-understand recipes (everything from "Melrose Avenue Chicken" to "Blackened Roadfish"!), charts and photographs, this book reveals how, with a little ingenuity and lots of tin foil, anyone can create a tailgate feast on the way to the stadium. Witty, preposterous, and great highway fun, according to the authors, the more than 35 recipes not only work—they're delicious. And when you try them, you'll find out what "cooking with gas" really means.

➤ *Successful engine cooking comes down to these two questions: How far are you driving? and When do you expect to be hungry?*

➤ *The traffic accident of the future will involve some boob who, peeling a memo off his on-board fax machine, doesn't see the lady in the next lane taking a Pop-Tart out of her micro. No such risk with car-engine cooking. Since you can't check to see if your dinner is done without getting out of the vehicle and looking under the hood, it's no more dangerous than pulling over to change a tire—a lot less dangerous, in fact, since you don't get to pick the location for a flat tire.*

➤ *When you start cooking on fuel-injector housings, there's an important caveat: You have to come to grips with the critical issue of hood clearance. If there's too much clearance, your food is going to fall off. And if there isn't enough, you're going to slam down the hood and squash the packages, break the foil, and make what can only be described as a big mess (The game hens, by the way, flattened just enough, rather like a pressed galantine; this probably helped them cook as well as they did.)*

➤ ***Recipe: Hyundai Halibut With Fennel***
Distance: 55-85 miles. New England fishermen used to call big halibut "doormats." For this recipe, get your steaks cut from one that looks more like a floor mat. At home or on the road, lay halibut steaks on 4 pieces of buttered foil. Sprinkle each with oregano, lemon rind, and minced garlic. Add a generous layer of fennel slices and sprinkle with wine or vermouth. Wrap tightly. Cook 1 hour, depending on thickness and cooking location.

Bicycling Science
Frank Whitt & David Wilson
1982; 360 pp.
$13.50 from:
The MIT Press
55 Hayward Street
Cambridge MA 02142
(800) 356-0343

This in-depth exploration of bicycling science, written by two MIT engineers, is enough to satisfy anyone's technical appetite. It is a classical study of power and speed that analyzes every component of the bicycle's workings—wind resistance, the wheel, friction, physics of the rider—and explains the system as a whole. Lots of fun equations and analyses for those who want to know what's really going on in this deceptively simple machine.

Excerpts:

➤ *Should one walk or pedal up hills? Noncompetitive bicyclists have the option of walking up steep hills. Some prefer to do so, alleging that a change of muscle action is agreeable to them. Some bicyclists, however, prefer to fit low gears to their bicycles and to ride as much as possible. Whether it is easier to ride or walk up steep gradients is often debated among bicyclists.*

➤ *Friction between tire and road: If we assume that an appropriate force can be applied to the brakes and that the blocks or linings have been proportioned so that they will not fade on account of heating, the stopping capacity of the brakes depends directly upon the grip (or coefficient of friction) of the tires on the road. For pneumatic-tired vehicles, this grip varies from 0.8 to 0.1 times the force between tire and road, according to whether the surface is dry concrete or wet ice.*

The Bicycle: Vehicle for a Small Planet
Worldwatch Paper 90

Marcia D. Lowe
**1989; 62 pp.
$5.00 postpaid from:
Worldwatch Institute
1776 Massachusetts Avenue, N.W.
Washington D.C. 20036**

Did you know that the United States has among the lowest gasoline sales taxes of any developed country—45% vs. 133% to 355% for many European countries—and that we have one of the highest rates in the world for miles driven per person? The U.S. is poorly structured for bicycle use, but examples from other countries and successful communities in the U.S. show what kind of policies make for successful reduction in the use of cars. Developing countries, for example are now faced with the dilemma of promoting motor or people power for their growing populations. An interesting and informative read, this book puts our unquestioned use of automobiles into a global perspective.

Excerpts:

➤ *Dutch officials realized that fostering cycling would not only improve the urban environment but also enhance the transport sector without having to pave over historic town centers or spend large amounts of public money. Between 1975 and 1985 the national government spent some $230 million to construct cycleways and parking . . . Highway construction expenditures, by contrast, began to decline; by the early eighties, funding for bicycle projects exceeded 10 percent of capital spending on roadways.*

➤ *From the 10-speeds of Boston to the black roadsters of Beijing, the world's 800 million bicycles outnumber cars by two to one—and each year bike production outpaces automobile manufacturing by three to one. Bicycles in Asia alone transport more people than do all of the world's autos.*

Please Help Us To Improve This Guide

This guide offers you access to the best resources we are aware of. No doubt, better or complementary resources exist. When you come across these, or find errors in this book, please let us know by sending in this page with your comments, corrections, or suggested additions. If a friend would be interested in this book, please use the enclosed order form on the next page. Thank you.

Comments, corrections, and suggested additions:

_____

_____

_____

_____

_____

_____

_____

_____

_____

_____

_____

_____

_____

_____

_____

_____

_____

_____

_____

_____

_____

_____

_____

Detach and mail your comments to:
Rocky Mountain Institute
Attn: The Efficient House Sourcebook
1739 Snowmass Creek Road
Snowmass CO 81645-9199
(303)927-3851, FAX: (303)927-4178

Other Publications by Rocky Mountain Institute

H-1	"Visitor's Guide" Description/Tour Guide of Rocky Mountain Institute headquarters plus a where-to-get-it list of technologies (22 pp)	$5.00
E86-9	Energy Unbound: A Fable for America's Future (a popularized, updated, expanded version of Soft Energy Paths) (399 pp)	$20.00
E89-17	Least-Cost Energy: Solving the CO2 Problem, 1981, 1989, second edition (191 pp)	$15.00
E91-10	"If it's Not Efficient, It's Not Beautiful" *Fine Homebuilding* article, Spring 1991 (1 p)	$1.50
E91-12	Practical Home Energy Savings (48 pp)	$8.00
E92-9	**The Efficient House Sourcebook** (166 pp)	$15.00
W91-18	"Water-Efficient Technologies: A Catalog for the Urban/Residential Sector"—Second Edition, 1991 (200 pp)	$25.00
W91-26	"Water Efficiency for Your Home: Products and Advice Which Save Water, Energy and Money" (24 pp)	$1.00
W91-27	Water Efficiency: A Resource for Utility Managers, Community Planners, and Other Decisionmakers (114 pp)	$15.00
ER89-36	Energy Casebook (60 pp)	$15.00
ER91-7	Food & Agriculture Workbook (124 pp)	$15.00

Order Form

✂ ---

Pub #	Cost	Pub #	Cost	Pub #	Cost
	$		$		$
				TOTAL	$

NAME _____

ADDRESS _____

CITY STATE ZIP _____

___ Please enter my name and address on RMI's mailing list so I can receive the RMI newsletter three times a year. ($10 donation requested)

Detach and mail this order form and your check or money order to:
Rocky Mountain Institute
1739 Snowmass Creek Road
Snowmass CO 81654-9199

If you have any questions, call (303)927-3851. Thank you.